AFRICA CALLING

AFRICA CALLING

A Medical Missionary in Kenya and Zambia

John W. Gerrard

The Radcliffe Press
London · New York

Published in 2001 by The Radcliffe Press
6 Salem Road, London W2 4BU

In the United States and in Canada
distributed by St Martin's Press
175 Fifth Avenue, New York NY 10010

ISBN 1-86064-659-X

A full CIP record for this book is available from the British Library
A full CIP record for this book is available from the Library of Congress

Library of Congress Catalog card: available

Typeset in Sabon by Oxford Publishing Services, Oxford
Printed and bound in Great Britain by MPG Books Ltd, Bodmin

To my wife, Betty,
who means so much
to me and our three sons,
Jon, Peter and Chris.

Contents

Maps and Illustrations

Maps

Illustrations

Some Ancestors and Descendants of Jonathan and Jane Gerrard (née Lee), recorded in greater detail on the Gerrard Family Tree

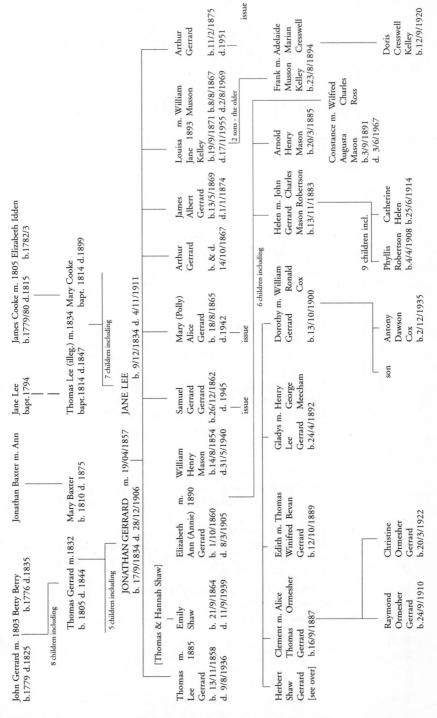

John Gerrard m. 1803 Betty Berry
b.1779 d.1825 · b.1776 d.1835

Jonathan Baxter m. Ann

James Cooke m. 1805 Elizabeth Idden
b.1779/80 d.1815 · b.1782/3

8 children including

Thomas Gerrard m.1832 Mary Baxter
b. 1805 d. 1844 · b. 1810 d. 1875

Jane Lee
bapt.1794

Thomas Lee (illeg.) m.1834 Mary Cooke
bapt.1814 d.1847 · bapt. 1814 d.1899

7 children including

5 children including

JONATHAN GERRARD m. 19/04/1857 JANE LEE
b. 17/9/1834 d. 28/12/1906 · b. 9/12/1834 d. 4/11/1911

[Thomas & Hannah Shaw]

Thomas   m.   Emily
Lee   1885   Shaw
Gerrard
b. 13/11/1858 b. 21/9/1864
d. 9/8/1936   d. 11/9/1939

[see over]

William Henry Mason
b.14/8/1854
d.31/5/1940

Elizabeth m. 1890
Ann (Annie)
Gerrard
b. 1/10/1860
d. 8/3/1905

Samuel Gerrard
Gerrard
b.26/12/1862
d. 1945

issue

Mary (Polly) Alice Gerrard
b. 18/8/1865
d.1942

issue

Arthur Gerrard
b. & d.
14/10/1867

James Albert Gerrard
b.13/5/1869
d.1/1/1874

Louisa m. William
Jane 1893 Musson
Kelley
b.19/9/1871 b.8/8/1867
d.17/11/1955 d.2/8/1969

2 sons - the older

Arthur Gerrard
b.11/2/1875
d. 1951

issue

Herbert Shaw Gerrard
b.16/9/1887

Clement m. Alice
Thomas Ormesher
Gerrard
b.16/9/1887

Edith m. Thomas
Winifred Bevan
Gerrard
b.12/10/1889

Gladys m. Henry
Lee George
Gerrard Meecham
b.24/4/1892

Dorothy m. William
Gerrard Ronald
Cox
b.13/10/1900

6 children including

Helen m. John
Gerrard Charles
Mason Robertson
b.13/11/1883

Frank m. Adelaide
Musson Marian
Kelley Cresswell
b.23/8/1894

Arnold
Henry
Mason
b.20/3/1885

Constance m. Wilfred
Augusta Charles
Mason Ross
b.3/9/1891
d. 3/6/1967

9 children incl.

Doris
Cresswell
Kelley
b.12/9/1920

Raymond
Ormesher
Gerrard
b.24/9/1910

Christine
Ormesher
Gerrard
b.20/3/1922

son

Antony
Dawson
Cox
b.2/12/1935

Phyllis
Robertson
b.4/4/1908

Catherine
Helen
b.25/6/1914

Children of Herbert Shaw Gerrard

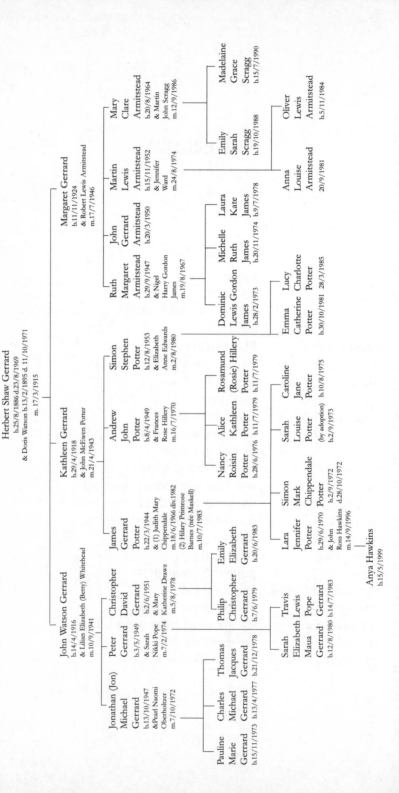

Glossary

chikwikwe	locusts
gitara	doctor
kafundu bantu	man who skins people to see what is inside
Kazunumozo	Mrs Hardheart
kubanda	to name or to trample down
langa	look
matatu	local taxi
mazungu	white person
miraa	hallucinogenic drug obtained from bark or leaf of a tree
mohau	non-alcoholic brew
muga	witchdoctor/friendly greeting
mukirangi	the great one who knows a lot
muragi	diviner with magical powers
mwalinu	teacher
mwigithan	conciliator
Njeri	powerful council
Ngu wezu Njelende	It is Gerrard
rugongo	autonomous group
twa fwa nkoshi	we are dead from meat hunger
ushibalwazhi	father of the sick
wa nkwata chiwena	a crocodile has got me

Acknowledgements

I am indebted to my grandfather for having saved so many of my father's letters and for returning them to him. Above all I am grateful to my wife for her advice and help, for without these the book would never have been written. I am grateful to my sisters, Kathleen Potter and Margaret Armitstead for help and support, to my sons Chris and Peter (and Peter's wife Nikki) and my nephew Jim Potter for their contributions on their work in post-independence Anglophone Africa, to my nephew John Armitstead and Christine Budd for the light they shed on the Maua Methodist Hospital after independence, to my cousin Raymond Gerrard with whom I shared a happy holiday in Zambia in our teens, to my cousins Catherine Bennett who shared her extensive knowledge of our forebears with me, and Doris Baker who drew the family trees, and who was named after my mother to show the esteem with which my parents were held, and to Antony Cox for sharing the fruits of his genealogical studies with me. I owe a special debt of gratitude to Margaret Bell for describing the years she and Stanley spent at Maua and for allowing me to read relevant parts of Stanley's MD thesis, and to Barbara Dickinson of Maua for news of its recent expansion. I am also grateful to Bob Williamson for suggestions and editorial help, to Ed Sebestyen for helpful maps, without them the African names would have been meaningless, and last but not least to Jenni Martin who was ultimately responsible for my writing this book.

Introduction

I was born on 14 April 1916 in Northern Rhodesia, now called Zambia, on an isolated mission station called Kasenga. It was seven day's ride by ox-wagon from the nearest town and the railway. My father, who was a medical missionary, delivered, circumcised and christened me. He later married me to my wife, Betty Whitehead. My playmates were black African children. My first language was that of the Baila people whom my parents had come to serve. I helped them to master it.

In 1920, five years after my parents had first left England, they returned and stayed with my grandparents in a large, capacious house in Swinton on the outskirts of Manchester. They brought with them their two children, my sister Kathleen and me. A year later they returned to Kasenga, leaving us, my sister and myself, in the care of my father's eldest sister, Auntie Winifred. Three years later I went to a preparatory boarding school for boys. When I was separated from my parents I wrote to them regularly every week, and they wrote to me, but I never kept their letters and they never kept mine. I saw my father every four years when he returned to England for a year's furlough, but we did not see a great deal of each other for I was at a boarding school for most of the time and he had to travel round the country lecturing about his work in Kasenga.

My parents returned to England for good in 1941, just in time for my father to marry Betty and myself. The war separated me from both Betty and my parents for most of four years, and when I was demobilized Betty and I were busy building our own home and bringing up our own family, three delightful little boys. After the war, when I had completed my training, paediatrics, I joined the staff of the Department of Paediatrics at the University of Birmingham. In 1955 I was asked to head up a new Department of Paediatrics in the School of Medicine at the University of Saskatchewan in Saskatoon, in the heart of the Canadian Prairies. The opportunity seemed too good to pass over. We packed our trunks and started new lives in Canada. My parents never complained. They may even have been pleased that we, Betty and I, for it was a mutual decision, had accepted the challenge the move offered, even though it meant that after years of separation we would be as far apart as we had ever been.

When my parents settled down in England, letters they had written from Africa to their own parents were returned to them by their father who, being a very methodical man, had filed and kept them. When my parents died the letters were passed on to me. For too many years they lay untouched and unread, safely stored in a box. When I, in my turn, retired, I turned to these letters and discovered a father I had not known fully when he was still alive. Attached to these letters were notes made by my father about his own grandparents. With the help of my two sisters, Kathleen Potter and Margaret Armitstead, three cousins, Catherine Bennett, Doris Baker and Antony Cox, and the support and guidance of my wife, Betty, as well as the encouragement of a writer, Jenni Martin, I have done my best to weave a tapestry based on the lives of my forebears, my parents especially, and the activities of my sons and nephews. The background for this tapestry has been the times in which my grandparents grew up in England 150 years ago, the tribal customs of the Baila and Ameru among whom my parents spent the best years of their lives, and the changing face of Africa. I hope this saga of our family will mean as much to you as it has to me.

1

My Forebears

I was born on a small mission station on the banks of the Kafue River in what is now called Zambia, but was then called Northern Rhodesia. My father, Herbert Gerrard, always called Bert, had grown up in a devout Primitive Methodist household, the eldest of five and the first of two sons. He started his education in the local council school and completed it at a boarding school, Elmfield, in York. He was expected to go into the family business, a burgeoning construction company. His grandfather had built the company up from scratch and was its chairman. His father was the managing director. My father started his training in the carpenter's shop but later felt called to be a medical missionary. He went to Hartley College to train for the ministry and to Manchester University for his medical education. In addition to obtaining his Bachelor of Medicine and Surgery, he was awarded in 1910 a bronze medal for his prowess in practical histology.

After qualifying as a medical doctor he went to the Royal Infirmary in Hull for further training in 1913. While there, he went on Sundays to a Methodist church where his eye lit on a family, which consisted like his own of two boys, Will and Gerard, and three young girls, Florence, Doris and May. He was frequently invited to their home. The three girls were keen table tennis players. Flo and May for a long time could not understand how it was that Doris, whom they could usually beat, always managed to beat my father. This was, I think, an early example of ping-pong diplomacy.

1

My mother, born on 13 February 1895, was only 18 when she first met my father, 19 when she was engaged and just turned 20 when she married him. She came from a well-known family; her father was an engineer and at one time the harbour master of Hull. He invented a device for trawlers for lifting loaded nets on board. One of her forebears, Henry Watson, had been granted the Freedom of the City of Kingston-upon-Hull in 1818; another was said to have played cricket for Yorkshire. She was a good student and athlete, running and playing hockey for her school.

Almost immediately, Doris and Bert fell deeply in love. He took her to see his parents in their home in Swinton. Both loved her. On one occasion Doris slipped into her bedroom and was surprised to find her future mother-in-law fingering and examining a nightdress she herself had made. Caught unawares, she said she had been examining her needlework and had found it flawless. Doris was a very good seamstress.

The day after they were engaged my father penned the following letter to his love:

Royal Infirmary,
Hull,
June 5, 1914.

My Dear Doris,

You see I am in a hurry to get my first love letter written, if you except [the] letters [I sent] home when I was at boarding school, which our headmaster used to teach us to call love letters.

I have been wondering what sort of a night you have spent. Although I sang you a lullaby before I left, I am afraid it wasn't sung with the imagination which would charm sleep to your eyes if you felt wakeful. Were your thoughts too busy Doris to let sleep come readily? Still they were happy ones, weren't they? When I got in last night I went and visited the isolation ward, and the nurse said, 'You don't look so tired tonight Dr Gerrard.' And I thought I could tell her a good reason why. I sent a line home before going to bed and gave them the good news. I shall try and send them a longer letter today, and tell them some of the good things, though I cannot tell them all about their new daughter and my dear wife that is to be.

Doesn't it seem strange that when a wonderful thing like this happens, the world goes on just the same? Here I am going on with my casualties today and you'll be running in the races as though nothing so momentous had occurred. Yet there is a big difference for us two, love, if for no one else. I feel gloriously happy today. May God keep us true to one another, dear and spare us for many years of happy work together. As we get to know one another better during the next few weeks, I feel we should grow to love one another more and more. May your slumber be sweet and deep to-night.

With heaps of love from yours ever, Bert.

At the outbreak of the First World War in August 1914, my father volunteered for the services. While waiting to find out if he were needed, he went as medical officer on a ship through the Mediterranean to Trieste, then in the Austro–Hungarian Empire. The purpose of the trip was to return the Austro–Hungarian diplomatic corps and bring back the British one from Vienna. It was and is the custom to ensure the safe return of diplomats to their native lands on the outbreak of war.

When he learnt that the services did not need his help, he proceeded with his plans to become a medical missionary. He ordered medical supplies from Burroughs Wellcome and invitations were sent out for the wedding. On 17 March 1915, Bert married Doris in Clowes Chapel, Hull. Close relatives witnessed the ceremony and my father's uncle, William Musson Kelley, married them. A brief honeymoon at Ilkley followed. My parents then packed their two cabin trunks for the voyage and collected 38 additional trunks, cases and boxes containing their wedding presents, tropical kits, sheets, towels, blankets and food — sugar, salt, tea, coffee and other staples to last them for six months. They said their farewells to their watching families, boarded the *Aeneas* in Liverpool and, on 3 April 1915, sailed into the unknown while war raged in Europe.

We will leave them there while we look into my father's family background to understand the influences that shaped his life.

We can only trace our family back to the 1750s, to a John Gerrard, a shopkeeper, who was born in Lancashire at this time. He moved to Little Hulton, not far from Swinton on the outskirts of Manchester, in about 1800. He died in 1825, leaving property worth a little less than £200, at that time the value of a house. He had seven children, five of whom were boys. His second son John (1779–1825), who was first a weaver and then a shopkeeper, married a Betty Berry (1776–1835). John's second son Thomas (1805–44), who like his father was also first a weaver and then a shopkeeper, married a Mary Baxter (1810–75) whose father owned a tavern called The Miner's Arms. After being a weaver and then a shopkeeper, Thomas and Mary moved into the Miner's Arms and became beer sellers. It was here in a building constructed of solid blocks of yellow sandstone that my great grandfather Jonathan (1834–1906) was born and grew up. The building still stands, 180 Manchester Road, Little Hulton; it is now no longer a tavern but the home of Mrs Gibbons, though when she bought it, it was called The Toby Jug.

Jonathan was the second of four brothers. His father died when he was only ten years old, so his mother brought him up. He and his brothers grew up racing dogs, rabbits and pigeons, gambling and drinking. His brothers drank heavily; the eldest ending up penniless in the workhouse. Jonathan might well have followed his elder brother, for he admitted that he had a liking for drink, but when he was 15 a gentleman came up to him and said, 'What dost thi do with thi Sundays?' Jonathan said he went to church, but that was all. The gentleman continued to press him and eventually Jonathan gave in and went with him to a Primitive Methodist Sunday school. There he was converted. The experience transformed him and left an indelible impression, for 50 years later he could still recall it vividly.

His first job was as a pit sawyer, earning 10/– (ten shillings) a week, standing in the pit holding the lower end of the saw while his partner held the upper end, above ground. Then, encouraged by the gentleman, he apprenticed himself to a carpenter and, while with him, he met his future wife Jane. He must have been a little gauche for he did not know how to approach her. 'Get see her somewheer, and ax her if she will meet with thi,' his gentleman friend advised him. So he asked Jane if she would meet with him, and she said 'Yes'. He thought he was getting on wonderfully, but when he met with Jane, he could not remember what he said, but he remembered Jane's reply, for she was in no hurry. 'There's plenty of time to talk about those things,' she said. Although he was very disappointed he did not give up and she eventually yielded to his advances, and they were married in 1857; both were 22.

Jane's background was very different from Jonathan's. She was a lifelong member of the Primitive Methodist Church, attending services and Sunday school on Sundays and classes in the middle of the week. She never missed paying her weekly class money. Her mother, Mary Lee, née Mary Cooke, had been born in 1814 in Walkden, not far from Swinton. Her father had died when she was only 11 months old. What happened to Mary's mother, we do not know, but her paternal grandparents, the Cookes of Walkden, brought her up and when she grew up she was expected to stay at home and look after them for as long as they remained alive. Her grandfather used to say, 'Our Mary must never be married while I live.' But Mary fell in love with a coalminer, Thomas Lee, and the couple decided to get married secretly. The day before the day of the wedding her grandfather fell ill. On the eve of her wedding day Mary sat up with him till three in the morning; a few hours later he died. The next morning, just as she was pinning on her wedding skirt, she was told that he had died. 'We cannot be married today then,' she said, but her friends replied, 'Oh but you must; everything is ready, and it can be done quietly.' So she and Thomas Lee set off on foot and covered the three miles to Eccles parish church where they were married on 28 September 1834. Mary was 20 and Thomas 19. Their first child was Jane. She was born ten weeks later.

Thomas and Mary Lee had seven children in quick succession, but only three survived to marry and have children of their own. After only seven years of married life, Thomas, like many miners of those times, developed tuberculosis and died six years later. He was well respected by his friends and was visited regularly by Mr Waller, the vicar, no doubt because he was ill and his days were numbered. The vicar gave him the sacrament a week before he died and later said he had never seen a happier death. Although it was early January and the snow was deep, 200 people attended his funeral — the chapel and the chapel yard were crowded.

After Thomas's funeral, Mr Waller continued to visit Mary Lee, whose only income was 13/- a week for three months, followed by 9/- a week for three further months. Mr Waller asked her what she was going to do. 'I'll do my best,' she replied, 'and leave the rest with the Lord'. Mr Waller found washing for her, which brought in 4/6d. a week, enough for food and clothing, and arranged for Lady Ellesmere, a titled lady who lived nearby, to pay the rent of 1/6d. a week. After Thomas's death, Mary called on Dr Anderton of Halshaw Moor who had looked after her husband when he had been ill. She told him how she was fixed, but said she would pay him as soon as she could. A few years later he sent her a bill for £3.13s. She thought this was very reasonable. She paid him 1/- at a time until it was all paid.

To do her washing, Mary needed a mangle. One was available locally for £10, but this was beyond her means. Luckily a neighbour had one to sell for only £5, but did not want to sell it to a neighbour. One morning David Lee, a relative of Thomas's, providentially came into the house and said, 'What is it you are needing? I know you need something for I cannot sleep at night.' Mary told him she needed a mangle. 'Do you know where there's one to sell?' he asked. She said she did, but the owners were not willing to sell it to a neighbour. David said he could manage that and went and bought it, even though at the time he was unemployed. He gave it to Mary and said she must pay him back when she could, and if she could not, never mind. About a month later he came to see her and she offered him a sovereign. 'Nay,' he answered, 'Yo haven't saved this.' But she later paid him every penny of the £5 that it had cost him. Some time later, when David had lost his own wife, he asked Mary Lee to marry him. 'Nay', she replied, 'not as long as my children will stay with me.'

Her eldest daughter, Jane, went to an old woman's school where she learnt to read. She later went to night school and learnt to write. She read with great keenness. She could write her own name and a letter in an emergency, but it was a big labour to her. From the age of nine she had to help her mother bring up her brother and sister, and when she played with them she would hold one child in one arm while playing with the second child with the other arm. Her father taught her to weave on a handloom when she was 11 years old and she weaved at home. When she was 13 she left for service to a Mrs Brookes. She worked from seven in the morning to seven in the evening earning 9*d.* a week plus her meals. She had to make porridge for her master and take it to him at his work at 8.00 a.m., and then make breakfast for their two boys, help with the washing and cleaning, and fetch water for the household from the well each day. She carried 24 quarts (six gallons) in a big can on her head, and two quarts in either hand. She also had to walk two miles for flour from a shop where the price was lower than at their local store. When she left Mrs Brookes the two lads were very upset. Mrs Brookes said she was sorry

Jane was leaving, 'Our lads were going to buy you a dress,' she added. 'If tha was my girl I don't know what I should feel like; tha'll never be good for nothing. Tha carries too heavier a weight on tha head.'

Jane left Mrs Brookes for a better-paid job, earning 1/– a week for a family that kept a grocer's shop, and sold tobacco. She had to be very exact. 'Tha monno give short weight, nor overweight,' were her instructions. She also had to keep the house clean. 'Na then, Jane,' she would be told, 'use that middle finger.'[1] It was the longest and could get into the dirty corners. There were also mice in the house.

After this she went to work as a weaver in Holdsworth & Gibbs Mill, Moorside, Swinton. She had to get up at 4.30 a.m. and walk three miles to the mill to start work at 6.00. She ran four looms and worked until 6.00 p.m. She then had a three-mile walk home for tea. On Tuesday evenings she would go to the preaching service. She joined the church when she was 14 and never missed the weekly collection. Her class leader was James Berry. Jane later said:

> He was a very nice man, but he made a mistake. He went to a brothel and was caught. He was turned out of the church. His wife was a very simple minded woman. I think he was dissatisfied with his wife. It was a pity. He was a good man. There was a lot more earnestness about people who confessed they'd been converted those days.

It was while she was working at Holdsworth & Gibbs Mill that Jane was knocked down by a jet of steam from a burst steam pipe and was badly scalded. She did not realize at first what had happened and thought that the mill had been blown

---

1. Doris Baker suggests that the middle finger was used to remove the last scrap of tobacco from the tobacco jar, so that none was wasted.

up. She hurried down one of the alleys on her hands and knees. An overlooker (as they used to call an overseer) Thomas Cook, stopped her and said, 'We must carry you home.' 'No, don't,' said Jane, 'It will upset my mother so much.' Mr Cook, in his simplicity, hurried off to her mother and told her such an alarming tale that she thought Jane had been killed. Soon afterwards Jane was carried in. The scald was a severe one, across her shoulders and down to the elbows. It caused a great deal of pain. The skin peeled off until the flesh was quite bare. In a month she was back at work. This was much too soon, but as she was getting 12/– a week while she was at home, she could not 'for shame' keep away from work any longer. Some 40 years later she still suffered from the effects of the scald, every change in the weather troubled her.

When Jonathan and Jane married they made their first home in Moorside, Swinton. They were both 22, though Jonathan was the elder by some three months. Jonathan was a joiner, looking for work wherever he could find it, mending wagons at the colliery, for example. On one occasion he disagreed with his foreman and was sent packing. He discussed his prospects with Jane who suggested he should try to improve his skills. So, for 12/– a week, he was apprenticed to a builder in Pendleton. To enable him to do this Jane continued weaving at the mill. A year later he started working as a foreman to a builder, Joseph Speakman. A few years later the latter asked Jonathan to join him in his business as a partner. Jonathan at first refused, but 12 months later, when Speakman begged him to join him, he changed his mind and they signed an article of agreement whereby they agreed to work together for ten years, forming the company of Speakman & Gerrard. This was in 1864, but after three years they agreed to separate. Speakman kept the works in Eccles, Jonathan the works in Swinton; the latter consisted of a one-storey joiner's shop with room for eight or ten joiners and a stable for four horses. Jonathan later said that at that time, 'I had not a piece of timber; I had not a steer or a saw bench or a tool. I had no debts and I had virtually no money. I borrowed some money from the Building Society and began to build.'

Jonathan had more land than he needed for his work, so he built four houses on some of the land, and sold them. An invoice dated 7 April 1881 illustrates the type of work he was doing at this time.

For Mr Ireland's funeral

21 Mount St.,
Worsley.

J. Gerrard.
Joiner, Builder and Undertaker,
Dealer in Timber, Coffins, Furniture & etc.
Funerals furnished.

To coffin (oak) 30/– less 10/–	£1.00.00
Shroud, & white gloves, & white tie	7.06
Funeral fee at church	10.00
22 1 lb loaves, current, each 4½ pence	8.03
3 dozen cakes	2.06
Settled	£2.8s.3d.

Jonathan continued, 'I went on at my own slow pace and am going yet. I am not much carried away with anything in this life, I can assure you I am thankful I have been taught this lesson, that if I have anything it has either been given to me or lent to me.'

In Swinton, Jonathan at first concentrated on woodwork at his yard in Long Street next to his home in Mount Street. He did his best to turn out flawless work. On one occasion, when some closet seats were being loaded into a pony cart, he came into the yard, saw the seats and, finding that they failed to please him, fetched an axe and broke them all up — only the best workmanship satisfied him.

Jonathan's business grew steadily and, in 1885, although he himself was only 50, he drew up an agreement for partnership with his two sons, Thomas Lee, aged 25, and Samuel aged 21. The introduction to the agreement is touching in that it shows how completely they trusted each other. It reads, 'Whereas the said parties have agreed to become partners in the said business of Joinery, Building and Undertaking, it is (in consideration of the mutual trust which they hold in each other) agreed to become partners.' The capital owned by Jonathan at that time was £1710, by Thomas it was £240 and by Samuel it was £38. For subsistence they agreed that Jonathan should receive 48/– a month, and Thomas and Samuel each 36/– a month. They also agreed that at the end of each year Jonathan would be paid £45 for the rental of buildings, each partner would be paid 4 per cent interest on his investment in the firm, and Jonathan would receive four-tenths of the year's profits and Thomas and Samuel each three-tenths. It was at this time that the business was first called J. Gerrard & Sons. To confirm the change in the name of his business, Jonathan wrote to his customers on 6 February 1885 thanking them for their confidence over the previous 20 years and soliciting their continued confidence in his partners and the new firm.

We do not know whether Thomas was already courting Emily Shaw or whether the added security he must have felt on being made a partner made him think of matrimony, but we do know that he wasted no time in introducing Emily to his parents. He had met her in a Primitive Methodist church in London, which he was visiting on business. On 21 June, four months after being made a partner, Thomas and Emily, my grandparents, were married in Hammersmith. Jonathan and Jane were not there to witness the ceremony, but Thomas did not mind because he had in his pocket a letter from his father explaining their absence and adding:

Notwithstanding the absent feeling occasioned by the thought of Thomas' apparent absence, we are proud to have such a son united in marriage with one so amiable and good as we believe Emily to be, and so likely to be a helpmeet to him through life.

We have the pleasure of thinking Thomas has always been a dutiful and loving son, and have no doubt that he will make an equally good husband.

You will commence your new sphere of life with better opportunities and advantage, abilities and prospects than we did.

We have formed the highest opinion of Emily, and consider her a suitable person for Thomas, and shall henceforth look upon her as our daughter.

We sympathize with Mrs Shaw in her apparent loss of Emily, but would remind her that while we obtain another daughter she gains a son.

And now dear children we commend you to the Lord etc. We all unite in wishing you much happiness and prosperity, your affectionate parents.

Jonathan.

Emily came from Yorkshire stock. Her father, Thomas Shaw, was a spinner and overlooker (overseer) in a worsted wool factory. He died three months before Emily was born, so her mother and maternal grandparents brought her up. She, like Thomas, was a loyal member of the Primitive Methodist Church, and it was natural that they should meet there. They made their home in 21 Mount Street, next door to Jonathan and Jane, and this is where my father was born. Some 22 years later, in 1907, they moved to Norfield, a relatively palatial home with a garage, greenhouse, kitchen garden and lawn, with two staircases, one for the family and a second smaller one at the back of the house for the servants, a dining room, library, two drawing rooms, one downstairs and one upstairs (the latter being reserved for Sundays and special occasions), bedrooms and bathrooms. Coal fireplaces were present in most of the rooms. I remember, a few days before our first Christmas in England, sending letters to Father Christmas that were wafted up the dining room chimney, carried on the rising smoke from the friendly fire. My sister Kathleen developed measles while we were staying there; she was isolated in a back bedroom and a sheet, heavily soaked in disinfectant, was hung over the doorway to keep the germs out of the rest of the house.

Granny was a well-organized hostess; she had to be, for Norfield had frequent visitors and on Sundays the visiting preacher was nearly always invited for dinner after the morning service. Each morning Granny would meet with Kate, her big, friendly cook, and with Hannah, her petite, slender maid to decide on the menus for the day. If the car and Rogers, the chauffeur, were available, she would often drive into Manchester to shop. She chose her clothes with care; they were always made to measure and were elegant but not ostentatious. Kathleen remembers her on one occasion canvassing the views of all her daughters and daughters-in-law before purchasing material for a dress. Granny had a particular concern for my mother who might, she felt, despite two successful pregnancies, be tempting fate if she were to have a third in the heart of Africa. She sent her the latest contraceptive information as well as a douche.

In summer Granny loved to drive to the countryside, Derbyshire or Cheshire, for a picnic or to drop into a favourite hotel. Though not physically active when we knew her, preferring to sit and watch her grandchildren playing in the streams or scampering across the fields, she was always serene and cheerful, and had a welcoming smile. She was a perfect helpmate for Thomas, running the house smoothly and apparently effortlessly while he gave all his attention to his own affairs — the business, church and civic duties.

To return to J. Gerrard & Sons, the business continued to expand steadily even though contracts were limited to an area within a five-mile radius of the works. The firm specialized in churches and by 1890 it had built six Primitive Methodist chapels (Gerrard's Chapel on Manchester Road, Swinton, was completed in 1891), one United Methodist and two Congregational churches, as well as a house for a general practitioner, Dr O'Grady, whom my wife Betty remembered because his practice was adjacent to her father's and the two worked closely together. The firm's first really big contract, £73,000, was, very appropriately, a home for inebriates built in 1902.

At the turn of the century, probably because Jonathan's son Thomas was now managing director, the company assumed a new complexion. First came the installation, in 1900, of J. Arthur Gerrard, Jonathan's youngest son, aged 25, as the fourth partner. The second was the expansion of the company by the addition of new departments. Since all four partners were basically carpenters and joiners, when contracts were submitted it was necessary to contract out much of the bricklaying, plumbing and painting. Jonathan had noted that another building company, Cubitt's, had brought under its roof a broad spectrum of subsidiary companies and, in 1901, he decided to do the same. He drew up agreements with William Richardson, the owner of a bricklaying company, and J. E. Bailey, the owner of a painting company, to incorporate their businesses in his enterprise. In return, he made Richardson a partner and the manager of the new bricklaying department and Bailey the manager of the new painting and plumbing departments. J. C. Robertson, an outstanding joiner and carpenter who had become a member of the family by marrying Jonathan's granddaughter Helen (Nellie) Mason, joined the company in the same year. It was also the year in which J. Gerrard & Sons became a private limited company. The following year the firm moved to new and larger premises on Pendlebury Road, Swinton. All the partners were non-smokers and non-drinkers, but John Robertson actually smoked when he joined the company. He used to tell his children that one Sunday Jonathan asked if he might walk home with him after the service. We do not know what he actually said to John Robertson, but we do know that he never smoked again.

When Jonathan died unexpectedly on 28 December 1907 at the age of 73 of pneumonia, caught while visiting one of his buildings under construction, he, with the help of his three sons, had transformed a one-storey joiner's shop and a four-horse stable into a thriving building enterprise. Its own buildings were valued at £25,000 and instead of turning out coffins and toilet seats he was building churches, schools, halls and fire stations.

The business, however, did not consume all his energies. For 12 years he was deeply involved in local politics and for all his life with the Church. He was drawn to politics when he became aware that some members of the Swinton and Pendlebury local council were thought to be feathering their nests at the expense of the ratepayers: pipes had cost £100 more than the market price and the council was £8000 in debt. Jonathan decided to enter the political arena and was elected to the council in 1871. His first move was to propose to the board that the 'books, plans, papers and other documents belonging to the board' should be made available to those on the board. His proposal was roundly trounced, and thrown out as being quite unnecessary. When Jonathan later tried to see the documents, he was told that they had been transferred to the City of Manchester and were not available.

Jonathan noticed that, following board meetings, other members often stayed behind after he had left. He wondered what they were discussing and decided, after leaving one meeting, to stay in the courtyard where he could look through the window and see what was transpiring. A member of the board noticed his figure flitting in and out of the shadows and, claiming that he thought he had seen a burglar, went out to the courtyard, seized Jonathan by the collar and dragged him, so he said, protesting vigorously into the boardroom. Although Jonathan said his designs were innocent and that he came willingly into the boardroom, the board declared that his actions showed he was unfit to discharge his public duties and banned him from further meetings of the board. However, Jonathan continued to make his views known by trumpeting them through the keyhole with a megaphone. His struggle to make the actions of the board public were eventually settled in his favour in a London court and, following this, he returned to Swinton to a hero's welcome. When Jonathan was first elected to the board he had 11 opponents and no supporters; when he retired 12 years later, he was chairman with 11 supporters and no opponents.

His work for the Primitive Methodist Church meant more to Jonathan than all his other achievements. Though Jane was brought up in the Primitive Methodist Church, Jonathan had been an Anglican until the age of 15, when he was converted to Methodism while attending Sunday school in a Primitive Methodist church. After he married, he and Jane attended the same church. The Primitive Methodists were followers of Hugh Bourne (1772–1852), a flamboyant, charismatic Wesleyan Methodist local preacher who delighted in open-air meetings and so riled the Wesleyans that he and his followers were expelled from the conference. The first Primitive Methodist church was opened in the Midlands in 1811. When Jonathan and Jane moved to Swinton, they found the four walks to and from their church in Wardley each Sunday (for Sunday school at 9.30 and 1.30 and for services at 2.30 and 6.00) very time consuming, so when an opportunity arose to buy a property on Manchester Road — a building that had been used by the Presbyterians — for the princely sum of £200, Jonathan bought it. The congregation later built its own church, opened free of debt in 1891, and its own Sunday school, opened in 1897. In all these activities Jonathan was the prime mover; the church for many years was known locally as Gerrard's Chapel. Jonathan was the Sunday school superintendent from 1871 until his death in 1907. The school opened with four teachers and 13 scholars; 60 years later there were 21 teachers and 253 scholars.

Looking back in 1902, Jonathan recalled, 'My mother kept a little grocery shop and served beer, and I served beer, but I resolved, when converted, not to do so. On June the 9th, next, it will be 50 years since my dear conversion.' From that date onwards, he was a staunch teetotaller. He had a strong sense of what was right and what was wrong, and was not afraid to stand up for the right. Mr Gillibrand described Jonathan as, 'a man of a quiet and unassailable character, of sterling honesty, and sterling purpose and unassailable integrity'. He liked humorous stories and had a very happy disposition, but he rarely laughed outright. My cousin Raymond tells that his mother's cleaning lady said that Jonathan used to pick her up when she was a little girl and put her on his shoulders as he carried her happily to Sunday school. In his later years it is said that he had difficulty in controlling the children.

When he died, the funeral service was held in the church he had built. His son, Thomas, sent out the following letter:

> Swinton,
> Manchester,
> January 3, 1907.

Dear Sir,

It is with sincere regret that we inform you of the death of Mr JONATHAN GERRARD, Chairman and Founder of the Company, which took place at his residence, Swinton, on Friday last, December 28th.

He had had two or three severe colds during the year, which had laid him up for a time, but was feeling very well again, when he contracted a chill while visiting one of the buildings in course of construction. Pneumonia set in, resulting in his somewhat sudden death. He had attained the age of 72 years. He had all along been a tireless worker and a man of great perseverance.

What his hand found to do, he did with his might. He was for 12 years a member of the Swinton and Pendlebury Local Board, for one year as Chairman, and was for several years on the Board of Guardians.

He was highly honoured among all who knew him as a man of unswerving loyalty to conscience, upright in life, generous to a fault, and a true friend of the poor and oppressed.

Yours sincerely,
J. GERRARD AND SONS LTD,

T. L. Gerrard, Managing Director.

Hundreds of people, including the president of the Primitive Methodist Conference, the Reverend G. Parkin, attended his funeral. The mourners left the church to the strains of Chopin's Funeral March played on the organ by his 20-year-old grandson Clement Gerrard, a future director, managing director and chairman of J. Gerrard & Sons.

When Jonathan died, Thomas Lee Gerrard was 51 years old and the managing director of J. Gerrard & Sons, which he and his brother Samuel had helped his father to build. What was Thomas's contribution to its success?

Thomas was known to our family as Grandpa, to many of our relatives as Uncle Tom, and to those who worked with him in the firm as Mr Tom. He was born on 12 December 1858 in very humble circumstances. His mother was trying to make ends meet as a weaver in Gibbs Mill, while his father, who had been an odd-job joiner, was apprenticed to a carpenter to improve his skills. Having brought up her own family, his grandmother, Mary Lee, was now helping his mother with hers so that she could go out to work. When he was old enough, he went on weekdays to the local elementary school and on Sundays to Sunday school; it was a long walk to Sunday school. When Thomas was 12 he was able to go to a new Sunday school and a new church, acquired at his father's instigation nearer to their home. When he signed on for Sunday school he was proud to know that he was the first scholar to register. The following year he stopped going to the day school, education was not compulsory after the age of 13, and started working full time for his father in the carpenter's shop, and on Sundays he started teaching in Sunday school.

In Thomas's hands the business continued to grow steadily. As it increased in size, relations became more formalized. In 1892 Jonathan had been elected chairman and in 1900 Thomas was elected overall managing director. His youngest brother, J. Arthur, became a partner six years later, in 1906. Thomas's son Clement joined the firm in 1904, and his nephew Laurie A. Gerrard in 1906. As the work of the firm had increased greatly, in 1902 they moved to new premises on Pendlebury Road. The move meant that they were not only working in new buildings but also with the latest and best equipment. Almost overnight the firm became the best equipped and most modern in the North of England. This was due in large measure to the foresight and drive of Mr Tom, coupled with the support of his new (1901) partners, Richardson and Bailey. The firm was now able to spread its wings and to tackle contracts, such as the inebriates' home, that would previously have been beyond their capability.

Mr Tom took one additional vital step; he insured the firm and all its buildings. Jonathan had never insured it, believing that the good Lord would see that it came to no harm. Grandpa's faith was every bit as strong as his father's, but he also knew that accidents could happen and he insured against them. This was fortunate because one night in April 1914, just four months before the outbreak of the First World War, the buildings caught fire. The fire, which probably began in the boiler room, started soon after midnight and, fuelled by stacks of dry timber, it was spectacular, for the whole works with the exception of the offices and stables went up in flames. Two houses, one owned by J. Arthur Gerrard, the youngest partner, and the other by one of the office staff, also went up in flames.

I can still remember Grandpa describing how he was awoken with news of the fire and how he hurried to the scene of the conflagration to see his dreams going up in smoke. But before the flames had been extinguished he and his fellow directors, along with John C. Robertson, were already drawing up plans for the new buildings.

The First World War started on 4 August. By the end of the same month Gerrards were in their new buildings with the latest equipment and were ready to play their part in the war that was expected to end all wars. Initially, hutted camps for soldiers were in special demand and camps constructed by Gerrards soon dotted the English countryside, and were even seen in France and Salonika. Around Manchester, the parts for the huts were manufactured at the works and then transported by horse-drawn lorries to the site where they were put together and the huts constructed. The camps were needed urgently, horses were slow and so Mr Tom decided to use a motor lorry. Motor lorries or trucks soon replaced the horse-drawn lorries. The firm also switched from wooden to metal scaffolding and when, after the war (1929), Gerrards obtained the contract to build the Royal Hospital School in Holbrook, Suffolk, they used for the first time a 240-foot Insley mast with a 40-foot arm capable of lifting weights up to three tons, in the construction of the central 200-foot tower. The school was their first major construction outside the Manchester area.

Grandpa often said that it was harder to keep a large concern going than to build one up from scratch, but he managed to keep winning new contracts to keep his expanding firm busy. At one time it was said that Gerrards had built half of Manchester and owned the other half. This was a pardonable exaggeration, but I remember seeing billboards with J. Gerrard & Sons in bold letters all over Manchester. The growth of the firm is illustrated by a few simple figures. When Jonathan left Speakman in 1867, taking part of the business with him, Speakman had an annual turnover of £25,000 and employed between 20 and 25 men. When his son, Mr Tom, died 70 years later, in 1936, the firm had an annual turnover of £11 million and employed between 10,000 and 12,000 men.

In addition to his work for the firm, Grandpa was president both of the North Western Federation of Building Trade Employers and of the Manchester, Salford and District Building Trade Employers' Association. But his interests spread beyond the business world, for in addition to serving on committees on nursing services, education and the employment of juveniles, he was a member of the Lancashire County Council (from 1919) and later a Lancashire County justice of the peace and county alderman. He was also keenly interested in politics. He was a staunch Liberal, and a long time supporter of Lloyd George. I think he knew that Lloyd George was a bit of a scoundrel, but he continued to admire and support the man whom many called the 'Welsh Wizard'.

Grandpa was also a very loyal supporter of the Primitive Methodist branch of the Methodist Church, especially of the church in Swinton, which he had helped his father to build. He became a local preacher, preaching for the most part in the ten churches in the circuit. He kept a careful record of his sermons, in shorthand, making a note of the church in which he preached, the text and subject of his sermon, the number in the congregation and any comments made to him by his listeners when he shook their hands as they left the church. He was never ostentatious in his views, and if you had met him in the street, for example, you would have soon learnt that he was a successful businessman, but you would never have suspected that he was also a local preacher in great demand. When he started keeping a record of his sermons, in 1910, he was preaching half a dozen times a year, but from 1923 to 1933 he was preaching at least once, and often twice, every Sunday. He also played a part in the council chambers of his church; for one year he was vice-president of the Primitive Methodist Church, the highest office a layman could hold. He was a strong supporter of the move to unite the three Churches — Wesleyan, United and Primitive — and represented the

Primitive Methodist connection at this time. He was treasurer for many years of Hartley College, where my father and other aspiring ministers were taught, and he did his best to provide them with better salaries.

At home Grandpa was always cheerful and always had a fund of amusing stories, which he wrote down in a little book he kept in his waistcoat pocket. One story I remember was of a little boy who came home from school crying because the other children were calling him 'big head'. 'Ne'er mind lad,' his father consoled him, 'There's now't in it.' This was the only story with an unkind flavour I ever heard him tell; two more typical stories, handed down to him by his father are included at the end of this chapter.

My grandfather was generous to a fault. I have never seen him happier than when he was writing cheques for charities. In England at that time, to receive income tax rebates on donations it was necessary to promise to give the same amount for seven years. Grandpa was also very generous to his family. I am sure that he paid for my education, for my own father could not have afforded a boarding school. I am sure he helped other grandchildren. At Christmas he gave all his children and grandchildren the same present, a new £1 note in a Christmas card. A £1 note was a lot of money for a child in those days.

Grandpa always started his day by throwing open the windows, except when it was foggy, and breathing in the fresh Swinton air. He would then do his morning exercises. After breakfast, he walked, with short quick steps, to the works a mile or two away. His only other exercise was lawn bowling on the well-manicured lawn. On this lawn anyone who could bowl was welcome to bowl with Grandpa.

Grandpa never smoked and never drank alcohol. He was frugal in his eating habits and said that, after a meal, one should always feel ready to eat it all over again. When he had a meal downtown, when on business for example, he would return to Norfield delighted because he had spent less than a shilling on his simple lunch. He had one weakness, and that was Mars Bars. When he later developed angina and a meal or exercise could trigger his chest pains, he would often finish a meal with a Mars Bar, saying, 'I might as well be hung for a sheep as a lamb.' Another aphorism he frequently repeated and practised was, 'Look after the pennies and the pounds will look after themselves.'

Grandpa always went to bed at 9.00 p.m. If there were visitors at that time he would take his gold watch out of his waistcoat pocket, flip it open, look at it and say, 'It's nine o'clock and time for bed. Early to bed, early to rise makes a man healthy, wealthy and wise.' His visitors would depart and the rest of us would troop upstairs to bed. There was no television, let alone a late night movie.

He enjoyed good health, but was handicapped by angina for the last year or so of his life and was trying to regain his health while holidaying in Scotland when he died on 9 August 1936. The Swinton church and schoolroom could not accommodate all who came to his funeral. He had been a great businessman, a great servant of his community and church, and a great father and grandfather. The Reverend Rutter, who delivered the memorial address, said that all in all Alderman Gerrard could be described as Mr Greatheart. A font was later given to the church by his family. On that occasion my Aunt Winifred, his eldest daughter, compared Jonathan with Thomas, but what she said we do not know.

Two letters, written by my grandfather are in our family archives. These letters say more about him than I ever could, and are included at the end of this book. He was a man of great integrity who was loved and respected by everyone, by those who worked for him or with him, by those in Swinton who knew him, by his church, which he served so faithfully, and by his family.

He was a great inspiration to me. I was sorry not to be at his funeral. I missed it because I was hitchhiking and walking in Germany during my first summer vacation from Oxford.

* * *

Now let us turn to the stories told originally by Jonathan and Jane and repeated many times by Thomas.

The first story and Jane's rejoinder were first told to their family on Christmas Eve 1899. Thomas, who was forever repeating them, enjoyed them so much that he always chuckled long before he reached the punch line. Jonathan adored Jane but liked running down women. Jane loved Jonathan but enjoyed denigrating men.

* * *

A man married a farmer's daughter, but after a time he became dissatisfied with her because she always wanted her own way. The man went to her father and asked him to take his daughter back. The farmer said that his daughter was only like other women because they were all alike. The husband could not believe it, so the farmer said he would convince him. He would give him a basket of eggs and two horses, a black one and a grey one, and ask him to visit homes asking who was the master of the house. When he found a house in which the master was a man he was to leave a horse; and when he found one in which the woman was the master he was to leave an egg. Off the man went, thinking that he would soon be rid of his horses. However, as he drew towards the first house he heard the woman giving her husband such a dressing down and such a lecture that he thought it was no use making enquiries there, so he left an egg. He went on and called at home after home, but it was no use, the women were always master and his basket of eggs was getting emptier and emptier, and he still had the horses. At last he came to a house where peace and tranquillity reigned. He told the man and his wife his mission and they both agreed that the man was the master, so the visitor was pleased to leave them one of his horses. But a dispute arose. The husband looked over the horses, examined their teeth and felt their legs and declared the black horse to be much the better horse. The woman thought the grey one was the better. Her husband tried to show her different, but it was no use. At length the husband said that he knew the black one was the better, but for the sake of peace and quiet his wife should have her own way. To their chagrin the man who brought them the horses said he was sorry he would have to leave them an egg and not a horse.

* * *

Jane took up the challenge, and told her story, the story of 'Dick wi't leg'.

* * *

Dick was a tailor with a wooden leg who was rather fond of drink. He was noted for cribbing cloth whenever he had cloth to make into a suit. The parson at the church wanted a suit made from some good cloth that had been given to the church so that he could go into mourning after the death of one of the parishioners. The parson wanted 'Dick wi't leg' to make the suit. However, because he also wanted to ensure that Dick did not diddle him out of some of the cloth, he kept a strict eye on him. The Sunday after the suit was finished, the parson appeared in church wearing his new suit, but imagine his astonishment when he saw Dick wearing an identical suit. Somehow Dick had managed to double cut the cloth. In other words, while he was cutting out the parson's suit he cut out a second one for himself.

2

Why Africa?

During the lifetimes of my great grandparents and grandparents, and while my father was growing up, British newspapers were full of stories from Africa. People were intensely interested in the lives and travels of great explorers like Mungo Park, Speke and Burton. The liberal-minded wanted Britain to spearhead the effort to abolish slavery and the slave trade; and those of evangelical outlook wanted to bring the millions of heathen Africans into the Christian fold. Since the first years of the century Christian missionaries had been going out to the frontiers of the Cape Colony. All these different interests and ambitions became concentrated in the life and work of David Livingstone who lived from 1813 to 1873.

Livingstone went out as a medical missionary to a long-established mission among the Sotho tribes near the northern frontier of Cape Colony. From there he set out to explore the geography and tribes of the interior. The papers he sent back to England describing the lives of the tribes and the geography and natural features of the country were recognized as solid contributions to the literature on South Africa. Between 1842 and 1853 he went further north. He penetrated the Zambezi basin and was the first white man to see the Victoria Falls. He crossed Africa from coast to coast, from Mozambique in the east to Angola in the west and back again. In 1859 he established a mission on the shores of Lake Nyasa.

Livingstone also sent back to Britain detailed accounts of the

Arab slave traders. He described how they had penetrated from the east coast as far as the Congo basin. He deplored their power and influence, and found that they forced him to abandon the mission on Lake Nyasa. In the eyes of British people he became the heroic Christian crusader.

When he set out in 1865 to discover the source of the Nile, editors in both Britain and the United States kept their readers on tenterhooks. For years it seemed that there was no news of their hero, so in 1871 the *New York Herald* sent one of its most flamboyant reporters, Henry Morton Stanley, to find him. This he did at Ujiji in East Africa, on the eastern shore of Lake Tanganyika, and the words of his greeting, 'Dr Livingstone I presume,' were reported round the world. Although he was ill, Livingstone was not to be persuaded to leave. Faithful servants stayed with him and when he died they buried his heart in African soil and brought his body back to be buried in Westminster Abbey, in a great Victorian funeral in April 1874.

The scene was now set for the 'scramble for Africa' among the great powers. In South Africa, Cecil Rhodes, with his millions made from diamond mining and his political power in the Cape Colony, envisioned a road from Cairo to the Cape under British control. This meant preventing the Germans, Belgians and Portuguese from extending their influence in the interior. He did everything he could to encourage British settlers and traders to penetrate the Zambezi basin. In 1889 he founded his Chartered British South African Company to secure control of and develop the lands that now comprise Zimbabwe and Zambia. These territories soon became known as Southern Rhodesia and Northern Rhodesia respectively.

The British South African Company remained influential in Northern Rhodesia and continued to oversee the land reserved for Africans until 1924, when Northern Rhodesia formally became a British protectorate under crown trusteeship, looked after by the Colonial Office in London. My parents went out in 1915 and their letters for the first seven years were stamped with British South African Company stamps overprinted with the word Rhodesia.

I think that there can be no doubt that my father was inspired by the life and work of David Livingstone, for he became the first medical missionary to be sent abroad by the Primitive Methodist Church. Church-going British people felt a responsibility for the Africans who lived in the new territories that had come under British or South African rule during the previous 30 or 40 years. Church leaders, however, also felt a responsibility for the missionaries working in remote areas of Africa, often with their wives and families and far from any organized medical help. With this in mind, the Methodist Missionary Society decided to send my father and mother to African reservations in southern Northern Rhodesia. This was just as well because it was exactly where they most wanted to go.

We left my father and mother boarding the Blue Funnel Liner, the *Aeneas*, in Liverpool on 3 April 1915. Their families came to see them off, none the happier as it was wartime and they were sailing under escort. My parents were supremely happy, for my father was doing what he had always wanted to do and my mother wanted to be with him. As they sat in their cabin surrounded by flowers and gazing at the top of their wedding cake, they wondered what the future held in store. For the time being, they were on their second honeymoon and, fortunately, they were both good sailors. There were not many passengers on board, but they were friendly. During the daytime there were deck sports and in the evening they dined at the captain's table. Their trip was uneventful, though on several occasions the word got around that there were enemy submarines in the vicinity. They learnt later that all their silver and wedding presents were lost when the ship in which they were being transported was torpedoed.

My mother later described their arrival to my son, Jonathan:

> The view of Table Mountain and Cape Town as we approached delighted us, as did the variety of people on

the streets. In Cape Town we boarded the northbound passenger train on which we spent five days. There was one anxious moment for me, when Bert dashed out of the train at the last minute to buy some of the delicious fruit that we had seen being sold so cheaply in the station, as I hung out of the carriage window to watch for his return, it was with great relief that I saw him board the guard's van. I was having visions of being stranded in Africa, not knowing a soul, and my purse in Bert's pocket. All was well, and we settled down in our comfortable compartment with lots of books and papers. It was not long before I learnt that, whatever Bert had or had not, he always had a book in his pocket.

Meals on the train were excellent. We decided to have breakfast and dinner in the dining car, and to lunch in our compartment on fruit and wedding cake. I suppose we were too shy to pass more than the time of day with other passengers. We enjoyed watching the scenery as the train wound its way slowly up the plateau. Whenever it stopped for any length of time we, and the other passengers, walked outside to stretch our legs.

Travelling through the Kalahari was a dirty business. In spite of special dust screens over the windows, coloured stewards came more than once with dust pan and brush to clean up the compartment. They made up our bed at night and were attentive and courteous.

In Bulawayo the train spent the day. We saw the wide streets Cecil Rhodes had planned, wide enough for a span of oxen to be turned, but the place seemed hot and bare, and we were glad to be back in our familiar compartment in the train. As Bulawayo has grown it has become more attractive with its tree lined streets and variety of shops, parks etc.

The highlight of the journey was seeing the Victoria Falls, full at the end of the rainy season, and going over the wonderful bridge before we reached Livingstone, the

29

most important city in Northern Rhodesia. Many times during the journey north we recalled places and events in missionary history. We finally got off the train in Kafue, situated north on one of the Zambezi's large tributaries, and put up at a small hotel there. We must have looked young, pale and green, and one hard baked settler as good as told us that we weren't likely to last long in so rough a country.

To our great comfort and joy there was a note at Kafue to tell us that we were expected, and that a trader would contact us and take us by river from Kafue to Kasenga. He arrived the next day and bought stores. There had been high jinks at the hotel. The men, who had had lonely weeks on isolated farms, drank more than they should, and we were told had a merry time dancing on the tables in the hotel. There was only one woman there, the proprietor's wife.

After a couple of nights there, we travelled down the Kafue in three boats lashed together. I believe that the middle one with a cabin would have been top heavy on its own. One of the boats was given over to several Africans, a cheerful crowd. Our cabin had two camp beds with mosquito nets; we also had deck chairs and a small camp table under an awning. In addition to the supplies of food brought by the owner, tea, coffee, sugar, flour etc., chickens were bought from Africans at sixpence each, whenever the boat was tied up for the night. The river was in flood, and sometimes almost doubled in its tracks. We saw little villages on patches of high ground and small companies of Africans. Crocodiles basked in the sun on exposed places, and sometimes the snout of a hippo was visible. From time to time we saw Africans in 'dugout' boats, added out of solid tree trunks, gracefully propelling from a standing position. They looked very precarious to us. The country was very flat, known in our time as the 'Kafue Flats', hardly a tree was visible. There was continuous sunshine throughout the day. Occasionally, on the north bank across the river, we had glimpses of low hills.

In this manner we travelled along for four or five days until we reached Kasenga, our destination. On the bank was a company of Africans to greet us, no doubt forewarned by the bush telegraph. One of the special things that stuck in our minds was, after greetings were over, the Africans said, '*Twa fwa nkoshi*'. We are dead from meat hunger. No doubt they were heartily sick of the mealie (maize, Indian corn) porridge, which was their staple diet, eked out by sour milk and occasional wild spinach from the bush a few miles away. To greet us with the Africans was an industrious missionary, a South African, who was transferred to another of our mission stations after a few months, and a European nurse, Miss Barlow, who had come from England the previous year. She was learning the language, and lived with us happily during our first year. She was a good talker, we were shy at that time, and found her an asset when the odd trader called. There was a Christian African teacher, called Joshua, who could speak English, who was brought from South Africa by the Rev E. W. Smith when the latter was allowed north after being detained by the Boer War. Joshua was a great help when interpreting at first. He later married Nachiloba, the very attractive young daughter of Paulo who had helped Edwin Smith in the preparation of his great work, *The Ila Speaking Peoples*. We were sorry not to meet Edwin Smith, whom we passed on the high seas, on his way home to take up the appointment of Secretary of the British and Foreign Bible Society. His wife, Namusa, (mother of kindness), was much loved. Not only did Mr Smith leave us an excellent bungalow, gauzed to keep the mosquitoes out, but a well laid out garden with orange, lemon and grape fruit trees. These no doubt helped us to keep well.

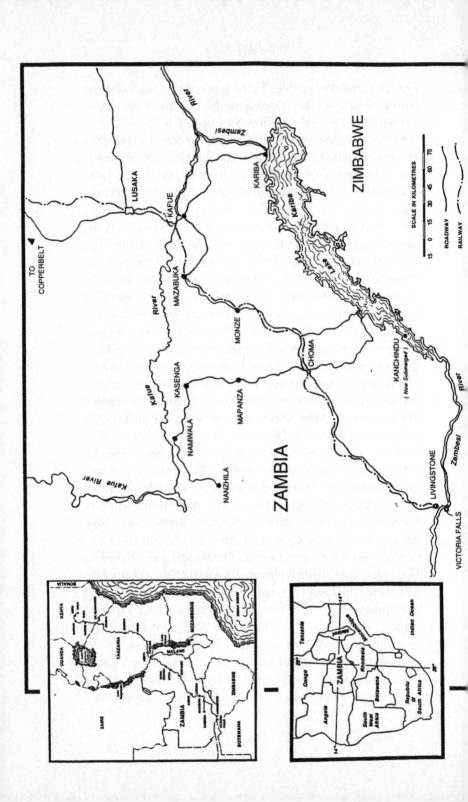

During the rainy season mosquitoes were like snow outside the house after dark, breeding in the nearby flats that the river flooded. Vegetables were difficult to grow. Our groceries came twice a year, brought from Monze on the railway 100 miles away by ox-wagon, a seven day journey. We took our daily dose of quinine, 5 grains.

We settled down very happily in our new home, and began to learn the language. I had a good ear, and my husband's great interest was in the different structure of the language. He really needed to talk, both for his medical work and his preaching, and we were both eager to get to know the people. And how kind and well mannered they were when we must have made many great howlers, saying one thing when another was meant, due to wrong inflection. Solomon, Mrs Smith's old cook, a cheerful man about my husband's age, who had served more than one missionary, was our cook and friend, and a keen local preacher on Sundays. I remember him once saying that I 'katached' him, bothered him. This, looking back, I surely did, being young and ignorant and not understanding. He continued to serve us faithfully, and his church and family for some years, till he helped another missionary's wife. He was still alive, though almost blind, when we visited him in the care of his son Edwin, in 1969, who still writes to us. We were all mutually delighted to see each other. His wife, Ruti (Ruth) who had helped to clean up after John's and Kathleen's births, had died some years previously.

3

Customs and Beliefs in the Baila and Ameru

When my parents reached Kasenga they found themselves in a society that, for many generations, had had its own well-established code of conduct and articles of belief. These had been passed down to the people by word of mouth, for they had no written language. The men, women and children knew what was expected of them and did their best to maintain the traditions their forebears had passed on to them. My parents spent their first 19 years (1915–34) in Zambia and their next seven years (1934–41) in Kenya. In Zambia they spent their first 16 years at a mission station called Kasenga, where they served a scattered population on the high grasslands bordering the Kafue River, north of the Victoria Falls. They spent their last three years in Zambia at Kanchindu on the banks of the Zambezi River below the Victoria Falls. Kanchindu no longer exists, for it and many other little villages disappeared under the waters of Lake Kariba when the Kariba Dam was built. In Kenya my parents lived at Maua in lush, hilly country, serving a thickly populated region 300 kilometres north of Nairobi, near Meru and not far from Mount Kenya.

The lifestyles of the Africans in Northern Rhodesia and Kenya were in some ways very different. The Ila surrounding Kasenga were mainly cattle herders living in scattered villages growing and mostly living on maize (Indian corn), whereas the

Ameru around Maua herded mainly goats with some cattle and had a much more varied diet of fruit, vegetables, corn and millet. The structure of their societies, however, and their traditional beliefs were very similar, with one big difference, the Ameru practised female circumcision whereas the Ila did not. Edwin Smith had studied the customs of Ila people, Dr Stanley Bell, who followed my father at Maua, studied the Ameru. In describing their customs I have been guided by Dr Bell.[1]

The Ameru lived in villages headed by a chief and governed by a council of elders, all men. The men usually had two or more wives. A brief description of their customs and traditions follows.

The great desire of all women was to marry and have children. When a woman married, she was provided with a hut of her own, each wife with a separate hut. Near the end of her first pregnancy, a wife's husband would build her a temporary hut near the village, to which she, accompanied by several older women including her husband's (but not her own) mother, would go when her labour started. After the delivery of the baby, the cord would be cut, either with a sharp blade of grass or with a sharp stone. The baby was then put to the breast. In addition to the breast, it was customary for the mother, from an early age, to chew food, such as a banana and, after masticating it thoroughly, to pass it on to her baby by pushing it into its mouth with her tongue. The baby would be wrapped in a piece of goatskin or blanket and would sleep with its mother, nestled up against her warm body. The mother would remain in her temporary hut for a week and would be brought food each day by her attendants. A week after the baby's birth she would move into her own permanent home. In the case of a first pregnancy, this would be a new hut. It was then that the baby would be washed for the first

---

1. 'Clinical Epidemiology in Meru District, Kenya', by Stanley Bell MD, DTM&H. Thesis submitted for the degree of Doctor of Medicine, University of Durham, January 1955.

time. While continuing to breastfeed, when the mother returned to her own hut she would assume her normal duties of tending the garden, going to market, and fetching wood and water while her husband's mother watched over the baby. Baby boys were welcomed more eagerly than baby girls, singletons more than twins, and fraternal twins more than identical twins. The child's hair would not be cut until he or she was two years old, at which point the father's mother would shave the toddler's head, leaving only a little tuft of hair on the crown. Until this time the parents were expected to refrain from intercourse. The little boys often wandered about naked, though from the age of three they usually wore a cloak of goat's skin. The little boys helped to look after the goats and cattle.

Little girls were treated just as lovingly as little boys. They also wandered round naked until they were two to three years old, when they would be given a goatskin skirt cut away at the front and sides. When they approached puberty, they would wear a garment made of skin that covered their bodies and was fixed above the breasts. At this time their ear lobes would be pierced and a thorn inserted to keep the opening patent. The opening was stretched gradually by inserting pieces of wood of increasing sizes. Girls also wore beads and bangles around their ankles and neck and hanging from their ears. Long before this, as soon as they could walk steadily, they would be given a gourd to fill when they accompanied their mothers each day to the spring or stream to collect water. They also quickly learnt to collect twigs to carry home for the fire.

Initiation at puberty was probably the most important moment in the lives of boys and girls. For the week before the ceremony, groups of boys who were due to be circumcised would walk in single file wearing feathered headdresses and strings of bamboo sticks hanging over their backs and chests, singing as they walked through the villages, while girls sang and danced to cheer them on their way. The witch doctor, the tribe's traditional healer and spiritual guide, would choose the day for circumcision. Early in the morning a group of warriors would take the boys to a stream, where they would wash themselves before returning to a nearby open grassy place where they would sit in a row, stark naked, with their knees drawn up and widely separated. Groups of women would be singing and dancing nearby, but would be shielded from the candidates, who might number one or two but who often numbered more, by a screen of older men and warriors. Each candidate was also supported by two warriors, who would kneel behind him and hold his shoulders. When all was ready, two youths would call the circumciser. The latter, who would be an older man wearing a headdress and ornaments and with his face painted with white chalk, would run towards the crowd accompanied by two assistants. After one or two preliminary dashes towards the dancing women, who would run away, the circumciser and his two assistants would enter the circle in which the boys were sitting. One of the attendants would then open a snail gourd from which he would take a small knife to give to the circumciser. The latter would then approach the first candidate and, very deftly, take the foreskin, cut a neat hole through the upper part of it, pull it down and then thread the head of the penis through the slit, like pushing a button through a button hole, nicking the dependent skin on either side and pinning the flaps together with an inch long thorn provided by his second assistant. The circumciser would then move on to the second boy. The whole procedure would last less than a minute; it sometimes took only a few seconds. There was little if any bleeding.

As soon as the operation was over, helpers and elders from his clan would cover the boy so completely with pieces of banana bark that he would scarcely be visible. A closely packed group of men and youths who surrounded him would then together perform a slow shuffling dance to the boy's own village, chanting all the time, while the women raised screams of pleasure as they danced around them. The boy would then be taken to his mother's hut, which she had vacated. On the first day, the warriors who supported him while he was being circumcised would remove the thorn from the foreskin. Two or three days later, his friends would take him to his own hut. In the not so distant past he would have remained in this hut for six months, but when my parents were at Maua, it would be for only three to six weeks. During this time he would be taught how to treat his relatives, elders and other warriors, and receive instructions on the customs relating to sexual behaviour.

When the time came for him to leave his mother's hut, his father would be asked to give him a new name. His father usually suggested two or three names and the boy would choose the one he thought best pleased and honoured his father. This was the name to which he would respond in the days ahead. When the time came for him to leave his hut, his mother would shave him completely and, amid great rejoicing, he would move into a communal hut with other warriors of his age. While living in this hut he was now expected to keep physically fit. He would also attend dances and, when he did so, he had to dress up. His hair would be treated with red clay mixed with fat to form a pigtail and he might also wear a lion's mane round his face, bells on his legs below the knees and round his ankles and in one hand a spear, with a ball of feathers on its tip to make clear his peaceful intentions, and in the other a decorated shield. His body would be decorated with chalk.

The young warriors had considerable sexual licence and in the evenings they would visit villages in which the girls were known to them. If a warrior were invited into a hut and the girl was with her mother, the latter would go out, leaving the couple undisturbed for the night. The girls were often still immature. As far as is known no precautions to prevent pregnancy were taken, but pregnancies were usually avoided, for warriors were not expected to cause unplanned pregnancies. It was thought to be a catastrophe if an uncircumcised or unmarried woman fell pregnant and, in such an event, she would usually hastily be circumcised and/or married. In England at that time, the women were just hastily married.

These visits often led to a warrior deciding to ask a young woman's father if he might marry his daughter. If the father consented, a 'bride price' would be negotiated and the time of its payment agreed. The initial instalment was usually paid before the marriage and the final one after the birth of the first baby. These arrangements were agreed to verbally, which sometimes later led to disputes over the details of the agreement. Such disputes were often brought to the attention of the elders whose judgement was final. Children were regarded as the father's property and when marriages broke down the father always took custody of them. A junior warrior in due course became a senior and then later an elder.

Elders formed the repository of wisdom in the community. When men showed evidence of maturity and sound judgement, they would be elected to the council, or even the powerful council, the *Njeri*, to share in its deliberations. An elder would wear a goatskin cloak. His village would consist of his own hut, the huts and stores of his wives and an enclosure for the goats. It was considered unlucky for him to mention the number of his children. His food, which his wives prepared for him, usually contained plenty of meat, for his larder was regularly fortified with goats received from the litigants he had fined or as bride prices when his daughters married. He did not cultivate his garden, this was the duty of his wives, but when new land was prepared, he would help to clear the underbrush, hew down trees and prepare the soil. He also looked after his yams, his *miraa* trees, of which more anon, and his hives; these were usually placed in the fork of a tree. All these were passed on from one generation to the next. His wives were responsible for brewing his beer from fermented honey or cane sugar. In old age, the retired elders would revert to a second childhood, tending the goats and cattle with the young boys.

According to Ameru custom, no child should be born of an uncircumcised woman. Female circumcision was therefore

something to which all girls had to submit.[2] For a period of
two to four weeks before the time of initiation, the girls would
be relieved of their usual duties. They would be decorated in
their finest clothes and given a thin leather skirt, shortened in
front, and an elaborate feathered headdress. Groups of girls,
like the boys, would wander round the villages in which they
were known, dancing and singing as they went. Dances were
held during the evenings for two to three days before the
actual ceremony, to which young warriors and older women
came. On the day of the initiation, women glamorously
dressed in their best clothes would begin to gather soon after
sunrise. The older women had broad bands of white chalk
across their heads to show their joy and support for the girls
who were going to be circumcised. My mother, who witnessed
such a ceremony, described it as follows.

> On Friday morning Naomi and I went to see a girl who
> lives quite close to us circumcised. The girl was at school
> at Meru, but was brought home for the occasion. No
> men were allowed to see the ceremony. There was much
> singing and dancing by girls and women before the oper-
> ation. The girl then cast off her garment, sat down on a
> clean banana leaf, and was held very tightly by two
> other girls, and the circumciser did her deed with an axe
> head taken from a filthy bag. The girl was not allowed
> to cry or look sad. She was given just about a minute
> after the operation to sit. She was then made to stand
> up. Her legs were quivering, and blood was trickling
> down them. She showed herself to the company, and
> then walked off to her own hut where she would be
> confined and fed for about three months. When I asked
> some of the women if she wouldn't have a lot of pain,

---

2. My father said that any attempt by missionaries to ban the custom of
   female circumcision only emptied the churches.

they said she would be all right again in five days. One wonders how such a strange custom originated.

Dr Bell, in his thesis written a few years after my parents left Maua, said that the circumciser used a knife and made three incisions, the first removed the head of the clitoris and the next two the labia minora. In some instances part of the labia majora may also be removed.

On the day following the circumcision, the women who supported her came, accompanied by others, to wash her. It was from them that she learned what role she would be expected to play when she married. While in the hut she would be brought fattening foods. Once her wounds had healed, she would receive potential suitors in the evenings and at such times her mother would go to another hut. At this time, if one suitor paid particular attention to her then negotiations between the two families would begin. Formerly, the young woman would leave her hut when she went with her bridegroom to his village. In Dr Bell's time, however, it was becoming commoner for her to return to her own village before arrangements were made for her to marry.

After the initiation ceremony some girls kept their original name, whereas others chose a new name when they left their village to move into the husband's. A newly married woman tended to avoid eggs and fowl in her diet, for it was believed that they militated against pregnancy. Also, she did not wash regularly, but from time to time would go to a nearby stream to wash while other young women poured water over her. However, she never washed her 'clothes'. Intercourse was encouraged during the ten days following the end of her menstrual flow and was avoided for two years after the birth of a baby. Girls, from a very early age, were taught to carry on their backs very heavy loads, supported by a strap round their foreheads. Loads weighed up to 120 pounds and were often carried for long distances. Her duties included tending the garden, carrying produce to and from the market, and bringing wood and water to the village. If her husband had a large garden and she had a baby and possibly other children to look after, she would not be averse to her husband looking for a second wife with whom she could share the work. A wife of marriageable age who had lost her husband was taken as a wife by her first husband's brother. If she were too old to bear children she would probably go to live with one of her sons.

Beliefs and Taboos

The Ameru, like Africans elsewhere, had a very strong belief in the spiritual world, and any disease that afflicted them was ascribed to the anger of ancestors in the spiritual world. They avoided contact with excreta, for they thought it was harmful and for this reason they did not like communal latrines; they defecated in the bush, avoiding their own and other people's faeces. For the same reason they avoided contact with the dead. If anyone were ill and seemed about to die, he or she would be placed in a temporary hut some distance from the village and, for as long as the person remained alive, food would be brought to him or her. When the person died the hut would be pulled down over the body; the hyenas did the rest. The government was trying to make them bury their dead, but it was an uphill battle. It was difficult to persuade nurses in hospitals to handle either faeces or the dead, and those who did undertake this work were often from the lowest social orders and had to be paid 'danger' money.

Miraa, beer and snuff

At one time, only the elders and their guests chewed *miraa* or drank beer, though all adults, men and women, took snuff. *Miraa* was obtained from the bark of twigs from the *miraa* tree. Trees were the property of elders. The bark contains an alkaloid, which, according to a government analyst in Nairobi, has some of the properties of ephedrine and some of cocaine. Chewing it takes away the appetite and relieves fatigue. The truck drivers who drove from Nairobi to Ethiopia during the Second World War used *miraa*. Formerly, its use was restricted to elders, but it is now indulged in by all and sundry, especially young men, and is the source of a lucrative trade between Meru and Nairobi, and Nairobi and Saudi Arabia. As with *miraa*, only the elders who controlled the amount of beer brewed, and their guests with whom they shared it, would consume beer. Today, however, beer is freely available and, when used to excess, adds to the disruption of the family. Snuff, carried in little gourd containers, is shared by all, men and women, and appears to be harmless.

* * *

Kasenga, the mission where my father and mother found themselves, was situated on a low rise not far from the south bank of the Kafue River. This river is one of the Zambezi's largest tributaries and, after meandering in a leisurely way across the high veld, it plunges into the Zambezi valley to join the great river nearly 400 kilometres below the Victoria Falls and 40 kilometres below the Kariba Dam. The village of Kasenga was a few miles from the river itself. During the rainy season, in the summer, the river overflowed its banks and, for many miles, flooded the surrounding veld. At these times the mission was inaccessible unless one was prepared to wade knee deep, and sometimes waist deep, through miles of water. At the mission station my parents took over the small bungalow, well gauzed to keep out the mosquitoes, left by their predecessor Edwin Smith.

Edwin Smith was a remarkable man. His father had been a missionary in South Africa and Edwin was born there, at Aliwal North, in 1876. He returned to England for his education at Elmfield in York, where my father and uncle Clement also went. In 1897, he was accepted for the ministry and, in the following year, returned to South Africa as a missionary to Basutoland. In 1902 he led the pioneering mission to the Baila, establishing the mission station at Kasenga. There he put the Baila language into a written form, compiled a grammar and dictionary and translated most of the New Testament. With Captain Dale he co-authored a monumental two-volume book, *The Ila-Speaking People of Northern Rhodesia*. He returned to England in 1915 and my parents were disappointed to miss him when their boats crossed on the high seas. He served for a year as a chaplain to the armed forces in France. In 1916 he was seconded to the British and Foreign Bible Society, which he served with distinction for 23 years. After retiring, he spent four fruitful years with the Negro Colleges in the United States, fostering African Studies. Africa remained his lifelong passion. He also wrote more than 20 books. *The Ila-speaking People of Northern Rhodesia* was a milestone in anthropology and his *Aggrey of Africa*, written with great understanding, was widely read; I still have a copy on my bookshelf. He received many honours, including the silver medal of the Royal African Society and an honorary doctorate of Divinity from the University of Toronto. He was a remarkably energetic, gifted and productive person, and he left the bungalow, with the orange, lemon and grapefruit trees he had planted, for my parents. He died in 1957 at the age of 81.

My mother planted a garden by the river where she grew vegetables and maize — Indian corn — the staple component of the African diet in that district. Fresh water was brought from the river to their house each day in a big metal drum drawn by oxen. The mission station had two houses, one, already mentioned, for my parents, and one for Miss Barlow, a lively nurse who was never lost for a word. The station also had a dispensary, three schools, one in Kasenga and two in nearby villages, and three houses for the three African teachers. One of these, Joshua, whom Edwin Smith had brought from South Africa, was the only African who could speak English. The station also employed a cook, Solomon, inherited from Edwin Smith, six African preachers and ten Africans to do daily maintenance work on the mission. The dispensary and my father served an area of more than 3500 square kilometres containing 24 villages.

Although Kasenga itself was isolated — it took five days to reach Kafue 160 kilometres to the east where the railway crossed the river of the same name and three days to reach the nearest mission station but when the various sects came together at conferences, Anglican, Catholic, Seventh Day Adventist, Presbyterian and Methodist missionaries were represented. The various missions and missionaries came from England, Holland, France and the United States and they all had different approaches. One, for example, had a small station but concentrated on training evangelists (of whom he had 30) to send into the surrounding villages; in this way he had managed to increase his fold by 1000 members. The Catholics had the most sophisticated station. They not only had priests but also bricklayers, carpenters, farmers and cooks, as well as a reputation for being very kind and hospitable to all who visited them. My own father enjoyed the company of them all, but obviously kept in particularly close touch with his Methodist colleagues, the Shaws, Prices, Fells, Buckleys and Slaters, not only because they were all working together, but also because their wives all came to him for the last two months of their pregnancies and did not return to their homes until their babies were well and gaining weight. My mother also got to know them intimately, for though she was not a trained nurse she was one of the first to have a baby (me) in Africa and knew the sort of problems that arose. Oddly enough, relationships seem to have been very formal in those days, for my parents always referred in their letters to their colleagues, apart from the Slaters, as Mr or Mrs so and so. The Slaters were always called Arthur and Pearl.

My father's task at the mission was to look after the dispensary, deal with medical and surgical emergencies, supervise the work of the schools, train teachers and preachers, and make regular surveys of the villages in his district in order to get to know and win the confidence of the chiefs. Without the help of the chiefs, the children would be kept working in the fields and away from their classrooms and sick patients would continue to go to their own witch doctors. To do all these things he and my mother had first to learn the language. This they did very successfully and it played a great part in winning the hearts of the Baila people. Their teacher was Joshua aided by me, for when I learnt to talk I was fluently bilingual and was sometimes able to help my parents.

Ten years after my father first came to Kasenga, he put his thoughts on learning the language down on paper. He was marooned at the time by torrential rains and floods, which had made the road to Kasenga impassable. He wrote:

> The missionary is usually very handicapped in preaching the gospel in a foreign tongue. He may know enough of the language to give the essence of his message without gross grammatical errors, but his limited vocabulary debars him often that freedom of expression and variety of illustration, that are so helpful and necessary when constantly occupying a pulpit. Further, with the best will in the world to speak correctly, his accent remains foreign, and must often make it difficult for his hearers to follow him. Constant practice, quick ears and an ability to imitate, added to some training in phonetics, are necessary if he is to gain a freedom of speech easily followed by his congregation.
>
> I was fortunate to be confined in Kafue with a student who lived in a village only ten kilometres from Kasenga and whom I knew well, as I had treated him for wounds to his arm, which he had received in an attack on some lions. One of the words we tackled was *kubanda*. It has two meanings: to name and to trample down. Shaamwali said they were different words; one was *kubanda* and the other was simply *kubanda*. What was one to make of that? Well, there was a difference, but it was only one of intonation. And there are many words in Baila with only that

difference. Not only so, but each word has its own intonation. Often Shaamwali was puzzled by a word I gave
him. When he tumbled to what it was, it seemed I had
given it the wrong intonation, a little difference in pitch.

The Baila, like all the Bantu, have a great wealth of
proverbs and proverbial sayings. To know them and to
be able to quote them aptly, whether preaching or in
other circumstances, is a great gain. Some of those
Shaamwali gave me are as follows.

'A bad thing knows the mouth.' That is, taste a thing
before you condemn it.

'The morrow brings other things.' You don't know
what tomorrow has in store, therefore do it now.

A man may be described as 'an antbear who makes
burrows for others'. The antbear, in its search for food,
makes large holes in which sleep jackals, hyenas, snakes
etc., who are thus saved the labour of making their own
burrows. So is the man who spends the money he has
earned in paying his friends' taxes, buying their clothes,
or providing the marriage dowry.

The saying, 'To mourn like the Bacazhi,' has a legend
attached to it. The Bacazhi were so overcome with grief
when a beloved chief died, that they decided to eat no
more, and said, 'Let us throw away our grindstones.'
They threw them into the river, but when hunger
overcame them, they regretted their rash act. So one who
neglects essential duties and spends much time in mourning, is said to mourn like the Bacazhi.

Similar teaching, it seemed, was conveyed by a sen-
tence of which I had a note: 'It is I who cause to fall on a
bad place'. These words, Shaamwali explained, were
said by a cow to a man who said he was not going to dig
his garden, he was going to live on the milk of his cow.
The cow addressed him as above, adding, 'Just when
there is famine I will wean my calf,' when, of course, his
milk supply would stop.

In investigating some words I came across native folk beliefs. A kind of greenstuff was taboo to one who had eaten 'rain medicine'. Rain medicine, Shaamwali told me, was made by taking some of the flakes made from a tree struck by lightning, mixing them with some other things, and putting them in a small horn. The owner of this horn will be awoken when it thunders. He then goes out of the house, blows quietly on his horn, and the thunder and lightning, but not the rain, cease.

I had a note that a word 'to put a child on the back' also meant to give a woman medicine that she might have children. The following sayings were discussed with Butaapa:

'Steal at night, and the night itself sees you.' Butaapa went on to say in explanation, 'Nothing is hidden from God. If you say you will steal at night and no one will see you, you will be seen. If a man is suspected of being a thief, you may leave him alone, for if he really is a thief, it will one day be known. If people find him out, it is not the people only, but God who has shown him up. A thief does not live long, or a liar, nor a witch; they are few who do such things and live long. God does not sleep, he is the owner of the whole earth.' And Butaapa went on to say how this had been known from long ago, and was common knowledge. All this and more he said eloquently and with much conviction. Certainly the people are not without faith, and we may say, of our work, that we have come 'not to destroy, but to fulfil'.

This language study presents many difficulties; in Shaamwali's words, when the meaning of a word had quite baffled me, 'Baila is a long way off'. But it is worth all the effort to learn it, for it helps to bring one nearer the hearts and minds of the people, and enables one more effectively to divine the word of truth.

Another problem arises when the same word has a different

connotation in the two languages. At one time my parents noticed that they were not getting any cream from their milk, so they sent their cook, Sianza, to the cattle kraal to spy out the land. He caught a herd boy pouring milk from a milking can into a bucket partly filled with water, and this is why they had so little cream. My father also had trouble with his brick makers when he was building his new two-storey home. He caught them cheating him. For a week each gang said it had made 1000 bricks a day. They counted them by making 25 lots of 40 bricks each. My father counted the lots but not the number of bricks in each lot. He let a week go by without checking the bricks, but then found that instead of there being 40 bricks in each lot, there were fewer than 30. When this was discovered, they added some of the previous week's bricks to make the numbers in each lot up to 40. At such times the Africans seemed incorrigible.

On another occasion my father had a little business with a man called Herbert and was dismayed when Herbert told him he was cheating. This naturally irked my father, for he was always scrupulously honest and, though under most circum-stances he would have refused to deal any further with the African, on this occasion he decided to discuss 'cheating' with him. He learnt that the word did not suggest double-dealing in Baila, as it did in English. It is second nature for the African to 'cheat', but cheating to them means driving a good bargain. It is good business, and no one is offended if he is found out. Herbert told my father that if he put too bad a meaning to cheating he would tie his own hands.

Although the young man who diluted the milk with water and the bricklayers who pretended they had made more bricks than they had were cheating in my father's eyes, in their own eyes they were doing nothing wrong; they were just being smart.

In my parents' work it was vital that they should understand the full meaning of all that the Africans said to them and that they in their turn should be able to convey to them all the implications of the Christian message. Language played a key role in their work and that they were able to sprinkle their speech with local idioms and sayings testified to their own sincerity.

4

Medical Work

When my father and mother reached Kasenga there was an almost audible sigh of relief from all the missionary wives. They knew that pregnancy at the best of times was a hazardous undertaking, but on an isolated mission station with no antenatal care it could be disastrous. My mother was the first of the wives to have her baby in remotest Africa and, though my delivery was uneventful, soon after my birth my mother developed a fever. The commonest cause of a fever following the birth of a baby at that time in Europe was puerperal sepsis, and in the days before antibiotics this was often fatal. Also, as a result of the fever, my mother lost her milk. There were no prepared formulas in those days; there was not even a feeding bottle for babies on any of the mission stations. Luckily, my father found malarial parasites in my mother's blood and quinine, then the only known remedy for malaria, quickly brought her temperature down. Her milk supply returned and my father was able to relax, knowing that all would be well. In due course, he circumcised and baptized me. Later, 25 years later, he married me to my wife Betty.

The next missionary wife to seek my father's attention was Mrs Buckley. Her husband was stationed at Kanchindu, deep in the Zambezi valley, more than 300 kilometres from Kasenga. Towards the end of her pregnancy she was carried in a hammock all the way to Kasenga. The delivery was uneventful and the baby thrived. Next came Mrs Kerswell from Namwala and Mrs Shaw from Nanzhila. My mother had all her three children, a boy and two girls, in Africa. All missionary wives expecting a baby were brought to my father when they were seven months pregnant, and they stayed until the baby had been born and was well established on the breast.

Not all babies were brought to Kasenga. One missionary wife who was frail and fragile had been advised not to become pregnant, but she did. While pregnant she became desperately ill and sent for my father. She died before he could cover the 40 miles across the veld on his bicycle to reach her. She was the only white fatality associated with pregnancy of which I am aware.

Although having babies was very important to African women, their pregnancies were often hazardous. During a trek to an outlying village, one of my father's teachers asked him to see his second wife, a young woman he had recently married, because she was expecting her first baby and was having spells of abdominal pain. My father described the episode as follows:

Her husband had calculated, as best he could, the length of her pregnancy and thought that she still had another month to go. He did not think the pains she had experienced one night were related to her pregnancy. The pains persisted intermittently all the next day, so in the afternoon three women, including Ruthi, herself the mother of five, and a woman with much experience in Native Midwifery came to help. These women realized she was in labour, but were rather premature in their ministrations. It would have been better for her had she been allowed to rest. At a very early hour the next morning Shazambwe called on me, and said that his wife seemed to be very tired, and was making no progress. We walked over to his home, half a mile away, in the moonlight. Having been associated with the mission for many years, Shazambwe had built himself a house with corners, but apart from that it was no better than many native huts, in fact it was worse than many of them. The sky was visible through the ridge; there were holes in the walls, and the floor was very dusty.

We went into the larger and inner room which was lit by a hurricane lamp and a small fire which smoked at times. A double bed took up most of the available space. Shazambwe's wife sat on the floor leaning against a woman who supported her back, while another woman sat in front of her, her feet against her buttocks, and holding the ends of a cloth that went round her waist. At each pain she pressed hard with her feet and pulled on the cloth while the patient strained. A girl was lying asleep on the floor, and the other two women each had a baby who was inclined to be fretful for lack of sleep. The room was full, but Shazambwe managed to find a place for a deck chair for me to sit on. Affairs were proceeding normally, and there was nothing for us to do but wait. Shazambwe's wife was very tired, and dozed when she could, but soon after my arrival the pains became stronger, and she took heart. Her husband and Ruthi encouraged her to 'bear down', or scolded her if she stopped to take a breath. Just about dawn the baby was born, and it gave a lusty cry and settled another of Shazambwe's anxieties. One of the women held it, a small greasy atom, blinking at the light, till the afterbirth came away, and the cord could be cut. To hasten this event Ruthi, encouraged by the patient herself, poked a porridge stick down her throat and made her retch.

When all was happily over, the mother and father were pleased to have a baby girl, and the mother's long vigil was over. As I walked home the eastern sky was aglow with the sun, which was just beginning to rise above the horizon.

Not all deliveries ended as happily as the above; only too often the mother died and the baby would be left with no one to care for or feed it. A few years after my parents came to Kasenga they were on trek, visiting the villages in their care, when they came to Kampenzele's village. Kampenzele, the chief, was a good and kindly man who did his best to help his folk. They were worried when my parents arrived because one of their women was having a prolonged labour. Later the baby was born, but the afterbirth was delayed, so they asked my father to see her. For a while all seemed to be well, but then she suddenly died. My parents left on the following day, but before leaving they asked the chief if he would like them to rear the baby. There was no milk for her and no one in the village was prepared to look after her; her prospects were bleak. The chief was pleased with their suggestion, so my parents took the baby home with them. My father took a piece of his rubber stethoscope tubing, threaded it through the cork of a medicine bottle, and made up a formula using the condensed milk they had been adding to their tea. They reached Kasenga two days later. Topsy, for this is what they called her, weighed about five pounds at birth, which was the average weight at birth for most African babies at that time. She had a rocky start but thereafter thrived and, as a young girl, was later able to return to her own village.

Their next motherless baby, a boy, was brought to my parents from a village 14 miles away. He was four days old when two women brought him to Kasenga. My mother quickly bathed and dressed him, while my father prepared his bottle, this time using a rubber fountain-pen filler borrowed from Arthur Slater, for a teat. They were told the baby's name was Moonoke, the local word for mourning, but my parents called him Moses; it seemed more meaningful and reminded them of the first adopted baby in the Bible. Moonoke did not pass urine for some time after his arrival, so my father circumcised him and, after a bottle, he passed urine freely. My mother was still looking after Topsy, who was two, so she had her hands full. A teenager of mixed race called Kasale, who was helping her, was so full of tribal beliefs that she felt sure that Moses would die because a pregnant woman, a fateful omen, from his village had visited him. Fortunately, he thrived and many more motherless babies were brought to my mother. All returned later to their own villages.

On a different occasion, when visiting a nearby village, my mother was asked to take care of another motherless baby. She was only too pleased to do so and asked one of the African women who was with her to carry the baby back to Kasenga. She was reluctant to do so, but eventually acquiesced. My mother later asked her why she had not wanted to carry the baby. 'Because any woman who touches a baby whose mother has died in childbirth will never have a baby of her own,' she replied. This woman was and remained childless. She never had a baby of her own. She was barren and ascribed this to having touched the motherless baby. This was a sorrow that weighed heavily on my mother's heart for the rest of her life.

Kasenga had a dispensary and every morning my father would see patients from the surrounding villages. At first they were reluctant to come, not believing that such a young man from England could rival their own traditional healers. When they went to their chiefs for advice, they would be given non-committal replies — wait and see. And this they did, but when they saw men who had nasty ulcers that would not heal (yaws)[1] return cured, cured by a needle (injections of neoarsphenamine), they started to come, usually in twos and threes, but one day an excited dispensary assistant came running over to my parents to say that a cavalcade of patients had just arrived. It transpired that one of the men associated with the mission, who lived many kilometres away, had told his chief that my father could really help sick people. The chief was so impressed that, though he lived 90 kilometres away, he decided to see my father himself. He set out on foot, spending

---

1. Yaws were troublesome ulcers, which, like syphilis, were caused by a small spiral shaped organism, or spirochete. Neoarsphenamine, given by injection, was, at that time, the best treatment for syphilis; luckily it was also remarkably effective for the treatment of yaws.

the nights at villages on the way. At each village he would sing my father's praises and at each village sick people joined his cavalcade. When he reached Kasenga, his retinue had swollen to 30. This was the cavalcade that the dispensary assistant had seen. The mission had nowhere to accommodate them, and had to build temporary huts in which to house them while their complaints were attended to. One elderly patient, who came alone, was so delighted with his response to treatment that, when he went home, he asked my father to give him 10/– so that he could buy himself a new wife.

One chief, too ill to walk, was carried, and arrived begging to be made better, but was grieved when he was sent home untreated, for there was no treatment for his illness. He was carried home by the local ambulance service, a hammock carried by prisoners from the gaol in Namwala, where the government offices were located. My father was seconded to these same government offices when the flu epidemic swept through Africa after the First World War. Everyone seemed to go down with the flu and many died. The first to die in Kasenga was an African who had been a porter with the British forces in East Africa during the war; he was hale and hearty one moment and dead the next. The government had advised everyone to remain outside as much as possible, so while my father looked after the government sick in Namwala, my mother camped out in the open with her children at Kasenga. Luckily, they all remained well. One chief, Siatwinda, in the Zambezi valley near Kanchindu, who had 15 wives and 34 children, made everyone in his village stay outside from sunrise to sunset and no one died in the epidemic.

When the epidemic had subsided my father returned to Kasenga and to his usual routine. Among the patients who came to see him was a woman with a huge abdominal tumour. She had walked several miles with her husband, hoping my father might be able to help her. My mother, describing the incident to us later, wrote:

'Bert decided that she had a large ovarian cyst. To remove this in England, certainly in the old days, would have meant a major operation with the help of a couple of doctors and nurses. The cyst was of such a size that it was likely the woman would die if nothing was done. Bert thought and prayed hard before deciding to operate. The relatives wished for this, and they and the patient agreed. On the day appointed our deal top dining room table was scrubbed, and this, with a single bed, and sterilized dressings, were taken into our little spare room, which was the operating theatre. When all was ready the patient said she had decided not to be operated on. This was one of the rare occasions when Bert put his foot down, and said she was to have the operation, and she was cleaned and made ready with Joshua and myself sterilized and gowned as assistants, Joshua, the only African who could speak English, to give the chloroform, and I to hand Bert the instruments. As far as I remember Joshua never turned a hair, but I had to dash out onto the verandah after a while. At last it was all over. People had gradually gathered outside the window to see what was happening, gazing with astonishment. The woman was put to bed in the prepared bed in the room where Bert and I nursed her for a few days, and where her husband visited her. It didn't seem more than a couple of weeks before she walked home. And we never saw her again. This operation earned for Bert the name of Kafundu Bantu — the man who skins people to see what is inside.

Most of my father's operations were not planned; they were responses to emergencies, usually accidents. One such accident led to the loss of a young man's leg. On this occasion my father was visiting the Prices at Nanzhila. When he came out of their little church on a Sunday morning he found a young boy, lying in a canoe, waiting to see him. The boy had been

bitten by a crocodile and then dragged by oxen for 65 kilometres across the veld in a canoe to Nanzhila. When he
reached Nanzhila his foot was dead, shrivelled up and with a
fetid smell. His story has been well told by Mr Price who, at
that time, was stationed at Nanzhila.

'*Wa nkwata chiwena!*' — a crocodile has got me! With
this shriek of terror Chibuta called to his companions to
come and rescue him.

A youth of seventeen, Chibuta, with several companions of his own age, was spearing fish in the tall
reeds of a swamp left by the river after the rains. Rushing to his rescue, his companions beat off the crocodile,
and turned to their injured companion. The crocodile
had seized him by his foot and with one powerful snap
of his jaws had completely severed the leg bone, leaving
the foot hanging by a few lacerated shreds of flesh and
tendon. Messengers set off to the village, and the boy
was carried to his father's hut.

The men of the village gathered to discuss what should
be done, and they decided to take the injured youth to
the nearest white man, some 65 km away at Nanzhila. A
stretcher was improvised from poles and blankets and
Chibuta was dragged on his stretcher in the canoe for
three days by oxen. During this time he must have suffered great pain of body, as well as mental strain from
the shock of his experience.

It is strange how things often work out for the best. It
so happened that on the day that Chibuta was carried
into the Nanzhila mission station, Dr Gerrard, who at
that time was in charge of the hospital at Kasenga, 60
miles away, was in Nanzhila as he had come in response
to an urgent call to see Mrs Price, who had been ill for
some time and was not getting any better. Dr Gerrard
had set off post haste, and so had arrived in time to treat
Chibuta. When he first saw him, his foot was dead,

shrivelled and tied to the rest of his leg with dirty rags; it smelled awful. He decided he would have to amputate it below the knee. In more civilized areas an operation of this magnitude demands all the conveniences and equipment of a modern surgical theatre. In this case there was neither the theatre nor the equipment. Being only an outpost dispensary, Nanzhila's surgical equipment comprised a few scalpels, needles, ligatures and most fortunately a moderate supply of chloroform, but there was no operating table, no sterilizing equipment, and no trained nursing staff. But in Africa necessity is often the mother of invention. A carpenter's bench can be made to serve as an operating table, saucepans can be used for sterilizing instruments, and missionaries, with only an elementary knowledge of nursing, can turn this knowledge to good account in time of need. In the capable hands of Dr Gerrard a successful amputation was performed, using a carpenter's saw.

The doctor's work called him back to Kasenga so Chibuta was left in my hands. His wounds made good progress and in due course completely healed. His recovery brought a new problem. What was to be done to enable him to get about. Cases were known where people who had lost a limb were condemned to crawling on their hands and knees as the only means of locomotion. To consign Chibuta to such a fate was unthinkable, so a crutch was made, and in a few days Chibuta was able to move about. Great was his gratitude when he was able to resume the activities of his youth, curtailed though they were.

Then came a day when Chibuta first realized the extent of the handicap of the loss of his leg. It was a Sunday morning, and he had attended a service in the mission church. When the service was over, the children of the congregation ran and jumped and chatted outside. Chibuta remained in his seat at the back of the church, his face bathed in tears. Mrs Price asked him why he was crying, half wondering if something had gone wrong and that he was in pain. But he reassured on that score. Reluctantly he revealed what was in his mind. 'I am crying because of my sorrow,' he said. 'I have realized that I will never again be able to run and jump and join in games with my companions, as I once did.'

But in spite of his limitations Chibuta became quite active, and the time came when the call of his own folk and village became insistent, and he asked to be allowed to go. But that crutch did not seem to be sufficiently versatile to help a one legged youth negotiate the African bush-paths. Necessity was once more the cause of inventiveness. After a good deal of patient labour, with many unexpected difficulties, I was able to fit Chibuta with a wooden stump. He was too modest to call it a wooden leg, though a wooden leg it was to Chibuta, and with it he was able to get about, relieved of the need for one hand always encumbered with a crutch. Before he set off for his own village Chibuta came to say goodbye, and to thank me for all that I had done for him. 'But there is one thing I am sorry for, Sir,' he said. 'And what is that?' I asked. 'Well, I am a black boy, and my new leg is white,' he replied. A coat of blacking soon solved that problem; it also satisfied his pride in his colour.

Crocodiles, however, caused fewer injuries than lions. Lions were numerous and often heard at night, but they did not disturb the Africans as long as game was plentiful. When it was not they turned to cattle, and when they did so, the Africans would go after them armed only with spears. The Africans were intrepid fighters and many were brought to my father having been brutally mauled. The lions were nocturnal creatures and were rarely seen during the daytime; no one worried about lions when the sun was up, but there was one occasion when the postman, carrying His Majesty's Mail, was accosted by a lion in broad daylight. All he did was to shake his bag of letters in the lion's face, telling him that they were His Majesty's letters and must not be disturbed, and he ambled away, which was fortunate, for the bag contained letters from England for my parents. But lions could be seen at night, as my sister Kathleen once experienced on returning home from school for the holidays. After having been met by my father at Choma and while being driven home over the veld, it was late and night fell while they were travelling, she remembers the eyes of the lions shining like brilliant stars in the glare of their headlights. They saw two lions, one of which was resting in the middle of the road. The lion acknowledged their presence graciously, rose slowly and then walked sedately away. Another watched them from the edge of the road as they passed by. But in the daytime, despite the postman's experience, lions could be dangerous. One man who was brought to my father had been picked up by a lion by the shoulder and then shaken like a rat. The lion had then sat on him. He lay perfectly still and, to his amazement, after a little while, the lion got up and walked away. By the time the man reached my father his wounds were foul smelling and he was feverish, but once the wound had been cleaned he made a steady and uninterrupted recovery.

Although the Africans were impressed by my father's surgical skills, they were even more amazed by the miraculous power of his needle, for whatever their complaints, many came demanding to be 'speared'. When government representatives came to immunize their cattle against the tsetse fly, they were reluctant to comply, but said they would willingly let Kafundu Bantu — 'the man who skins people to see what's inside' — give the injections. They came to him with malaria, measles, deadly in the very young, pneumonia, gastroenteritis, malnutrition and leprosy. The 1933 edition of the Oxford Universal Dictionary defined the latter as 'a loathsome disease, which slowly eats away (and deforms) the body'. There was no specific treatment for leprosy until the advent of sulphonamides in the later

1930s and, because it was thought to be highly contagious, lepers tended to be ostracized and kept in leprosaria, isolated from society. My father's account of his visit to a leprosarium is given in the appendix.

* * *

Although my parents filled an important niche and were greatly appreciated and loved in Kasenga, there were times when they felt that their skills would be put to better use were the population thicker and the facilities better. So, when they were told that they were to move to Maua in Kenya, where the population was denser and where there was a new hospital with proper wards and operating facilities, they welcomed the change and the challenge.

No one could call Kasenga beautiful, but Maua was. It was surrounded on three sides by the green Nyambeni hills, but on the fourth side it looked down on the plain, stretching as far as the eye could see, 2000 to 3000 feet below them. The country was well populated, the total population of the area being 400,000. There were many potential patients. The Ameru seemed to be much more vital than the Baila in Kasenga, the men were more lively and often painted themselves and held ceremonial dances, often naked. The women, too, danced and sang, especially with the ceremony of female circumcision. The missionaries had tried to ban the latter, but this had only led to wholesale exodus from the church and of orderlies from the hospital.

The Ameru also had a rich heritage, full of traditional ceremonies, which provided a strong backbone and stability to their society. Everyone knew his position in the hierarchy and kept to it. Maua was never isolated, as Kasenga was each year when the rains fell. The rains in Maua merely turned roads into temporary quagmires, making travelling momentarily inconvenient. Their neighbours were not far away; Meru, the district headquarters of the Methodist Missionary Society, was only 55 kilometres away, and the bustling city of Nairobi, the capital of Kenya, was only 300 kilometres, a short day's journey, away. The nearest neighbour, a Catholic mission, was an hour's walk away. There they would find a welcoming cup of tea, or a little crème de menthe, distilled by the sisters for their priestly brethren.

The Methodist Missionary Society started its work in Kenya at the turn of the century. J. B. Griffiths, the general superintendent of the United Methodist Missionary Society in East Africa, wrote in 1914, the year before my parents went out to Northern Rhodesia, that his little dispensary was proving a boon 'to hundreds of suffering men and women', but they could not do all that they wanted to do because they had very little real medical knowledge. A medical doctor was sorely needed to provide medical as well as spiritual help. He repeated his plea four years later, but he had to wait until 1928 for the arrival of the first medical doctor, Dr H. W. Brassington. He opened the first hospital at Keigoi in the Meru district in the same year. The mission committee, after obtaining a government grant for £500, approved the building of a 50-bed hospital. The hospital was made possible by the generous gift of £3000 by Sam Berresford, a retired clerk in Chesterfield, a little town in faraway England.

The soil of the first site chosen was found to be of a poor quality. It would not provide sufficient support for the construction of a hospital, so it was moved to Maua. Reverend Brewer, a recent visitor to Maua, has told us that when construction started and wooden supports were planted in the ground, they would be removed each night by suspicious villagers and that the hospital, if it were to be built, had to be moved to a site further from the village, to an area where building was allowed to continue unopposed.

Dr Brassington found that many of the people were reluctant to come to him, for he was competing with well-established local doctors known as *muga*s, and potential patients were often reluctant to try untested Western remedies. Fortunately, the *muga* fraternity were not so firmly established that they had to pass exams before practising their own brand of medicine. My parents, when they arrived, developed excellent relations with their rival, the local *muga*. *Muga*s in Kasenga had never shared their art with my father, but Maua's *muga* was only too pleased to share his, not only with my father but also with my mother. When treating a very sick woman the *muga* first killed a goat and then marked the middle of the patient's forehead with the goat's blood. He carried with him a bag filled with small calabashes containing his supply of medicines. He never actually gave any medicines to the woman to drink, he just touched her lips and tongue with them, and she would then spit them out. The administration of the medicines was accompanied by a series of incantations designed to convince her that she would recover. My father discussed the work of the *muga* with Stephano, a local preacher. Stephano said the *muga* helped 'by helping the heart, not the body'. Perhaps he was right.

On one occasion a boy was brought, unconscious, to my father who, after examining him, turned to his parents and said that their son did not need medicine; he just needed rest. His parents were naturally disappointed and promptly took him off to the *muga*. That afternoon my parents went to the boy's home. They found him lying on a banana leaf, partly covered with a dirty skin, full of holes. The *muga* was grinding some medicines on a stone, which was circled by two strings of beads. Small sticks and feathers had been driven into the ground round the stone and two rows of string were wrapped round the sticks. The *muga* proceeded to rouse the boy by blowing fine particles in the form of a powder into his nostrils and into his ears. The lad struggled violently. The *muga* also put dabs of medicine like paint on the boy's skin in various places, the navel being one of them. He also gave the boy medicine, which his mother, who was supporting and holding him with the assistance of a man, spat into his mouth. The lad was violently sick and continued to struggle. These measures succeeded in rousing him. When we left, the boy was covered with a single skin and allowed to sleep.

Because my father was now in an area bristling with villages, he was often asked to see Africans in their huts, especially if they were too sick to walk or were in labour. He had a Chevrolet truck at his disposal, and was able to collect patients and bring them to the hospital. He quickly acquired a new name, *Mukirangi*, The Great One Who Knows a Lot. He could also have been called a family doctor for, whatever their problems, he was there to help them. The following extract from my father's diary describes, if not a typical day, at least a busy day in the life of the *Mukirangi*.

Last Sunday was a full day. It began at half past one in the morning, when Solomon called us and said his wife, Miriam, was in the maternity ward. She had run it fairly close, for all was over and we were back in bed two hours later. While Doris was bathing the baby and tidying up, I came home and we all had a cup of tea. The native women in this mission have developed a great liking for tea.

I was up for prayers at seven o'clock, and immediately afterwards buried a patient who had died in the night. We put the body on the stretcher, and using the old mission Chevrolet as a hearse, took the sanitary man and an orderly along to the grave, which had been prepared previously. If we can't cure patients we have to bury them ourselves, for the natives won't do it.

There is a good deal of sickness, mainly coughs, colds and ulcers, in the district just now; it is attributed by the natives to the long spell of dry weather. From nine to one o'clock there was a continual stream of patients at the Dispensary.

Immediately after lunch I went two miles down the hill to see a sick woman. She had a high fever and pneumonia. There was no hope of getting her into hospital and, apart from good nursing, there was not much hope for her.

When night came we were again called to the maternity ward. Damaris was in labour, and Miriam, who had only been confined that morning, was standing by. Again we were not kept waiting long, and by eleven o'clock we were back in bed. That meant three babies in our Maternity Ward, all girls. They are keeping Doris, my unpaid assistant, busy this week.

Some of the difficulties my father faced in his work with the Ameru are well illustrated by the following near tragedy that occurred in 1938. One Sunday afternoon, on returning from a walk, my father found two youths wanting to take him to a case. They said the patient, a woman, lived near the road and would come back to the hospital in the car, so he only took a stretcher, left his medical bag behind and drove off in the car with the two youths. After covering nearly ten kilometres, they left the car and went on foot down a path, the two youths in front carrying the stretcher, Itaro and my father behind with the former carrying a hurricane lamp because it was quite dark. As they walked, a full moon came up over the horizon. After about three kilometres they came to a narrow path through a plantation, in the middle of which they found the hut for which they were looking. Out of it came three elderly women, followed by a young woman, evidently in pain. They put the young woman on the stretcher and my father examined her. Her baby was dead and, from her answers to my father's questions, had probably been dead for a day or two. There was only her brother and Itaro to carry her, so my father sent the brother off to get help. Meantime, he realized that if he had a knife he might be able to help her. Itaro did not have a knife, so he went off to find one. He returned with a small double-edged African dagger, which he proceeded to sharpen on a stone. He later told my father that the owner of the knife had not admitted to having a knife at all, so he had seized his bag and looked for it himself. With the young woman lying on the stretcher and Itaro holding the lamp, my father did a craniotomy (pierced the baby's skull) so that the baby, who had been dead for a day or two, could be delivered. As soon as my father started to operate, he and Itaro were left alone. When the operation was over and the dead foetus had been delivered, my father asked for some water so that he could wash his hands. While he was waiting he said to Itaro, 'What about a piece of banana stem?' and he washed with the water from it. The old women then returned, but no one came to carry the young woman on the stretcher, so they gave instructions to the women, and then left for home. My father was told that no one would dare to touch her, but that food would be put on the ground near her. Her husband and mother, the only people who might have helped her, were away. She was most anxious to come to the hospital and, three days later, she struggled the three kilometres to the road, where my father met her and picked her up. Although they had left the stretcher for her, no one would use it or carry her to the road. The poor young woman had a rough ride in the car, even though my father crawled along in second and bottom gears. She was in an awful state when she reached the hospital, but soon smelled sweeter and made an excellent recovery. But this was not the end of the story. A little over a year later her husband brought her back to see my father and this time she was holding a baby in her arms and feeding him from the breast. 'And what is the baby's name?' my father asked. '*Gitara*' (doctor), his proud father replied, 'In gratitude for all you did for us.'

Not long after this a man brought his wife, who was in the first stage of labour, because he wanted her to have her baby in hospital where my father would care for her. He had heard how magnificently my father had cared for the young woman with an obstructed labour. When he was told that he would have to pay 5/– if his wife were to have her baby in the hospital, he was all for taking her home, nearly ten kilometres away. My father told him that the baby might be born on the road, so he gave up the idea and paid 2/–. The baby, a bonny little girl, was born that night at 1.00 a.m. The mother, who was an excellent patient, was the first patient from a village unattached to the mission to be admitted to the hospital for her confinement (March 1938). Some 50 years later eight babies were being delivered every day in a new, expanded maternity wing.

On one of my father's 'hut calls' to see a young woman in labour, her mother and several other relatives were also present and, though obviously worried, were reluctant to let my father examine her. But eventually they gave their permission and my father put on a rubber glove, added a little lubricant to his finger and examined her. Everything was in good order, so he told her and her mother not to be overly concerned, for her daughter would shortly have her baby and all would be well. The orderly from the hospital who had accompanied my father told her mother that the lubricant he had put on his finger was a medicine that would ensure that the baby had a smooth passage into the outside world.

On another 'hut call', again to see a woman whose labour was not progressing smoothly, my father had first to pick his way carefully through an enclosure where the cattle were kept before reaching the hut. Then, stooping low, he entered the hut in which his patient was lying. Having passed round a partition to screen the patient from public view, he found himself in almost total darkness, his eyes smarting from the smoke from a smouldering fire. When at last he was able to locate the patient, he had to make a small hole in the wall of the hut to let a little light in so that he could diagnose the problem. A small incision (an episiotomy) gave the baby an unobstructed passage. When my father returned to the hospital he sent an ambulance — the mission Chevrolet — for her, and she and her baby spent the next few days in the luxury of a hospital bed.

The babies delivered in the hospital were initially only those of mothers who were working on the mission. The first baby from the village to be born in the hospital was delivered on 26

March 1938, but it did not take the African women long to realize that giving birth to a baby was safer in hospital than in a hut, but at 5/– it was expensive. Almost exactly a year later, while my father, this time accompanied by a nurse called Joy, was making a hut call, again to see a woman in labour, a crowd of about 400 women gathered on a green grassy common near the market. The women, who were wearing their best skins, had strings of blue beads round their necks and had anointed their bodies with fat. Some of them had also painted white rings round their eyes, giving them a gruesome appearance, and they sang and danced. My mother who was watching them thought she heard the word *gitara* (doctor) repeated in one of their songs and wondered what had caused the celebration. Her question was answered when a young man from the mission came to tell her that the local council had met and had agreed to pay for African women to have their babies in hospital. The women were naturally delighted, but wanted confirmation of this from my mother. She was reluctant to speak to them herself, but asked the young man from the mission to tell them that it was much easier for *Mukirangi* to help them have their babies in the maternity ward than in the darkness of their huts. They continued to sing and dance for a considerable length of time; then, as it was Sunday, Cornelius, a local preacher, concluded the day's ceremony with a service. Strangely, the leader of the meeting was a man. Today the hospital has a 25-bed maternity ward, a gift from Germany, and an average of eight or nine babies are being delivered every day.

While the government wanted to change a number of local customs, including the people's refusal to bury their dead, it was only possible to make these changes with the prior approval of the chiefs and elders. Once this had been obtained, a meeting would be held and the new law or practice proclaimed. When the chiefs and elders agreed to allow their dead to be buried, a large meeting was held in Maua. The district commissioner, government clerks, chiefs and elders arrived and sat in the middle of a circle surrounded by well over 1000 local citizens, both men and women. A government clerk proclaimed the proposed change in the manner in which they were to dispose of their dead. A man with uplifted arms repeated the proclamation in a loud voice. A sheep and a bundle of little sticks were then brought into the centre of the circle, at which point the sheep was killed and its legs were broken. The proclamation was repeated, with the announcer holding up a little stick that had been dipped into the sheep's blood. As he finished, he touched the sheep on the neck and legs, saying that whoever failed to obey the commandment would die like the sheep. The people all responded, the men by beating the ground with sticks and the women by clapping their hands. The announcer then walked to an opening in the circle, still speaking, and threw the stick away, the people again responding. This was done more than a dozen times. The last announcement was to the effect that anyone who took part of the sheep to use as 'medicine' would surely die. The impressive ceremony was an essential step towards the burial of the dead.

This was only one of many changes accepted by or inflicted on the Ameru, which, in the course of three or four generations, had transformed a tribal society, if not into a Western democracy at least into a country with its feet well on the road to becoming one.

5

The Itinerant Missionary

To be an effective and competent missionary, my father had not only to be fluent in the local language but he also had to be able to travel, which might mean walking 20 to 30 miles a day. After reaching Northern Rhodesia, his first journey with my mother was on a boat travelling for four to five days westwards on the Kafue River from Kafue to Kasenga. Although the trip was exciting and enjoyable, he rarely used the river again. The local people walked everywhere; they never rode, for example, for they had no horses. If they had heavy loads to carry they used oxen and wagons drawn by oxen. Because they went everywhere on foot the veld was crisscrossed by paths, most of them narrow, just eight inches wide; only those that were much travelled were wider. They were never straight, but turned this way and that as they weaved from village to village. There were no signposts and few landmarks. When it rained, the paths frequently became muddy or were hidden under water; when the rains subsided, the grass would grow, often obliterating the path and hiding everything except the blue sky. On one occasion, thinking that he might have lost his way, my father climbed a fig tree to see if he could see the village he was hoping to reach. All he could see was an ocean of grass, but not many yards further on, he rode on his bicycle into the village he was seeking.

He made many of his 'hut calls' on his bicycle. On one occasion he went 16 miles to see the wife of one of his teachers who had just had a baby followed by a prolapsed uterus. He carried his medicine bag with him, but this and even he himself were often thrown off the bicycle by unexpected holes and bumps in the path. Once, just after the rains, cattle had been driven along the path and had churned it up with their hooves; this would have been impediment enough, but the sun came out and baked it hard. He had to push his bicycle nearly all the way. Once, when a group was threading its way through the grass single file, the leader stepped aside to pause for a moment and to let my father lead the way; he stepped into a well-camouflaged deep hole with muddy water at the bottom, an animal trap designed to catch wild animals, not itinerant missionaries.

Bicycles and feet were sufficient to cover relatively short distances, but if my parents wanted to visit other mission stations — the nearest was a three-day journey on foot (the railway was five days away on foot or by ox-wagon) or when they wanted to visit a series of villages and schools, they had to *trek*.

The word *trek*, like many other Dutch words connected with farm and veld life, gained currency throughout southern Africa during the Great Trek, when the Boers loaded their belongings onto wagons and, with their wives and children pushed (trekked) into the interior to seek new homes. Such long treks were no longer common in my father's day, for the railways had replaced the wagon trains, but there were still large parts of Africa in which the ox-wagon or porters were still the principle modes of travel. My father would use porters when he went on trek, but he would use an ox-wagon for the five-day journey to the line to put my sisters Kathleen and Margaret with their heavy trunks on the train to Bulawayo when their holidays were over.

Treks played an important role in his missionary activities, for it was then that he was able to visit the villages in his 'parish', get to know the chiefs whose support was essential if the local schools were to be a success, and conduct the informal services he liked to hold on such occasions. My father, like the other missionaries, always travelled with his wife. A day or two before going on a trek they would have to assemble everything they might need — camp beds, tents, cooking utensils, food, chairs, a table and food. My parents once forgot to bring their tent and a bed, so had to spend the night sleeping under the open sky with one of them on the hard ground. With regard to food, though they always tried to be self-sufficient, they could often buy chickens, milk, ground maize (corn), occasionally sweet potatoes, and groundnuts (peanuts). They always took plenty of salt with them because the porters could exchange this for food in the villages.

Eight or more oxen would be harnessed (or inspanned as they called it) to a wagon that had been loaded with baggage early in the morning of the departure. The driver would line the oxen up in a long trek chain and, if they were well trained, they would meekly accept their yokes and form up two by two. Then, while a man held the leading pair in place, the driver would crack his long whip, give a fearsome yell and off the oxen would go. Nevertheless, progress was slow — two to three miles an hour, or about 15 miles a day.

My father once travelled with a Mr Taylor, an American missionary with the Macha mission, who was astonishingly skilful at driving oxen. He put some Yankee bustle into it too. When tired of the usual slow pace, he would take the whip from the African driver, crack it over the oxen, make fearful yells and the whole team would take off at the double. With him my father had his first experience of negotiating a riverbed in the rainy season. His adroitness at getting across was amazing. One stream was a raging torrent over which he tried ineffectively to make a rough footbridge with trees. He then waited for the flood to abate a little and, after some exciting moments, managed to get them all, with their baggage, wagon and oxen, safely to the other side.

On another occasion, when travelling with a light ox-wagon, my father went down a bank that was so steep that the wagon stood on end; everything tumbled out and the back wheels spun vainly in the air. On another journey, this time with Mr Price, he started off with a whole wagon, continued with half a wagon and finished with porters. Trekking with oxen, which were always hired from the local village, had its drawbacks, but the oxen came in useful later when my father had a car that broke down, for the oxen brought it safely home.

When my parents planned a trek with porters rather than oxen, which they often did, a man would be sent out two to three days beforehand to engage about 20 men who would gather at the mission, where the loads would be distributed among them. Their own needs for the journey were minimal, a few spears, some pots and some blankets, which were usually cheap, dirty and much the worse for wear. When all was ready, the loads would be taken up and they would all set off along a narrow footpath, walking in Indian file. Singing often cheered the way, a shanty man alternating with the chorus, and when they were not singing the carriers would chatter away, exchanging gossip and news.

A long halt at midday when it was too hot to travel would break the day's trek. Towards sundown they would stop and set up camp near a village. Loads would be downed, the tent pitched, water and firewood collected, and fires kindled. If food in the district were plentiful, the women would come from the village with baskets of ground corn. If the carriers had been given salt to exchange for their own food, lively bargaining would follow. A woman would empty meal from a basket and receive a handful of salt in exchange. She would object to the smallness of the quantity and demand more; after some arguing, a meagre pinch of salt would be added to the amount originally offered and sometimes a little more might be given before she went away. Gradually, the camp would settle down. My parents would use their canvas bath and have a change of clothes, then supper, prepared by their cook. The cook often had to prepare the meal under far from ideal conditions, for sometimes there were no trees for miles around and apparently no wood for a fire, but the cook would find a few sticks and, with these and some dry cow dung, would make a fire good enough to boil some water and cook some meat.

After supper my parents would sit over the fire, maybe reading a little by the light of a hurricane lamp. Nearby would be the fires of the carriers, round which they sat cooking and eating their suppers. Beyond was the deep darkness of the veld and forest, and above the clear sky shimmering with brilliant stars. This was the most wonderful time of the whole day. After a hymn and prayers round the campfire, peace would steal over the camp. The carriers would curl up in their blankets, heads well covered and feet sticking out, while my parents would retire to their tent and camp beds, ready to fall asleep.

The next morning they would make an early start, and the miles would slip by more quickly in the cool of the day. On one trek, in the hot season, my parents rose at 3 o'clock each morning and would cover more than 80 kilometres in the course of a day and a half. Winter treks were the best for them because it was always dry, the paths were easy to follow and the veld was burnt clear. But there were times when they had to trek during the rains, and then they might be plagued by heavy rain and thunderstorms. Black clouds, lit up by sheets of lightning, would pile up ahead of them as peals of thunder urged them on. If they were fortunate they would reach their campsite in time to pitch their tent before the rains came down in torrents. After the rains the flats were flooded. There was water, water everywhere, and they would have to wade for mile after mile through water up to their knees, continually plunging into unseen holes and cart ruts, and almost losing their balance. Such treks were tiring and, on reaching dry land, they would be both weary and thankful to have completed the day's journey. After a good night's sleep, they would be ready for another day's trek.

My parents' most memorable trek was to Kanchindu, in the Zambezi valley, to attend a synod, a meeting the Methodist missionaries held to discuss and share their problems and, they hoped, to find solutions. They left Kasenga early on Saturday 17 May 1924 with two African delegates (preachers or teachers), two kitchen staff, 19 carriers and five young children, the latter being carriers for the two African delegates. My parents also took their bicycles, which were useful for crossing the veld. Each carrier's load weighed roughly 50 pounds (22 kilos). Some missionaries tended to overload their carriers, thus saving money on wages, but my father felt it was wiser to reduce the loads a little so that if a carrier fell ill the others could share his load; 50 pounds was a heavy load in the hot weather.

To get to Kanchindu, the company trekked for five days across the veld. If possible, they would camp near a village each night in the hope of obtaining food and water locally, but they also had with them 30 kilos of maize, to be held in reserve because there had been some crop failures, two sacks of water and enough food for a day, as well as salt to be exchanged for food for the carriers. At the end of the second day, a Sunday, in failing to camp near a village they were unable to round up any villagers to swell the congregation for their service, so they held it for their own company only. Stephano, one of the African delegates, preached. As they were pitching their camp that evening my mother noticed a veld fire in the distance. It did not seem to threaten them, but not wishing to tempt fate, they burnt a swath of grass round the campsite and then beat it out with branches, making a protective barrier should the fire come in their direction.

On Tuesday, day four of their trek, they reached Macha where the Shaws, who had set off from Nanzhila, joined them. On the fifth day they reached Choma, on the line, where the Kerswells joined them. The party now totalled three missionaries and their wives, several African delegates, a number of cooks, children and carriers, making a total of about 100 all told. Ahead lay two and a half days' trek on the plateau and two days' descent through the jungle down to Kanchindu on the banks of the Zambezi. On their descent through the forest, my father sat down and wrote a letter to his parents.

I wish you could see us now. We are camped in the forest. It is dark, but our camp is lit up by a dozen fires.

In front of our respective tents are seated the Kerswells, the Shaws and ourselves, having finished the evening meal. Some hundred natives are sitting around their fires, cooking their suppers, and chattering away, their black bodies and faces reflecting the firelight. Above, the foliage of the trees reflects the firelight and beyond lies a clear starry sky. It is a romantic scene.

We are almost at the end of such a trek as we have never had before. The Kerswells, Shaws and ourselves left Choma on Friday afternoon accompanied by 100 carriers, teachers and Kafue students. For two and a half days we travelled on the top of the plateau, with occasional views of hills and valleys in front of us. Then on Monday we began the descent. Sometimes we were climbing, and sometimes going along the ridges, but chiefly we were going down, following a rough stony path. After five hours we came to a halt at the foot of the hills. It was a wonderful trek for the Shaws and ourselves who have always lived on the Kafue flats. Poor Mrs Kerswell, who is getting very stout, was two hours longer than we were getting through. Our Baila carriers came through well, though the stones tried their feet; to carry a load of fifty pounds barefoot over the path we had travelled on was no mean achievement. Tomorrow we shall have a few more miles of rough going before we reach Kanchindu on the banks of the Zambezi. Mr Kerswell is now whistling us up for prayers, and our whole company will gather round his fire while we have a hymn and a prayer to bring an end to the day.

When we left Maed the nights became much colder. Before they became colder Mrs Shaw had sent some of her bedding back, but she has since regretted this. For some nights Doris and I have dispensed with our camp beds, and have slept on the ground, the carriers having first cut some grass to spread underneath. In this way we made one big bed, and have been decidedly warmer.

Now we are getting down into the valley the nights are
not so cold.

Sunday, June 1st, 1924. Kanchindu is a prettily situated
station overlooking the Zambezi. The Zambezi here lies in
a deep valley, and the land slopes from the hills down to
the edge of the river. The result is that it is cut up by
gullies made by the torrents which come roaring down
them when the rains fall. So much so that it was difficult
to find a level place on which to build a house. The houses
are perched on a ridge with gullies on either side.

On Tuesday 17 June, with the synod over, the Shaws and
Kerswells decided to return the way they had come, up
through the forest and on to the plateau. My father and
mother, who chose to see more of the Zambezi, climbed into
the mission's capacious metal boat. It was the same boat my
cousin Raymond and I were to climb into eight years later when
we went to Kanchindu with my parents. Five Batonga men
rowed them 25 leisurely miles down the river past numerous
crocodiles basking placidly in the sun. Their carriers, tired after
their long trek, then joined them. The most peaceful objects my
parents had seen were the many crocodiles basking happily in
the sun.

On the following day, Wednesday, they continued to trek
through the forest and, on the Thursday, they started to climb
up through the forest to the plateau where they had wonderful
views over the Zambezi valley. Their route passed near to Mr
Taylor's mission — he was the American who knew how to
handle a team of oxen. His mission buildings were built of *pisé
de terre* — stamped earth — and he was teaching the Africans
how to build with similar bricks. The following day, Friday,
my parents reached Choma and, instead of camping, they
spent the night in the luxury of a hotel. Its manager, Mr
McKee, was also the agent for the Ford Motor Company. He
had bought one Ford for himself and had sold two others. This
obviously impressed my father who had been told that the

Trojan, made by Leyland Motors in England, would be able to stand up to the wear and tear of the veld, for when he returned to Kasenga in 1926 after his next furlough, he bought a Ford, called a Tin Lizzie in those days. In Choma they also met Colonel Hart, a keen farmer whom they were to meet again on their way to Kasenga. Near Choma many farmers were growing cotton and tobacco.

My parents left Choma on the Monday morning and had an easy day's trek of 14 miles, camping near the house of a Mr Tully, and had a delightful afternoon cup of tea with him and his wife and sister. Later, after their evening meal and prayers with their carriers, when they were sitting round the fire, my father asked one of the carriers to push the logs on the fire together as the fire was dying down, and he went on to ask him how he should have said this in Baila. After telling him, the carrier added that the same phrase, pushing logs together to make a blaze, was used to refer to a man who provokes quarrels between other people. A very apt metaphor, my father added.

The next day they went as far as Colonel Hart's farm. He was one of the earliest settlers round Choma who had served in France 'for the duration of the First World War', and had then returned to his farm near Choma. He was an enthusiastic road maker. The local farmers and the government had shared — pound for pound — the cost of African labour. The farmers had given their supervision free. Colonel Hart's chief line was in pigs. His neighbour, Mr Tarr, whose farm they reached at sundown, concentrated on potatoes and onions, irrigated by water from hot springs. Mr Tarr, who had a troublesome stammer, was very kind and hospitable. Because he was so well liked, his stammer only brought him sympathy and understanding.

The next day they reached Mapanza, 17 miles nearer home. They should have done more on the previous three days, but there was no point in doing so because their present stretch was without water; there was nowhere else to camp. Father Deacon gave them a warm welcome and did all he could to make them comfortable; he also entertained them with stories, for he was a great talker.

My parents were thankful when they finally reached 'home' after the longest trek they were ever to undertake. The carriers, during the trek, had on one occasion demanded a raise in pay, but my father refused to buckle under to their demands, though he expected they would try to get an extra shilling on payday at the end of the trip.

While my parents were on their monumental trek, Bert's father and mother were on a Mediterranean cruise. They both commented in their letters on the zest with which the Greeks and Italians in their own countries, and the Baila in theirs, haggled over prices, and wrote of the pleasure that comes after a long time away when one returns to one's own home and one's own bed.

Almost exactly a year later, in 1925, my father went on another trek, this time without my mother because she was busy looking after her third baby, a little girl called Margaret. As usual, my father took his bicycle on this trek and, for the most part, rode ahead of the carriers so that he could spend more time with the Africans, one of whom was Topsy, now growing into a winsome young girl, and the teachers and chiefs. To visit the villages north of the Kafue River, he first had to cross it and when he returned, 11 days later, he had to recross it to reach home and Kasenga. He crossed the Kafue in front of his carriers and was making a beeline for home, wife and baby when Sianga his cook took him by the arm and told him that his carriers would be very disappointed if he were to return without them. So he waited for them to cross the river and, when they caught up with him, they put him at the head of the column and marched behind him, singing all the way. Had they known the words, I am sure they would have sung, 'Hail the conquering hero comes'.

Just as the railway put an end to trekking by the Boers, so the car put an end to trekking by the missionaries, but it introduced new hazards because drivers were not used to driving in the bush and, unlike carriers, cars could not easily be replaced. One missionary, it is said, when driving along a track that passed under an overhanging branch, instinctively ducked his head and was surprised when the branch sliced off the roof of his car. Father's accidents were just as unexpected, but luckily in those days accidents only damaged cars, never those who travelled in them. The hazards of depending on the car were brought home to my father on one occasion when he had promised Mrs Shaw that he would be present when her baby was due. Mrs Shaw was in Kafue, my father at Kasenga and the baby was due on Tuesday 5 March. Since my mother was in England that year with her children, my father left Kasenga with Mrs Stamp. Mr Stamp, though stationed at Kasenga, was at Kafue where Mrs Stamp hoped to join him. My father offered Mrs Stamp a lift in his car. They left Kasenga on Friday 1 March expecting to reach Kafue the same day, four days before the baby was due. On Saturday 2 March, my father wrote to my mother in England, who was looking after my two sisters and me, with a litany of woes.

Mrs Stamp and I are at Mapanza stranded with a damaged car. We did pretty well on Thursday till about seven miles from here. We stuck occasionally in mud; for the worst patch, this side of Mandondo, we had some half dozen boys to pull the car. Having passed Mbeza we thought all our troubles were over. Unfortunately I turned off the road into the grass to miss some mud, and hit a stump violently. We borrowed four oxen from a village near by and were pulled *backwards* towards Mapanza. It grew quite dark, and we zigzagged along the road. At the drift, a mile from the mission, we could hear the rumble of water over the stones, and we decided not to attempt the crossing in the dark. We took our belongings out of the car, and, with Butaapa leading, we walked to the Mission, where we arrived about 8.30. There was quite a company on the verandah, just finishing their coffee. We got a meal and went almost immediately to bed.

Next morning oxen brought the car here. Smith and I worked at it all morning, then he went sick. He had a small abscess on his arm, the result of a bee sting, and it was very painful. I laboured some more during the afternoon, and then decided the damage was beyond my powers to repair. Smith went to Choma on the motor bike with a wire for Kafue, telling them why we hadn't arrived. We are hoping that McKee will take us in to Choma, and that some one will be able to come by car for us from Kafue. The railway strike is still on. Wonder if we will reach Kafue in time for the confinement.

Then, from Kafue on Tuesday 5 March, he continued:

We have arrived! And just in time! McKee's mechanic, Davidson, took us into Choma on Sat[urday] afternoon. We had to get a wire to Mr Shaw to come for us, but the telegraph business was congested and there was nothing doing. Finally we again hired McKee's car, and set off 10.30 Sunday morning. Beyond Monze we stuck an hour in mud, and reached Mazabuka at 1.30. We stayed there the night. During the evening I called on the Fells, both seemed well, especially Mrs Fell who is decidedly plump. Their quarters are temporary and small, but quite comfortable. Next morning I roused Davidson and Mrs Stamp at 5.30 and we were off soon after six. We took a new road which goes through the hills to the east of the line. Sixteen kilometres from the Kafur River we reached a pass in the hills where the road was not yet cleared, though natives were at work under two Europeans. Mrs Stamp and I left the car, and begged natives to carry our belongings, and we set off to walk. Eight kilometres down the road a motor lorry overtook us. A Mr London and Mr Jack Bushinger, whom we know well, were on the lorry, and they gave us a lift. Before we reached the river a storm overtook us; we were drenched. The wire to pull the pontoon across the river broke, and we were stuck for nearly an hour on the river shivering with cold. Mrs London gave us hot tea, and a change of clothes. Just as we were ready to leave, Mr Shaw arrived. So ended all our adventures. We found Mrs Kerswell here, for Mrs Shaw had not expected Mrs Stamp to come and help with her confinement. I have since discovered that Mrs Curry also wanted to assist at the confinement, so we were not short of midwives!!! One will be enough.

Then finally, on Wednesday 6 March, he announced:

On Tuesday, March 5th, Mrs J. R. Shaw, was delivered of a daughter. Yesterday, about bedtime, it was evident things were happening, and by 11.30 all was over. Mrs Shaw was a little overwrought, and I was glad it was all over so soon. For the rest all went well — a perfectly normal confinement. The baby weighed 8¼ pounds. This was the first Mrs Kerswell had attended, and she felt a little bit at sea — didn't know quite what to do next, and even seemed to find the baby awkward to bath. Mrs Stamp, who is staying at the Currys, saw the lights and heard noises, and got Mr Curry to bring her over; we had almost finished by then. The baby promises to be a bonny one. Poor kid! It had a mosquito in its net straight away and couldn't get to sleep till Mrs Shaw took it in with her. I tremble a bit now to think that I had ever considered not coming, owing to bad roads and the strike. They would have managed, but they would have been very anxious. As it was I arrived only just in time.

My father's journey with Mrs Stamp to Kafue, though full of troubles, was not nearly as hazardous as their return journey to Kasenga. This, fortunately, Mrs Stamp graphically recorded when she wrote home as follows.

After leaving Kafue we got to Mapanza quite well, with only once getting stuck on the road, and then boys were near enough to get us out. We came over shaky culverts and unsteady bankings on the road, but we managed alright. At Mapanza they would not hear of us going on to the Trader's for the night, so we stayed there. His Lordship, the Bishop, was still there, and it was Friday. They say we always land there on meatless days, and it's being Lent, they do not go in for extras afterwards. I love their Angelus. Whatever they are doing at 6 a.m., noon or 6 p.m., they all stop, and stand facing East until the bell stops ringing. It is a very nice reminder I always think. Of course we always go to Evensong when there, and that is another thing I always enjoy. I shall soon know where to find my place in the Prayer Book, I have been so often. I convulsed the Bishop by telling him of our bread, made with the Eno's Fruit Salts, when last on trek. He said he would never again travel without them! They kept on telling us that we should certainly have to spend a night on the veld, the roads were so bad, and padre kept saying, 'But it is full moon Mrs Stamp.'

Despite the dreadful tales of the road, I fully expected to be home next night, and so we should have been had the roads been no worse than they thought they were, but Helas! Early on Saturday morning we got a slight shower, which proved to be the tail end of a storm that had been raging all night in the direction we were going. We stuck in mud and, time after time, I had to get out and push, and my feet simply sank in the stuff, and I had a job to pull them out, when once they were sodden and the mud had oozed through the lace holes. Doctor wanted me to let him do the pushing, and me to drive the car, but I was too nervous. When we had done 15 miles in one and three quarters of an hour to the Trader's, we hired oxen to pull us over the next vlei [a pool or area of shallow water], and also hired a boy. We had to wait nearly a couple of hours, while the people decided whether to let us have oxen, and what they would charge us, etc. I get awfully fed up with things like that. Doctor sat serenely on and said, 'Well we are in their country and we must just possess our souls in patience and bide their time.' I suppose we might have saved a quarter of an hour had we stood over them all the time, but with the sun bearing down on us, and we had no helmets, well it wasn't worth it, so we had an apple or two and sat waiting.

Noon saw us adrift, and then they told us their oxen had been working since dawn, and so must rest, so we had to wait another hour and a half! After that our troubles came thick and fast. We never struck a dry patch for many minutes together, sometimes Doctor had to block up the carburettor, and we ploughed through water like a ship at sea. Into holes and out with the car rocking like nothing on earth. Then the ox chains broke, and the poor beasts got the wind up, and ran loose, and the poor leader had to wade round in water nearly up to his knees to get them back. Just as he was getting them fastened, they would give a pull, and be off again. As they were then a long way from home, and we only about five miles from the nearest village, we let them turn back. When we got out onto a dry patch, we went another two miles and stuck in deep mud. We put the shovel on the mud, and the jack on that, and jacked each wheel, while we pulled palm leaves and stuck under. I wasn't much use for breaking the leaves, and the boy wasn't much better, but the Doctor worked until the sweat poured out of him, and finally we got her out, with the boy and I pulling. We did another quarter of a mile, and this time were in worse than ever. You see there is no negotiating [circumventing] these bad patches. Where you get water there is generally yards of swamp and mud on either side, and you just take your choice between the two. If the road has a sandy bottom, we make straight for the water, but if it is muddy, we take the mud and only hope we can rush it in bottom gear. By this time it was sunset, and we had to send the boy for help from the village. Doctor found a dry patch on which to light a fire, though not without difficulty, and burnt a new crepe-de-chine hanky, (Mrs Meecham's Christmas present to him), in the process of getting the kettle off the fire. I suggested to him then that he discard the tie that matched the hanky, before that got in the flames. He is an awful man for not knowing whether he has got on his best or his worst togs, and is just as likely to go out to dinner in a creased suit or a shirt with a hole in, as to go on a journey like ours in his best bib and tucker. Still, those are details.

Some boys soon came out, and we went on to the village. It was a brilliant moonlight night, and they said the road was good from there on, so we tried to persuade them to let us have oxen, and we would travel through the night, but they weren't having any. We spun a long yarn about getting home, but they calmly informed us that in any case we couldn't get farther than Maala, six kilometres from home, without a boat, so we might as well stop there. They gave us the school, (one of Mapanza's outschools), to sleep in. It is a mud building built like a church. Mrs McKee had given us sheets, pillows, mosquito nets etc. I desecrated the altar by putting my boots on it for the night, to dry the thickest of the mud off. I was really too weary to bother about it, but Doctor was most professional, and insisted on my drying my feet and putting on my mosquito boots. We made beds of the car seats, and put our suitcases at our feet, and hung our nets from the beams. What mercy we had them, or we should have been bitten to death.

It was a miserable night, but it would have been ten times worse but for the mosquito nets, or it might have rained and the roof would not then have sheltered us for long. I found afterwards that the Doctor had given me the longest seat, so goodness knows how he fared. I think Doctor must have thought he was talking to John or Kathleen, for he was most kind and considerate. A hyena serenaded us all the first part of the night, and of course there was no door to the school, so Doctor said, 'Now you try and get to sleep, and if you can't sleep, wake me and we'll talk, but don't lie there till morning worrying yourself to death about things that may never come.' Sleep, ye gods, fancy thinking about it. However, Doctor obviously did not sleep, for every half hour or so he told me the time, and by one thirty we abandoned the idea altogether, and he told me all about his student days and his oral exam for Hartley, and I told him of some of our experiences as a family, etc. At four o'clock we were so cold and fed up, and there was no water to make any tea, so we ate apples, and then walked round and round that blessed hut till dawn. As it was the week of our shortest day (6 o'clock to 6 o'clock) it seemed an eternity coming. You know how, after a weary day and a sleepless night, you feel so cold and depressed in the early hours of the morning, and Doctor said, 'This sunrise seems a long time coming,' and I said, 'Yes, but it's a comfort and a lesson to us to realize that no matter how much has gone wrong with us up to now, that the sunrise is a certainty.' I'll bet that Mr Price, with all his ravings about sunrises as seen from our upper verandah, was never more thrilled with the sight of one, than I was with that one, and Doctor was much amused when I told him so.

At dawn we set off after a cup of tea, some bread and butter and chocolates, and had a really good trip. The rest of the road was as dry as that from Mapanza to

Choma (no, vice versa). Of course we found water, but it was always negotiable. We got to Maala by 9 a.m., after having done 20 miles. Mr Spiropolis brightened our little lives, and fortified our little tummies with hot coffee, before we sailed into the Maala vlei. I had to take my choice, as there was no boat on the vlei. I could either wade a good three miles with water up to my waist all the time, or wade a mile with water nearly up to my chest, or do a good six with water generally up to my knees, reaching my waist at the river. I chose the former. I was about done in, and knew I could not do the six miles. I began to have qualms about the shorter distance, but knew it was no good putting the wind up Doctor by saying so. We had to leave the car, and there it must stay for a month or two. Two boys carried our suitcases, and we set off. Doctor took his shoes and stockings off, but I knew I could not stick my feet in that mud if I did so, so kept mine on. I was very tired when water was up to my waist, and could have gone to sleep in the middle of it, it was so nice and warm, but the sun was beating down fiercely on our heads. When the water reached my chest, we stopped every little while for me to rest, and when we got to the smaller river, the boys waded through, and the one boy loaded the other with the two lots of cases, rain coats, boots etc. and came back for me. Of course, we might just as well have been at sea, there was nowhere without deep water for miles. Doctor, up to his armpits, helped me onto the back of this youth and I prayed that the boy would not lose his footing. Water was up to his mouth when he had my seven stones (98 pounds, or 45 kilos) on his back, and Doctor came behind, up to his chin in it. As soon as it was no more than chest deep for me, the boy put me down again, as the other boy was yelling that he was dead with the weight of the cases. As mine was my expanding case, and full at that, he wouldn't be far off being dead. Through the next mile the water got less and less, until we got right out of it, within half a mile from home. It is like looking out to sea, looking from our front bedroom verandah.

When we got in home, Ernest, my husband, had just come from church, and was very surprised to see us. The letters we had sent by post had never reached him, as everything was disorganized by the strike. Mr McKee had sent a boy through, specially, asking him to send trek gear through to meet us, (which we were hoping to meet all the time), and gave the boy an extra two shillings to come through quickly. The boy had pocketed that, for the note has sifted through from hand to hand, and arrived here today, when we have been home four days. Ernest had written telling me to stay at the line, and that I was not to attempt to get home on any account until he fetched me. I have never had his letter. I believe, had we come a day sooner, and missed the 30 miles that had that heavy storm, that we could have done it as far as Maala in the one day. However, we are safely home, and very glad to be here. I had most of Monday in bed, and am just amusing myself this week mending the month's accumulation, and writing letters. You and Mrs Gerrard are coming in for a specially long dose. By Doctor's orders (that sounds fine doesn't it?), I have not to exert myself this week. He tells me today he thinks I am looking better than I have looked for a long time, and thinks that hard treks suit me. I tell him it's the apples we brought back from Choma (and I really have very great faith in the effect of an apple on me), but I notice they do not keep him away. He says he said his prayers when he saw me safely through that water. Well I'm glad I went, and was of use to Mrs Shaw, there isn't much I wouldn't do for her, but I hope, if she ever sends for me when any more babies come, it will be in the dry season.

6

Life in Kasenga

M y father's and mother's work among the Africans in Northern Rhodesia, now Zambia, although occupying most of their time and energies, was not their only responsibility; they also had their children to consider. They had been led to believe that their work in Africa would be relieved every four years by a year's furlough at home in England. This routine was interrupted first by the First World War, since it took a long time for shipping to return to normal when the war was over, and later by my mother developing breast cancer in 1939.

My parents first left England for Africa in April 1915. Their return was delayed by the aftermath that followed the end of the war and they were not able to leave Africa for England until July 1920. When they eventually returned they were given a warm welcome by their parents, brothers and sisters. My father was then kept busy preaching and lecturing about his work in Kasenga. He illustrated his talks with what we called a magic lantern — a projector that used glass slides to throw black and white pictures on a screen. My mother, Kathleen and I were put in a little bungalow on a hill called the Cloud, which was far from *The Madding Crowd* in Derbyshire. Although Kathleen and I were happy there, it was not quite what my mother, who had been isolated from her friends and relatives for five whole years, had envisaged. We did, however, spend some time with our grandparents in their homes at Hessle, near Hull, where my mother's parents lived, and at Norfield in Swinton, the home of my father's parents. The question that loomed foremost in my parents' minds was what they should do with their children, namely Kathleen and me. What would be best for us, our health and our education? And what could they afford? Auntie Winifred, my father's eldest sister, provided the answer. She had graduated from Somerville College, Oxford, was a teacher and was still single. She nobly volunteered to look after us. She took us to a little school called Little Felcourt in Kent where we started our education. I was five and Kathleen was three. My parents returned to Kasenga in November 1921.

Four years later they returned to England, leaving Cape Town on 21 July 1925 and bringing with them an eight-month-old baby girl, my sister Margaret. They found me happily ensconced, with my cousin Raymond, in a residential preparatory school, the Downs at Colwall near Malvern. That this was possible was undoubtedly due to the generosity of my father's father. Kathleen was attending a good day school in Altrincham where Auntie Winifred was teaching. When my father was due to return to Kasenga in August 1926 my parents decided, after much heart searching, that it would be in the best interest of their children if they were to remain in England, and if my mother were to remain with them. The separation put a great strain on both my parents, for they worked as a team and needed each other more, if I dare say so, than they needed us. My father returned to Kasenga and shared the work of the mission station with the Stamps. That the separation was putting a greater strain on my parents than I had realized was brought home to me when my father's return was unexpectedly delayed for a few weeks and my mother broke down and cried. This was the only time I ever saw her weep. When my father returned he came home through the Suez Canal, landed at Marseilles, and was reunited with my mother in Paris.

While my mother had been looking after us, Auntie Winifred, relieved of her responsibilities, fell in love with Uncle

Tom, a professor of mechanical engineering at Manchester Technical College. They had first met at the Great Western Street Methodist church. Their romance came to a head while we were all on holiday on the Brittany coast near St Malo soon after my father's return. They were married on 27 December 1926. They did not have a family of their own and would have been happy to look after us, but when my parents returned to Africa in March 1930, they decided to take Kathleen and Margaret with them and to leave me in the care of Auntie Winifred and Uncle Tom as I was so happy at Bryanston in Dorset, the public school to which I had graduated.

After landing at Cape Town, my parents, Kathleen and Margaret climbed into the train that took them back to Choma. On the way they passed through Bulawayo, and there they left Kathleen, then aged 12, at a fine residential school, St Peter's Diocesan School for Girls. The school was Spartan; the children all slept outside on verandas wrapped in warm blankets in wintertime when the nights were cold. In their free time in those days they were able to wander freely round the town.

At the end of the term, Kathleen took the train to Choma, arriving in the afternoon where our father met her. 'Shall we go all the way to Kasenga tonight?' my father asked her, 'or pause on the way for the night?' 'Go all the way,' she answered. Gone were the days of trekking and ox-wagons, except when there were floods, when oxen were still indispensable. That afternoon Kathleen remembers seeing much wild game, kudu, hartebeest and antelope and, after the sun had set, two lions, their eyes reflecting the headlights of their car. The next day her little sister showed her round her new home. 'If you ever want anything,' she said, 'just call one of the boys.'

On the mission station the girls learnt how much their mother contributed to the life of the mission. She was not only fluent in Baila, but she loved singing with the Africans and joining in their dances; she taught the women how to sew, obtaining colourful materials from England for them to use.

She was a keen gardener and loved planting trees. A fine avenue of eucalyptus trees stood as a memorial to her for many years. She also loved trekking with my father, visiting the surrounding villages and sharing in his work.

My father was not only a doctor and preacher, but also a builder and brick maker. He made bricks from local clay and fired them in a kiln he himself had made. He built their own two-storey house with a veranda protected by a screen from the mosquitoes, which were as thick as snowflakes in a snowstorm when the rains fell. In a corner of the veranda there was a little tree on which a chameleon rested motionless with its tongue ready to snap up any unwary fly that strayed in its direction. Apart from his own house, my father also built a little hospital, houses for the two nurses Miss Brown and Miss Booth, a house for a teacher, and various other buildings.

He spent much time mastering the local language, compiling a dictionary, and translating hymns and the New Testament, which the British and Foreign Bible Society printed, into Baila. Margaret remembers seeing him, with the help of local Baila speakers, pouring for hours over the translation, anxious that it should convey the right meaning. The church had been built previously, I think by Edwin Smith. The men sat on one side of the aisle and the women on the other. The men, who were in the habit of spitting, had sufficient spitting powers to project their spittle through their own but not the women's windows, to the dismay of anyone passing by outside, and continued to do so until they learnt that spitting in church was considered unseemly.

My parents respected the customs of the Baila. They preached chastity and faithfulness, but did not wage war against polygamy, believing that it ensured that women who lost their husbands would not be abandoned. It also encouraged good husbandry, for only when a man gained wealth could he afford a second or third wife. They did not condone wife swapping, a custom the Baila practised, or encourage dowries, but there was nothing they could do about them except set an example. Chief Mukamunga once visited them to ask Father if he could let him have 10/–, the amount his son needed for the dowry to marry the young woman of his choice. My father, even though he disapproved of dowries, offered him a hoe, which he had actually obtained for him, but the chief turned the offer down, saying he needed money. Eventually, my father gave him 5/–, but when he got up to go he also took the hoe with him. He himself had three wives, the first by choice, the second he had inherited and the third he had married, with the consent of his wives, the previous year. 'Do you have any problems?' my father asked. He replied with a wry smile, 'jealousy'. Jealousy usually arose in these households, my father discovered, over sleeping arrangements — each wife had her own hut.

The next day my parents, by chance, visited Mala, and there met the chief, Chikatakala, who had ten wives. His wives were seated around him while they all chatted. During a pause in the conversation my mother asked the chief if he had any problems with his many wives, specifically if there was any jealousy. The chief was very amused and so were his wives; they all laughed. Chief Chikatakala had bilateral cataracts and was almost blind.

My father sometimes helped the district magistrate, Gilbert Hall, to sort out people's marital problems. On one occasion, Macula demanded money and cattle from Machilanga, another member of the tribe, because the latter had had an adulterous relationship with his wife. The situation was particularly unfortunate because Macula was on probation as a potential Christian. Machilanga said that he was not to blame, for the woman had seduced him with her coyness. My father and Gilbert Hall were sympathetic until they discovered that the woman was not really Macula's wife. It was a hoax whereby Macula, after first obtaining support from my father and Gilbert Hall, hoped to wheedle money and cattle out of Machilanga.

Gilbert Hall, who was doing his best to stamp out the last

vestiges of domestic slavery in the district, asked my parents if they would take care of a slave girl who had run away from her master and taken refuge with a workman and his wife. After he had gone into her case carefully, he handed her over to my parents, asking them to look after her while he made further enquiries, or, he added, until a man turned up to marry her. My mother took her into the house, gave her a print frock and asked her to help look after my sister Kathleen, then just two months old and gaining weight at the rate of three-quarters of a pound a week. The slave girl was such a successful nanny that my mother was reluctant to let her go. Paulus, their local African preacher, told my father to marry her off quickly 'or there might be trouble'. Such women, it was generally agreed, were unsafe unless they were married. We do not know whom she eventually married, but she must have made someone a very special wife.

My father was once sent a leper called Monze, who was a prisoner at the gaol in Namwala. He was a diviner who was thought to possess magical powers and seemed to be a very nice fellow. He was in prison because in the course of his divining he had discovered that a certain man was a sorcerer and had said so. The man, who then complained of being unable to find anywhere to live, had killed himself. Monze had no compunction about what he had done and in fact thought that it had been a good thing. Had he been a politician in Canada, he would have said, 'I did nothing wrong,' but the law stepped in and imprisoned him.

Headman Mukombwe accompanied my father on one of his treks because he wanted to discuss his concern that so many Baila women seemed to be barren. He thought it was due to an increase in immorality among Baila men, which he ascribed to the influence of the white man. It was not that they were promiscuous, he argued, but that before the white man came, if a man were caught obtaining favours from a neighbour's wife he would have a hand or ear cut off and be disfigured for life, but when the white man came and administered justice, he was merely fined or in some cases only reprimanded — this seemed to condone promiscuity and licentiousness, or at least certainly did not discourage it.

Some of their Baila customs were harmless. On one trek my father noticed that one of the carriers always walked round any tree trunks or branches in his path, just as we might walk round rather than under a ladder. 'Why do you always walk round tree trunks and branches?' my father asked him. 'Because my wife is pregnant,' he replied, 'and if I were to walk over the trunks and branches, harm might come to our baby, and I wouldn't want that to happen.'

Like the Ameru in Kenya, the Baila in Zambia would refuse to touch anyone who seemed to be on the point of dying or who was already dead. Though it made life difficult for my father when he was running the hospital, some of their shibboleths had to be respected. There may be good reasons for not touching the dying or dead, infection and contagion for example, but it was pitiful to think of babies whose mothers had died in childbirth being abandoned and allowed to die. After bringing up Topsy and Moses, my mother had a particularly tender spot in her heart for such abandoned babies.

The message my father brought to the Africans, as far as I can tell from his letters, was based on the parables of Jesus, the Good Samaritan, the Prodigal Son, the Good Shepherd, encouraging them to love and trust God, believing that He really loved and cared for them and was doing His best to meet their needs, and that they in their turn should love and support one another. In one of his letters he said he was pleased that his message sometimes fell on fertile ground, for he had just come across a woman scouring the forest for fruits during a famine and she said to my father that she knew God was looking after her, for He even looked after the little birds and He would look after her.

Children on their way to church on Sundays used to sing with full-throated ease, 'We are children ob de King, Ebernelly King, Ebernelly King, we are children ob de King, singing as we churney.' A headman once asked my father if we made offerings to our ancestors. My father said, 'No, we worship God.' 'Oh,' he replied, 'so do we, but we think our ancestors will pray to God for us, but perhaps they are not in heaven.'

My father also helped them in more tangible ways. When my parents first arrived on the banks of the Kafue, the locals greeted them with, 'We are dead with meat hunger.' This seemed odd because the Baila have large herds of cattle, but they did not kill and eat them on a regular basis, only on special occasions such as when a chief or headman died. Then a 'cry' or funeral would be organized. If a chief died during the rainy season, his cry would be postponed till after the harvest. Funerals would take place one at a time so that the villagers could share in the celebration of one cry after another. At a cry there would be much dancing and singing, and young warriors with their spears would slaughter many cattle, so there was always much feasting. Because quantities were limited, however, only the elders consumed the home-brewed beer.

For much of the year, therefore, the Baila herded but did not eat their cattle, so were 'meat hungry'. My father, and mother too, were expected to hunt and bring home antelope, kudu or zebra from time to time. As Margaret remembers it, scrawny chicken was the only meat they had on the mission station and they soon tired of that, so they too were ready for wild meat. My father and mother were always ready to shoot a buck. Margaret remembers putting on her khaki shorts, shirt and bush hat and going out very early in the morning, crawling from anthill to anthill — they were scattered like little skyscrapers across the veld — for cover when approaching herds of wild game grazing peacefully on the open veld. African bearers would accompany them and, when my father was ready to shoot, he would beckon the bearers to remain behind an anthill while he himself crawled forwards on his stomach towards an anthill nearer the buck. Then he would fire and all the Africans would dance and sing, and tie the buck's feet together and hoist it onto a pole and carry it back in triumph to the village, where it would be shared among everyone.

On one of his treks my father was invited to shoot a leopard that would, the villagers were sure, come that night to steal chickens from a roost only 20 feet from where he had pitched his tent. At midnight he heard fowl squeaking some distance away. At 4.00 a.m. the fowl near his tent began to squeak and squawk. He quickly got up and put his head out of the tent, but by that time all was quiet. There was no sign of the marauder who paid three more visits before dawn and ran off with all the fowl. My father was sorry that he had not climbed up to a nearby platform after the leopard's first visit and given him a warm welcome when he returned.

Another source of protein was fish, though this was seasonal because the people did not seem to consume the fish in the river. When heavy rains fell, the whole veld would be transformed into numerous vleis. The Africans would dance around in the shallow water among the mudfish and, if they trod on any, the women would yell to the men to come and spear them and the fish would be cooked that evening. As the veld dried the fish laid their spawn and the eggs would lie dormant until the next rainy season when the eggs would hatch and a fresh crop of fish would emerge.

After the rains had fallen the grass grew and the cattle thrived, but when the dry season set in the cattle had to be swum across the Kafue to more fertile land further north. This was hazardous, for the river teemed with crocodiles, which were deadly, and with hippos, which were not. Twice a year there was tremendous excitement when the cattle swam the river. Margaret remembers how the whole mission, including her sister Kathleen, herself and most of the village would stand on the river bank while Africans, standing perilously in their narrow canoes, formed a protective shield on either side of the cattle as they tried to swim across the river. The crowds on the bank would scream and yell for all they were worth in an attempt to keep the hungry crocodiles at bay, but inevitably some cattle were lost. There would be a swirl of water and a calf or cow would disappear.

Veld fires were, however, more dangerous than either the river or the floods. In the summer, when the veld became tinder dry, severe and terrifying fires would sweep across the plain. Flames, fanned by the wind, would cross the veld as if pursuing the snakes and numerous small animals fleeing from their devastation. To protect the mission from such fires, a deep trench, like a dry moat, had been dug around it. It was always kept free from anything that might catch a spark and burn. Consequently, the veld fires that swept into the area did not reach the mission buildings.

Less common than veld fires, but equally destructive, were the clouds of locusts that sometimes descended on the area. One such cloud swept through the neighbouring forest while my cousin Raymond and I were spending several weeks of our summer holiday at Kasenga in 1932. My parents witnessed the devastation caused by several swarms, and my mother described one graphically to a group of Sunday school children in Lancashire. I can do no better than quote her description verbatim.

It was a day when my husband got up very early one morning, while it was still dark, and with the very first streak of light, was away in the car on a sandy track through the forest — for we had no roads — as he had an appointment with our Government official, our magistrate, who was also our nearest neighbour, 65 kilometres away. And a few hours later the Africans and I were wishing he had not gone away that day.

Everything looked as usual when he left. There were our two mission houses, there was the Compound, our Mission village of thatched huts and long, low-thatched dormitories for boys too far from home to return daily, and there was our long, pretty, old thatched church with no windows, but with window openings over which hung low thatch that kept out the sun on very hot days, and our school building, with the dispensary tucked under one end, and our maize (Indian corn) lands near the Mission Buildings.

Outside our church was one of our most prized possessions, our church and school bell! Most schools or missions that I knew had only a metal railway sleeper, suspended on a branch of a tree, and a piece of old iron with which to strike it. Ours was a real bell, to call people to work and scholars to school on weekdays, and people to church on Sundays. As people in the villages round about didn't know Sunday from a weekday, the bell was rung at an unusually early hour on Sundays, to tell the day, and again later on for service. But Sunday had its snags. Most boys liked bell duty, but occasionally there was a boy who didn't, or who was careless, or a bit shorter than others, who would give a mighty pull or two, when the rope would fly out of his hands and wind itself round the cross bar, out of reach, and there would be no more bell, and we would be left wondering whether we had or had not heard it. The next week we would get a boy who would go on and on until someone was sent to stop him. Consequently a missionary decided we should have a regular timing for our bell, and made a rule that every boy on bell duty should also sing through the hymn 'Onward Christian Soldiers', and when the hymn finished, so did the bell. I thought you would like to hear about that, though the special day I really want to tell you about was a weekday, not a Sunday.

It was about eleven o'clock in the morning; and the only sounds were of the teachers in school, or the crack of the whip of the ox-driver as he brought up the cart from the river with its 40-gallon drum of water for houses, school and hospital. Patients leaving the hospital clinic would stop by my garden for a word of greeting, and to give me news of the villages, and women coming from the river with babies on their backs and one, two or even three water pots on their heads, and never spilling a drop of water, would call a greeting as they passed.

When, all at once, there was a screaming and shouting, and all was pandemonium, as boys came rushing out of school, followed by teachers trying to form them into groups. Our bell started going for all it was worth, boys were blowing whistles and mouth organs, and drums in the villages round about were being drummed, mothers with screaming babies joined the throng, and boys rushed into my kitchen coming out clanging lids of pans on my pans, and everyone rushed at me shouting, '*Langa, langa*' (Look, look), '*Chikwikwe, chikwikwe*' (Locusts, locusts). The next cry was 'Matches, matches'. Not until I saw the face of the Head teacher, a very wise man, calling the same request, did I realize this cry was serious, and was given to understand that only noise and smoke deterred locusts. By the time I had obtained matches the advance guard was upon us. I lost time, more precious than I knew, by making everyone to whom I gave matches promise to give them to no one else. I was a very scared person. All buildings, with the exception of our own house, were thatched, and the consequences of a stray spark were quite terrifying. Ought I to have given out matches, or not? Only the teachers and I had money enough to buy them, and the teachers wouldn't be carrying theirs. Africans rubbed two pieces of wood together to get a spark, and that took time. I had lost time by stopping to extract promises from all to whom I gave matches, that under no circumstances would the boxes I had given them leave their hands, and I had only given them to responsible people. By this time the advance guards were on us. They are quite harmless creatures, they don't bite and they can't hurt humans; they merely damage gardens and, worse still, crops. Locusts are rather like grasshoppers, only bigger, and with thicker bodies, legs, and larger wings.

Before we knew it they were in our hair, on our faces, down the necks of our dresses and shirts and, as we had neither sleeves nor stockings, were simply all over us. But the worst feature was the darkness. They came in their millions. The day began to darken, and then became quite black, and soon the sun was quite blotted out. We were in the same position we are in here when a heavy snow storm is coming in, and we cannot see who is approaching us in the street, but instead of fog we had smoke.

The head teacher directed us all, and he and the menfolk lit little fires for a smoke screen all round our maize lands, and the women and I all round the smaller monkey nut (peanut) fields adjoining them. A few minutes earlier our monkey-nut fields had looked like so many little shamrock plants pushing up out of the sandy earth, but they were getting less and less. As soon as we saw a spurt of flame we dashed to put it out, and then another started elsewhere, and we would rush in another direction. It was very tiring, and every now and then we women flopped down and I noticed that we were not sitting on the earth, but on soft cushions of what looked like lawn mowings, (grass cuttings), which got higher and higher, they were the locust chewed leaves from our trees and crops. I wanted to ask so many questions, but knew I would never hear the answers for the din going on all around. Would this go on for hours or days? And did locusts sleep at night? Or did they work in shifts?

They had come on a very strong wind, and as the wind settled down so did the locusts. In about one to one-and-a-half hours the wind suddenly got up again, just a hurricane, and in a few minutes it had blown the locusts away over our buildings and river. Beyond our river lay two hundred miles of forest between us and the town of Livingstone. Our boys shouted their wishes that they would gorge themselves to death before reaching Livingstone! Be that as it may, the few that reached the town were met by chemicals.

As the sun began to show itself again, and we saw blue sky, we looked at the sorry sight of our stripped maize and monkey-nut fields, the skeleton of the rose-coloured bougainvillaea that had covered our house, and the giant fig tree in our front garden, that seemed, to us, to be holding out naked arms to the sky, asking for leaves to cover it. Miraculously they came in the spring. During the afternoon we were as a city of the dead, with no work, no school, and everyone doing as I was, listening for the sound of my husband's car.

Later, when everyone flew to meet it, my husband got out with, 'What's the damage?' The seniors thought we might have saved around a quarter of our crops. We walked silently round, and at the end, he said, 'You've done very well. I have come through villages where they have hardly saved a single cob of maize.' We all felt tearful, knowing this meant famine at the end of the year. It came. Boys who lived far away were too weak to walk to school, and those nearer came hungry. Old people were without food for a couple of days or more at a time, so that the children would have food. This meant more hospital patients etc., and until money came from England via churches and government, with its loss of time, we were short of stores along most lines.

Well now, I don't want you to think that we got locusts every year. Many years would elapse between them, and then they wouldn't always come to the same spot, but it is to help people in countries where these things do happen that our boys and girls have worked hard, and I'm proud to belong to the same church that they do. And I am sure that you are too. Aren't you?

When Kathleen and Margaret were living at Kasenga, and Raymond and I were there on holiday, we all witnessed the havoc the locusts caused. We knew how vast and dark the clouds of locusts were and what it felt like to be smothered by them. Locusts do not transmit any diseases, for this my parents were naturally thankful, but they were worried lest Kathleen and Margaret might pick up a 'tropical' disease that might be potentially dangerous.

Margaret developed typhoid while at school and, though she became ill, she survived and recuperated on a farm in South Africa. Kathleen developed amoebic dysentery. My father had been transferred to Kanchindu and when the holidays ended Kathleen and Margaret had to be taken to the line to be put on the train for Bulawayo. The car was laden with my mother and father, my two sisters, two trunks, petrol cans full of water for the car and a canvas bag full of cold, boiled water for the passengers, as well as spare cans of petrol for the car. When they left Kanchindu on the way to the railway at Choma they had to make a steep climb over a very rough track through the forest. The valley was hot and humid. The car boiled as it struggled up the steep hillside and, by the time they reached a stream, the car had used all the water, even the drinking water. Kathleen and Margaret were parched, so my father asked two white men who were on the banks of the stream if the water was safe. 'We've been drinking it and we're OK,' they said. So they drank it.

By the time Kathleen reached St Peter's a few days later, she was weak with diarrhoea and lapsed into a coma. When she came round four days later, my father and mother were at her bedside. She was still critically ill. She missed most of that term recuperating on the Cleute's farm in South Africa. This was the same farm at which Margaret had convalesced after her bout of typhoid fever. Luckily, both recovered completely.

My father had been transferred to Kanchindu from Kasenga in either late 1930 or early 1931, so it was while he was at Kanchindu that he heard he was being transferred yet again. This time it was to a little village called Maua in Kenya, for a hospital had recently been opened there and the doctor in charge was returning to England in 1934. My parents had felt from time to time that, though their work in Kasenga was well worth undertaking, the population was so thinly spread that his talents would be put to greater use were he in a more populated region and this Maua was, so they looked forward to the move with a great deal of anticipation. The Baila, on the other hand, did not want to lose him. They voiced their feelings in a letter to the Methodist synod held in Broken Hill on 29 May 1934. It read:

Chairman and Friends,
    We pray to you to hear the words of us people, who are in darkness in the country of Baila, North, South, East and West.

1. First of all we chiefs of Baila and the Christians here greet the whole synod.
2. We beg that Dr Gerrard shall not leave this country of Baila because it is he who has become our father. He knows all our diseases better than other doctors.
3. We beg that you, our masters, will hear the words of your servants which we send to the synod. We desire that Dr Gerrard be called the Father of the Baila.
4. We know that one must travel everywhere for the work of the Great God, just as Jesus travelled. Now we say that Dr Gerrard should carry the burden of our wickednesses till he leaves to go to England.
5. Members of the synod, we beg that you will send another doctor there where you send Dr Gerrard. Will you please send this word to the officers in England, that this is what the chiefs say in this country of darkness, Northern Rhodesia.
6. Members of synod, we know nothing, but we say that you should listen to these words of ours. We are always perplexed at the way you are moved about. Now we say that Dr Gerrard may be the mainstay of the Ministry of Baila.

7. We pray that on our missions also we may have a minister who continues till death in our country, that he shall bear the heavy burden of the Baila. We chiefs and all our people agree to this.
8. Now we pray that God's assembly will listen to our words and give to us Dr Gerrard, that he may live here always.
9. We pray that the assembly will write us a letter in reply.
10. The name of us chiefs will come on paper on which we have put our official stamps.

A month after my parents arrived in Maua, he received the following letter from Harry Mwanga. The letter speaks for itself. My father had been greatly loved and he was greatly missed.

Kasenga,
P.O. Namwala,
8/1/34.

To Rev. H. S. Gerrard,
Meru,
Kenya.

Dear Sir,

People whom you stayed with for a number of years and left them again after having done such a wide and tremendous work in healing all various sicknesses, and bringing most invalids to life who were about to meet death, are anxiously waiting for your arrival in their country again.

You had become a great father and healer among we poor Africans in our country. May I tell you this time that every time when I visit my parents in Maala, I am using to have all sorts of questions from old and young men and women about you coming back in the country you left, both of you. In short, all the people in the whole of Baila have their hearts bleeding for your departure into another country. Yet we know that people in Kenya are our fellow Africans, but we still have our hearts bleed bitterly for your departure.

By not exaggerating your popularity to both of you, my grief and of the rest is 100%.

This does not mean that we despise your colleagues whom you left in charge of the hospital.

I remember Mungaila the chief asked me eight times at least since you left the place.

Hoping you will be back in Africa after your furlough in England to a country called Baila.

I am yours most humble,
Harry Mwanga.

My father, many years later, learnt that the letter sent by the Baila chiefs to the synod in Broken Hill, had been forwarded to the Mission House in London, and that the latter had told the Baila chiefs that Dr Gerrard could certainly stay in their country, but only if they could support him financially. This they could not do.

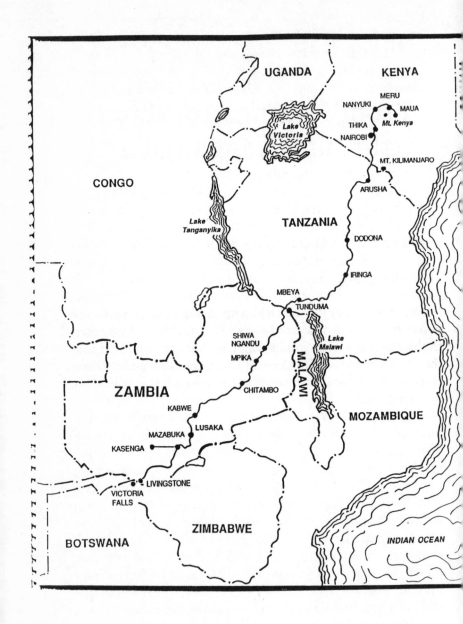

7

From Kasenga to Maua through Tanganyika

The move to Maua, while opening new horizons for my parents, meant that they would once more be separated from their children. They could not take Kathleen and Margaret with them, for their Ford would already be over-loaded with their own luggage, with all the cans of water and petrol that they would need to take, and with Andrew, their faithful servant who would travel with them. And, because they could not leave Kathleen and Margaret to fend for them-selves on the mission station, they had to send them home. So, Kathleen aged 16 found herself in charge of her younger sister Margaret, aged nearly 10, travelling to Cape Town where they boarded the boat for England and a new home. Auntie Winifred and Uncle Tom welcomed them with open arms and said that arrangements had been made for them, when the holidays were over, to go to Howells, a residential school for girls in North Wales, where their cousin, Christine, was already a pupil. The change in schools was a happy one for Margaret and she quickly settled in, but Kathleen found herself among a group of older girls who had already made their friends and she was also expected to play field hockey, a game she had never played at St Peter's. She missed the freedom that had been hers in Bulawayo and, of course, her parents.

My father and mother packed their model T Ford and, with Andrew, set off for their second journey into the unknown.

Their first had started when they stepped onto the Blue Funnel liner *Aeneas* in Liverpool 19 years before and had ended in Kasenga. This one began when they turned the ignition of their trusted but not wholly reliable car in Kasenga and ended when they reached Maua.

They started out on Tuesday 19 June 1934 and, having passed through Mazabuka and Lusaka, reached Broken Hill, the copper capital of Africa if not the world, 320 kilometres later. On the following morning, Thursday, they took the car to a garage for a final overhaul. They left on Friday afternoon and managed to reach Kapiri Mposhi by nightfall. There they found a good hotel belonging to an old settler, Mr Locke. When my father told him he had just driven from Kasenga, Mr Locke described how in 1908 he had travelled with ox-wagons through Nanzhila, a mission station not far from Kasenga, which my father knew well and had visited many times. He had been held up for a fortnight and remembered Mr and Mrs Price as a young married couple not long in Rhodesia. Mr Locke was a perfect hotel manager; the food was good and everything was spotlessly clean.

The next day, Saturday, my parents set off on a good road for Kalwa and the home of a couple of retired Scottish missionaries, Mr and Mrs Moffat. They passed through well-wooded country and crossed several streams, plus two rivers spanned by excellent bridges. They found the northeastern part of Northern Rhodesia very different from the veld around Kasenga. They stopped for petrol at a pump on Chirupula's estate, but the person in charge said he had none and instead served them tea in a large, rambling, two-storeyed house with a picturesque outlook. Having covered 362 kilometres, they reached Kalwa before sundown and were warmly welcomed by the Moffats. Mr Moffat was a grandson of the better-known Dr Robert Moffat, and had been born at Kuruma in the Cape Colony. His grandfather Robert, who had been born in Scotland in 1795, had had very little education and had moved to Manchester, England, where he had worked for a pious

110

merchant, James Smith. He fell in love with Smith's daughter, Mary. He also approached the London Missionary Society, which sent him to South Africa in 1816 at the age of 22. Four years later Mary followed him and they were married in Cape Town. Robert Moffat settled in Kuruma, near the Orange River. He was a man of great mental and physical powers, but was best known for his conversion of a Hottentot desperado, Afrikaner, for whose arrest and death the government in Cape Town had offered a reward of $500. Moffat had been warned that he was dangerous and should be avoided, but he nevertheless sought him out and, in less than a year, returned with him as meek as a lamb. The people were amazed. Moffat's mission was stationed at Kuruma, but he travelled widely. He also translated the New Testament into Sechuana, the most widespread of the African languages. He returned to England in 1870, was awarded an honorary DD by the University of Edinburgh, and died in 1883. His son, John, who was also a lifelong missionary in Africa, was born in Kuruma, in 1835. It was Robert's grandson who hosted my parents in Kalwa. The three generations of Moffats had served Africa for more than 100 years.

The following day was Sunday and, on being pressed, my parents agreed to stay. The Moffats had been at Kalwa for three years and had built a good brick house with a tiled roof for themselves, a church for the community and a compound for the workers. Their farm, which was well irrigated, consisted of an orchard, a wheat field, a vegetable garden, chickens and cattle. Mr Moffat was thoroughly enjoying his retirement, which Mrs Moffat had strongly recommended after 30 years of service to make room for younger people. On conducting the service in the church that morning, Mr Moffat spoke informally, as though he were carrying on a conversation with his congregation, and got a good response from them.

On Monday they set off at sunrise. Calling at Mills's store for petrol, they filled the tank from the pump for 4/9d. a gallon and bought an extra case of cans for 5/– a gallon. They knew that petrol would be more expensive further along the road and that supplies would be uncertain. After a few kilometres, they turned off the road to see the Scottish Church mission at Chitambo. After breakfast with Dr and Mrs Beveridge, they were shown round the mission comprising a girls' school with dormitories, a church and a hospital — all of brick with tiled roofs. Wherever my parents went they noted that Scottish missionaries were very good builders. When they left after a morning cup of tea, they noticed that the car was not pulling well. They thought at first that they were overloaded, but later decided that the engine was missing on one cylinder. Later, while lunching at a wayside rest hut, they discovered that a bolt was missing from the back spring. This, the engine trouble and the realization that they had only just started their journey cast a shadow over them as they limped along the road to Mpika, which they reached after sundown.

At Mpika they found a delightful hotel, the Crested Crane, belonging to Captain Smith. With Mpika being a stopover for aeroplanes flying from Cairo to the Cape and vice versa, Captain Smith had built a hotel to cater for that traffic. The lounge was floored with thick slates in various shades of pink, blue and grey obtained from hills a few miles away. Each bedroom had its own separate colour scheme with slabs of slate as washstand tops; all the woodwork was in local timber with the doors and furniture tastefully designed and well made. The setup reminded my parents of Sinclair Lewis's *Work of Art*; Mother was also reminded of the Bear Inn in Gloucester. My parents had covered 502 kilometres since leaving Broken Hill.

On the next day, Tuesday, Captain Smith hunted round for a bolt for the spring and, with the help of an assistant or two, he and my father fixed the spring. Captain Smith then found out what was wrong with the engine and soon put it right. He also told my father that he should be able to get a bed at Colonel Gore-Browne's place in Shiwa Ngandu, 160 kilometres further on. As it was noon when my parents left, 100 kilometres was all they could expect to cover that day. The road was rough, hilly in places, and they crossed many little streams. The trees and grass were green. At teatime they discovered that the bolt in the back spring was again missing. It was dusk by the time they saw Lake Young and knew they were near their destination. They drove up to the house with their headlights on and a man came out calling, 'Come in.'

They found themselves in a large dining room with a massive dining table and a great fire at one end. Their host, Mr Saville, was the manager of the establishment, the owner being away in England. He put my parents in a fine bedroom in which the manservant made a fire and provided them with hot baths and dinner. When Andrew saw my parents' bedroom, he opened his eyes wide and said he had never seen anything like it, not even in a town.

Next morning they had a chance to see where they were — in a mansion with terraced gardens and a magnificent view of Lake Young and the surrounding country. When Andrew brought their morning cup of tea, he said, 'We are unlucky; the front spring is broken.' Fortunately, Saville had the spring of an old Ford in the yard and he sent his African driver to look for it. He also found a steel bolt for their back spring. Africans and my father spent the morning effecting repairs and that proved to be the end of their car troubles. They had a look round the house — it had a fine library, lounge, bedroom suites and nurseries and, two storeys up, Mrs Gore-Browne's private room with a glorious view of the lake and hills.

My parents left after lunch and had a good run to the Scottish mission at Lubwa. There they found that Dr and Mrs Brown were expecting other guests, so had to put my parents up in an unfurnished house in which they slept on mattresses on the floor. They had baths and a good dinner and were just having coffee when the expected guests, Mr and Mrs Beveridge, arrived. My parents retired early.

Next day, Thursday, the mission bell was rung before it was light and while my parents were getting up Dr Brown gave them a call. He then went to the hospital to see his patients, returning to show my parents round the station. His own house was perched on a hill, with a fine panorama over the plain. He was building a beautiful church. He was a very active man and was ready to turn his hand to almost anything. My parents left before 7.00 a.m. and travelled through delightful country with numerous villages, picturesque streams and green woods. The last 16 kilometres to Mwenzo were along a country lane, off the main road and very rough and hilly. On reaching Mwenzo in the early afternoon, they drove up to the house of Dr Chisholm, with whom my father had travelled on the same boat in 1926. After tea Dr Chisholm showed them round the mission. It was well set out with the hospital as its chief feature — all in all a fine block of buildings such as my father might have built at Kasenga and an impressive church. A woman teacher and a Mr Fraser, the educationist son of Dr Donald Fraser, joined my parents at dinner. Before dinner they sat over a fire in an upstairs lounge. The house was a big two-storey building with verandas all the way round. They went to bed early.

The next day, Friday, they were up bright and early. They loaded the car and were off soon after sunrise. Dr Chisholm came down in his dressing gown to say goodbye. The road was rough for the first few miles but became smooth as soon as they reached the main road from Nyasaland, now Malawi. A mile further on they turned off to the right, joined the Great North Road, and crossed the border into Tanganyika, now Tanzania. They immediately found themselves on a wide, well-made road with magnificent views of mountainous country. The road was well maintained by the territory's Public Works Department and small camps had been set up for its work gangs every ten miles. The surface was good, streams were well bridged and they covered the ground quickly. There was a long steep descent into the small township of Mbeya, the centre of a gold-mining district made up chiefly of rather squalid Indian stores. They breakfasted at the hotel and then went through customs where, to their surprise and dismay, they had to pay 15 per cent duty on their trusty old Ford. The office closed before their business was completed and, while they waited, they went to the garage for oil and petrol, now little more than 3/– a gallon. East African coinage was only in shillings and cents, with 100 cents to the shilling. They sent Andrew off to the local market with a shilling to buy himself some food. He came back saying that it was far too much and that he wanted coins with holes in them. My father gave him some ten-cent pieces and followed him. He found Andrew standing with a copper in his hand considering the purchase of four large, cooked sweet potatoes. His purchase completed, a woman carried his potatoes to the car for him. At 2.30 my parents returned to the customs and immigration departments, and left about half an hour later. They were told that a Mr Cormack kept a hotel about 96 kilometres along the road, and there they intended to spend the night.

A few miles outside Mbeya the road began to climb the Mporotos hills, reaching a height of more than 2300 metres before it began to descend again. The views of the hills and plains were magnificent. The road itself was a fine bit of engineering, cut out of the hillsides and winding round their contours; some of the gradients were steep. Indians used the road to transport large quantities of material from Dodoma to Mbeya. My parents found an inn at Chimala, which was near a stream and reminded them of Derbyshire. A traveller for an engineering firm and an inspector of mines joined them for dinner. From the inspector they learnt that there was no petrol to be had for the next 280 kilometres and they had only five gallons in their tank. He suggested they should ask his driver (he had a hired lorry) as he had several cases of petrol on board and could replace a case at Mbeya. The man, an African, was rather reluctant, but finally agreed to sell my father a case. Their companions told them of the Lupa gold fields near Mbeya where there were 600 men digging, besides women and children. An amazing road had been made that rises to a height of 3100 metres and from which the aeroplane carrying the mail could be seen as it passed below.

Arrangements for a bath at the hotel were rather primitive, but the dinner was excellent — soup, pork, four vegetables, stewed cape gooseberries and cream, and coffee. They had a comfortable night.

They made an early start on the Saturday morning. The road was good and, as they had done for the whole journey, my mother and father took it in turns to drive. They covered 190 kilometres before stopping at the Sao heights for lunch. There, at an altitude of more than 2000 metres, a man and his wife ran a farm with a charming cottage in which to accommodate travellers, but my parents went on to Iringa, which was approached by a steep road cut out of the face of the mountainside. The town had two good hotels, an excellent garage, government offices and extensive Indian and African quarters. They arrived in time to have a new front spring put in the car before the garage closed. The hotel was very comfortable. They had luxurious hot baths, sat and read papers in front of a huge wood fire, and had a good dinner. The night was cold.

Having left immediately after breakfast on Sunday 1 July, they covered nearly 50 kilometres before beginning a 15-kilometre descent down a winding road that clung to the wall of an escarpment. My mother, who was driving at the time, had to drive very carefully, keeping close to the inside of the road when rounding corners. Below them they could see a vast, arid plain, but not the Serengeti. When they reached it, they found it was dry and barren, the only vegetation being thorn and baobab trees. It did not change for nearly 100 kilometres, when they reached a shallow river with an African hotel nearby. There they lunched on bread, marmite and apples from their food box. Barren as this country appeared to be, they saw lots of cattle and sheep, though what the animals found to eat was a mystery. The road then began to climb once more and by the middle of the afternoon they had reached Dodoma, a station on the Tanganyika railway, where they found a hotel. The Greek proprietor was having his afternoon nap when they arrived, but an African roused him. He found a room for them and gave them a refreshing pot of tea. They then wandered round Dodoma and were surprised to find a beautiful but small cathedral, donated by an Englishwoman in memory of her brother. The cathedral was an octagonal stone building with a dome from which it was lighted. All the appointments of the church were simple and beautiful. They returned at 7.00 p.m. for an English service. There were 17 in the congregation and they sat in the choir stalls. From the altar steps Canon Banks preached a simple harvest festival sermon.

On Monday they had an uninteresting journey to Kondoa and Irangi. Their guidebook had claimed there would be a hotel at the latter, but all they found were a few Arab and Indian stores and some government offices. They filled up with petrol and had tea in an untidy little room at the back of an Indian store, whose owner was the only person in Irangi who could speak English. They continued on to Babati, where they found one or two stores and a hotel left in the care of an African, but there was neither food nor bedding. They had expected to spend the night there, but as it was still only about 3.30, they decided to carry on for another 160 kilometres to Arusha. Between Kondoa and Irangi they had passed through some fine scenery, mountainous, green and well wooded, climbing to almost 2000 metres. They also saw some wild animals and Andrew was greatly interested in some giraffes and ostriches. Just after sunset they saw three lions only 50 yards from the road. My father was driving at the time; my mother told him to hurry on, which he did, so they did not stay to admire them.

The road had been rough, so they were glad when, as darkness fell, it improved and they could risk going at a fair speed. They could see enough to realize that the country was flat and treeless, but as they entered Arusha they saw palm trees, and banana and coffee plantations. Arusha lies at the foot of Mount Meru, and has become a great coffee-growing centre because of the constant precipitation of rain and mist the mountain causes. They found what they described as a very 'posh' hotel, with a palm court, swimming pool and immense dining room. It rained heavily during the night and my mother worried lest Andrew, sleeping outside in the car under a cover that was full of holes, should develop pneumonia because he already had a cold. They discovered the next morning that the poor man had had very little sleep and that his cold had not benefited. Presumably, Andrew spent all his nights sleeping in the car and we think he obtained his food either from local markets or from the kitchens of the homes and hotels in which my parents stayed. We wonder how many years would pass before he could share the same sort of accommodation as his master and mistress.

On Tuesday my parents had breakfast at their hotel in Arusha and with it came a copy of the weekly edition of the *East African Standard*, the first newspaper they had seen since leaving Broken Hill. At about 10.00 a.m. they left well-watered Arusha behind them and entered dry and arid land. The road was thick with larval dust and full of potholes; with the wind behind them they were shrouded in dust. They had to go carefully, often in second gear; the engine overheated and the water in the radiator boiled away. From the lower slopes of Mount Meru, with the mountain itself hidden in the clouds, it took them an hour or more to reach better country. On the previous day they had seen the peak of Mount Kilimanjaro gleaming in the setting sun above the clouds. As they left Mount Meru they again saw Mount Kilimanjaro, this time on their right. Andrew had never seen anything like it and was filled with astonishment. He would have been even more astonished had he known that when Britain, the colonial ruler of Kenya, and Germany, then the colonial ruler of Tanganyika, were originally drawing the boundary between Kenya and Tanganyika, Mount Kilimanjaro was naturally included in Kenya. When the Kaiser heard that the only two snow-capped African peaks were both being given to Kenya, he immediately sent a telegram to his grandmother, Queen Victoria, suggesting that as Kenya already had one snow-capped mountain (Mount

Kenya), Mount Kilimanjaro should be given to Tanganyika. Relations between the two being cordial at the time, Queen Victoria agreed and this is why Kilimanjaro is now in Tanzania.

At about noon they reached the Tanganyika (Tanzania) border at Longido. Here my father had again to pass through customs. The clerk, as at Mbeya, was an African. My father had hoped to get back the duty he had paid on the car, but there was nothing doing; all he got was a paper that exempted him from paying further duty in Kenya. It was windy and the road was dusty. As there was no suitable place for lunch, they drove through the gate out of Tanganyika and into Kenya, making for Namanga at the entrance to the game reserve. On the way they saw many zebra, as well as giraffe and antelope of various kinds. At Namanga there was a rustic hotel with a big garden. The manager gave them a pot of tea and a big plateful of ham sandwiches for the modest sum of 2/–. Soon after leaving Namanga they entered open country and saw herds of all sorts of game and many ostriches. They had also expected to see elephants, but their hopes were not to be realized.

As the sun was setting, they reached Kajiabo and found accommodation in a large house. It had been built originally as a sanatorium for men who worked at a low-lying salt lake some miles away. It was delightfully situated and very commodious. They had a large bedroom with an adjoining bathroom. It was in the charge of Africans who served excellent meals. In the visitor's book my father noticed one Murray-Hughes, a name familiar to him as someone who had been at Kasenga in his predecessor's time. After dinner, he asked the two other men who were present if one of them were this gentleman. Indeed, one of them was this same Murray-Hughes and my parents were soon giving him the latest information about the Namwala district, and about Doogan and other people he had known. My father asked him if he knew Mr Mortimer, who was to be his contact in Nairobi. On hearing that Mr

Mortimer worked in the government Lands Department, my parents lost no time in finding him when they reached Nairobi the next morning.

On Wednesday 4 July, my parents covered the last 14 kilometres to Nairobi. The road was excellent and macadamized for the approach to the city. As they entered it they found both the Lands Department and Mr Mortimer who gave them a guide to take them to the post office and bank, and on to his own home. There they found letters from home and a very kind letter from Mr Hopkins, the chairman of the Meru district. The Mortimers had arranged for them to stay in a house belonging to the mission. They had lunch with a Mr and Mrs Beaton who lived next door and they then put all their belongings in temporary quarters. They had tea and dinner and a quiet evening with the Mortimers. Mr Mortimer had entered the ministry in England in about 1910. He developed rheumatoid arthritis, resigned from the ministry and went out to Kenya. When my father saw him, he had a very good post with the government. His arthritis was still a handicap, but he managed an occasional game of tennis.

On Thursday morning, my father visited the immigration department, obtained car and driving licences, did a number of odd jobs and visited the hairdresser, as did my mother. In the afternoon Mr Mortimer took them a few miles out by car to the Jeanes School at Kabete, but they did not see much of it because the head was busy. That evening they all went to the cinema and so ended a long and eventful day.

On the road north out of Nairobi on Friday 6 July, they passed through beautiful country, hills and valleys, the slopes of which were all under cultivation. They stopped at Thika for morning tea, and from the hotel veranda had a view of a very pretty waterfall. Beyond Nyeri the country was flat and open on the lower slopes of Mount Kenya. At Nanyuki they stayed at the Sportsman's Arms, a delightful hotel facing the mountain. It had been open for only a year and was very popular, particularly with those who loved trout fishing and other sports. It was well appointed, with electric lights, excellent bathrooms, and splendid lounge and dining rooms. Mount Kenya was hidden by clouds when they arrived, but when the sun was setting the clouds vanished and they were able to see the peak in its pink mantle of snow.

On Saturday, a perfect day, they continued their journey. The road climbed gently but steadily to a height of over 2500 metres and then wound its way through the Meru forest, where they passed a sawmill, a hallmark of Western civilization, which supplied timber for the construction of European-type houses: there was no clay with which to make bricks. They reached Meru at about 11.00 a.m., and there met Mr and Mrs Hopkins. Mr Hopkins was the chairman of the Kenya Methodist missions. Arthur Hopkins, who was three years older than my father, came of good Methodist stock, for both his father and grandfather had been Methodist ministers. He himself had wanted to break new ground; he wanted to be a missionary. He went out to East Africa for the first time in 1918, to Ribe near Mombasa. He was twice invalided home, but was sent out a third time in 1928 to replace R. T. Worthington, the chairman of the Kenya district who had suddenly and unexpectedly died. Arthur worked hard to establish interdenominational harmony and was so successful that he was known as *Mwigithan*, the conciliator. The very kind letter they had received from him when they reached Nairobi had moved my parents. When he welcomed them to Meru, they looked and felt as fresh as if they had only left Kasenga that morning. Surrounded as it was by lovely green hills, the mission came up to their expectations and, what was more important, the land was well populated.

My parents spent the rest of the day at Meru mission (or Kaga as it was called) and went on to Maua, 50 kilometres away, on the following day, Tuesday. Halfway there the road began a long ascent and, at its summit, they came across a flourishing African market. They later learnt that such markets were popular in that district. The road then gradually descended into Maua, which was to be their new home. There, Dr and Mrs Brassington greeted and welcomed them after their 21-day journey of a little more than 3000 kilometres. He was the doctor in charge of the Berresford Memorial Hospital. The hospital was the gift of a Mr Sam Berresford who had donated £3000 for its construction.

Sam Berresford, a member of the United Methodist Church, was born in 1848 and died in 1935, a year after my father and mother started to work in the hospital he had donated. Little had he realized how much his hospital would mean to the village of Maua, or how much more rewarding it would make my parents' medical work there. Sam had been a clerk in an ironworks in Chesterfield, a pretty town in England known for its twisted spire, which, from whatever angle it is viewed, is still crooked. Its message is clear; however perfect we may try to be, we all have kinks and blemishes. Sam had been a staunch member of the United Methodist Church, had a fine voice, sang in the choir and often took solo parts. He married Martha Lawson. Her father had a shoe shop at 2 Glumangate, and when she and Sam married their first home was above the shop. They later moved to 18 Avondale Road and had three sons, John born in 1873, Thomas in 1875 and Harold in 1881. After Martha died in 1908 he remarried, we do not know whom, and a fourth child Patricia was born in 1911, but sadly died when she was only five years old.

The first United Methodist Church missionaries to go to East Africa were T. Wakefield and J. Woolmer. They landed in 1862 and the Meru mission opened in 1912. The church wanted to increase its work in that part of the world and, in particular, to add a medical arm to its mission. It was in response to this that Sam Berresford generously gave £3000 to building and equipping a hospital at Maua. Sam's second son, Thomas, had hoped to be a medical missionary, but died before completing his training. It was the money, Margaret Bell recalls, that Sam had put aside for his son's training that he used to build the Berresford Memorial Hospital.

Dr Brassington was appointed to Maua in 1925. The hospital, nestled in the Nyambeni hills, was opened in 1930. Built of local stone with a shingled roof and concrete floor, it consisted of three buildings. The central block contained the entrance, waiting room, examining room, treatment rooms and dispensary; the second block consisted of two 25-bed wards, one for men and one for women; and the third housed the kitchen and two storage rooms.

At the end of the first six months, Dr Brassington submitted his first report. He had seen 1580 patients, 24 of whom he had admitted to the hospital; two had been moribund on arrival and had died, one of tuberculosis, the other of malnutrition and worm infestation. The remainder had infections such as dysentery, malaria and severe skin infections; one had a hyena bite. All would have died had there not been a doctor and a hospital in which to treat them. Of the outpatients, yaws accounted for two-fifths; malaria, dysentery, scabies, bronchitis, worms and constipation accounted equally for the rest.

Sam Berresford, who was ultimately responsible for much happiness in Chesterfield and Maua, must have had some sadness in his life, for the plaque at the entrance to the hospital commemorating his gift was given in 'loving memory of his mother, Sarah, who died in 1873, aged 62, his first wife, Martha, who died in 1908, aged 58, his eldest son, John, who died in 1919, aged 47, his second son Thomas who died in 1897, aged 22, and his daughter, Patricia who died in 1917 at the early age of five. He never mentions his father. He was survived by only one of his four children and his second wife.

8

Teaching and Preaching

When I was growing up between the two world wars, many if not most of my generation believed that the world was gradually becoming a better place in which to live and that it would soon, as we often sang in church, 'be filled with the Glory of God as the waters cover the sea'. We believed that England, through the League of Nations, had an important role to play in replacing war as a means of settling disputes with arbitration and sweet reasonableness. Many of us also thought that, since the League of Nations was a child of Western and therefore Christian civilization, it was our duty to carry the Christian message to the people we innocently called heathen. We also knew it was important to raise the standard of living of the working, underprivileged classes, but we knew that this alone would not build a heaven on earth, for we did not live on bread alone. Tomás Masaryk, president of newly formed Czechoslovakia, expressed the spirit of the times when he said that history tends towards Jesus, suggesting that following the teachings of Jesus and spreading the Gospel to those who had never heard the Good News, would accelerate this trend. I am sure my parents believed this too.

Two world wars, the holocaust, the atom bomb, hundreds of minor and not so minor wars and skirmishes and the zest with which men, and it is almost always if not always men who are to blame, were slaughtering their neighbours, usually their nearest neighbours, with weapons of increasing deadliness, have made it quite clear that if history is not tending towards Jesus, many, many people, among them some who call themselves Christians, are doing their utmost to thwart this trend.

However, this belief in the importance of the Christian message and the need to make it known to those who had never been exposed to it was the driving force that kept my parents working in Africa, with a few interludes at home, for 26 years.

To carry this message, my father had to learn to speak to the Baila and Ameru fluently in their own languages and to translate the New Testament and a number of our better-known hymns into Baila. When he was transferred to Maua, he found the Gospels had already been translated into Kimeru; the Acts and the rest of the New and all the Old Testament followed later. To gain access to the Bible, which contained the heart of his message, the Africans had to learn to read. To learn to read they had to go to school. This is why missionary schools formed such an important part of the missionary's work. The missionary, in this case my parents, demonstrated that the message could be translated into action in their daily lives, and especially in their response to the Africans' call for help. Mr Groves, a fellow missionary then back in England, once asked my father how he was delivering his message to the Africans in Northern Rhodesia. This was his reply.

I am pleased to accede to Mr Groves' request and send you a letter about our work here, the more so as you yourselves are taking a special interest in this station. I hope I can write something which will help to make the contact between us a little closer.

There is an occasion which brings particular joy to the heart of a missionary, for then he sees the fruits of his labours, though at the same time it is the beginning of other responsibilities. Of one such occasion I would tell you in this note.

On a recent tour of our schools I came to the village of Chilumba. It is well situated, facing west, as do all native villages, and looks away over rolling, forest-clad country. Its houses are arranged in a row of semicircles along the hillside, the chief's own group occupying the centre. Across the open space before the chief's quarters is a teacher's house, alongside which passes a broad road leading to the small thatched building which serves as church and school. I say small, but it is really an ambitious building for a native village, being oblong in shape, with walls of unburnt brick. The people did all the work themselves, except the actual laying of the bricks, which was done by a trained native sent by the mission.

Chilumba is the foremost of our schools, and its history shows how such work may grow. Thirteen years ago a boy from there, Kausu, applied to enter the school at Kasenga. Under present rules I should not have admitted him, for he had once been a scholar at our Namwala station; his home was nearer there; and he ought to have gone back there. However I had been only a few months on the field, and was wanting scholars; the mission was not as well organized as it is now, and Kausu, or Jeremiah as he became later, was admitted. Before brothers and friends from the village joined him in school, Jeremiah himself, out of school hours, worked in our house, where one of his duties was to nurse occasionally our baby boy. His idea of soothing him when fretful was to prop him up on his knees, and, holding his head between his hands, rock it from side to side, and sing to him. He it was who gave my wife a nickname *Kazunumozo*, Mrs Hardheart, a name which, in spite of itself, came to be used with affection by Jeremiah and others.

Jeremiah had reached the top of the school when the Institute was opened at Kafue, and he was one of the first batch of students. When he came out, three years later, I was on furlough, and Mr Price stationed him at his own village. There were difficulties in working among his own people. One of which, he told me later, was that they took advantage of his earning a regular salary, and got him to help them out with their taxes, so that he was sometimes hard put to it to clothe himself decently. Then he was a prophet in his own country. But the appointment was justified. Young as he was, he won his own people, and gathered almost all the adults of the village into a catechumen class. Further, as boys in the school became fluent readers, they passed on to Kasenga for further schooling. So practically the whole village, young and old, came under the influence of the mission. Jeremiah has taught at other schools since, but he laid a good foundation, and others have carried on the work. Hence I enjoyed that Sunday as one of the happy occasions of a missionary's life.

It had been a stormy night, and the rain continued until well on into the morning. Then it cleared, and the bell rang, and the folk trooped down to the little church. Before the service began I noticed a little incident. Some women looked through the church windows, a remark was made, and a number of men walked out of church. These same women then entered, and the men returned. It was some native taboo which they wished to avoid. Then, before the service began, we found it necessary to put outside some fowls, which were part of the offertory. The service itself was engaged in earnestly and reverently. Before it closed we had to receive six more members. The previous quarter Mr Price had baptized thirty. Now these six knelt down for the same sacrament. Briefly its significance was explained, prayer offered, and then, as water was sprinkled on their heads, they received their new names, 'Thomas, I baptize thee in the name ...' 'Martha, I baptize thee in the name ...' and so on. And so a few more were gathered into the fellowship of the church of Christ.

Before closing, I might tell you a little of the medical

side of things. The other day I received an urgent message from a chief to go and pull a tooth out. He had set out that morning to come here, accompanied by wives and friends, but he was old and ailing, and, after two miles, had been compelled to turn back. Twelve miles to go and pull a tooth out seemed a tall order, but I got out the motor cycle and went. The only obstacle on the road was some mud in a vlei, trampled into a black slime by cattle, and both going and returning I was fortunate in getting help to push the cycle through. The chief and I retired to the back of a hut, some women were told to make themselves scarce, and then I removed the molar which had kept the old man awake the last four nights. Before leaving I dropped a suggestion that had been in my mind, namely, that he and his fellow chiefs might contribute a few cattle to the hospital so that patients might have milk. He quite agreed, and told me to speak to the others about it.

Yesterday I had to operate on a woman with elephantiasis. Coming before it was far advanced, she made my job easier. Also I was working single handed, the orderly, Samson, being away attending some men wounded in a fight. The woman put her baby, a fretful, ailing child, on the floor of the hut, while she came in for her operation. Afterwards she and her baby lay comfortably in bed in the ward.

There is a very old woman, Nakasokolo, a one-time slave, who lives in the hospital quarters. Bent with age, skin all wrinkled, of unknown age, she is still not without vigour. She has delusions that folk curse her and throw stones at her, and the other day she called me, 'Come on Jelende [Gerrard], there is one of your sick folk cursing me.' And her tongue went at a tremendous pace. Patients gathered round and tried to calm her, saying that the offender had gone away. They know her well, and treat her kindly.

The medical missionary has an advantage over his non-medical colleagues in that he can often help those who need him in a tangible way; he can even at times save lives, which my father was able to do. He never turned a patient away, but when he could not help he would say so. My mother helped him in this work; the two worked as a team. My sister Margaret remembers accompanying my mother day after day as she took a bowl of specially prepared rice pudding to crotchety old Nakasokolo, no longer befriended by her own people but still loved and supported by my parents.

When he arrived, my father both supported already established schools and opened new ones, supervising the teachers' work and making sure that the children were encouraged to attend. School meant more than reading and writing; it included an introduction to the teachings of Jesus and to the stories in the Old and New Testaments, and it began each day with prayers. The teachers often put new life into old stories. One teacher used to take his class outside and, while standing on a high rock as if on a tall mountain, would re-enact the story of the Temptation so vividly that many of the children would remember it for the rest of their lives.

The teachers were paid from mission funds. Their salaries at first extended from January to January, but because funds were limited and the children took time off each spring, the boys to help their fathers herd and the girls to help their mothers in their gardens, the mission decided to stop paying the teachers during the holidays, causing some distress which was eventually settled amicably. The schools required constant vigilance. The quality of the teaching was judged by the children's response and attendance at school was assured by the cooperation of the local chief. One scholar was so thrilled with being able to read that he borrowed a reading primer from Mr Price, and when he returned to his village he taught his friends how to read. Their response was so enthusiastic that, not long afterwards, a school was established in his village. Those who wanted to receive higher education after completing the equivalent of grade six at the mission school were sent for further training to a high school at Kafue and, on completing this, were ready to teach or pursue other occupations.

The importance of mission schools in the education of Africans cannot be exaggerated. For example, Kenneth Kaunda, who was born in Northern Rhodesia in 1924, played an important role in obtaining his country's independence (as Zambia) and in 1960 he became its first president. His father had been a teacher, as had his mother, who was in fact the first African woman teacher in Zambia. Kaunda himself went to a Scottish mission school and also taught. At one time he worked for Gore-Browne in whose home my parents spent a night on their way to Maua. When Kaunda worked for him, Gore-Browne was a member of the Northern Rhodesian Legislative Assembly and it was at this time that Kaunda was first introduced to the complexities of government. Harry Nkumbula, the first leader of the opposition party in the Zambian parliament also started his education in a mission school, the school my father supervised at Kasenga. He was my father's houseboy in the late 1920s while my mother was looking after my sisters and me in England.

Nelson Mandela also went to a mission school. He was born in 1918 in the little village of Mvenzo in the Transkei. He had royal blood in his veins, for his uncle was the king. Like all African boys he grew up herding cattle and, when he could, playing with other boys. In his village there were two Mfengu brothers, George and Ben Mbekela, who had escaped from the Zulu wars and whom Mandela's father had befriended. George was an ex-teacher, and Ben an ex-policeman. Both had been to mission schools, and both had been baptized and were Christians. Their faith rubbed off onto Mandela's mother, but not onto his father. His mother was baptized and christened Fanny. George, who often talked with Mandela, told her that her son was very intelligent and should be sent to school. She passed the suggestion on to his father, who was agreeable but said that his son should be properly dressed. With this in view he fixed him up with a pair of his own trousers, cut off just below the knee and tied round the waist with string, for they were far too big. The school, a Wesleyan Methodist one, was just over the hill in the next valley. At his first class, the teacher, Miss Mdingane, gave each of the children an English name. She told Mandela that his was Nelson and Nelson he has remained to this day. The rest of Nelson's story is beautifully told in his autobiography, *Long Walk to Freedom*.

Julius Nyerere, who in 1961 became the first prime minister of an independent Tanganyika and in 1964 the first president of Tanzania, the country formed by the union of Tanganyika and Zanzibar, also started his education in a mission (Catholic) school. He was born in 1922, the second son of the fifth wife of his father, who was a well-known chief. He had three brothers and four sisters. His father had a total of 22 wives. Nyerere went first to a Catholic missionary school, Mwisenge, and then to a government high school where the emphasis was on fair play, sportsmanship and, as in some English public schools, fagging, when junior boys had to do jobs and run errands for senior boys. Nyerere was baptized at the age of 22 and christened Julius. He went on to study at Makerere College, Uganda and at Edinburgh University before returning to Tanganyika to work for the independence of his country, which he achieved without the loss of a single life.

Jomo Kenyatta, who was born in 1894, also started his education in a mission school. His grandfather, a Kikuyu, had been a *muragi*, a diviner with magical powers, and his father the leader of a small agricultural settlement. At the age of 10 Jomo became seriously ill with a jigger infection of his feet, which was treated successfully surgically in a Scottish mission hospital. This was his first introduction to white people and missions. When he recovered, he ran away from home to become a resident pupil in a Scottish mission school. In 1914, at the age of 20 he was baptized and given the Christian name of Johnstone; his family name was Kamanu. He later changed his name to Jomo Kenyatta. From 1929 to 1946 he spent all

131

but one year in England, working mainly on farms, but also attending a Quaker school. He studied anthropology and wrote an important analysis of the Kikuyu tradition. My father recognized him in the Sherrat & Hughes bookstore in Manchester and chatted happily with him. He played a major role in obtaining independence for Kenya and was imprisoned during the Mau Mau uprising, but was released in time to become the first prime minister, in 1963, of an independent Kenya. A year later he was made president of the one-party Republic of Kenya.

Not long after, speaking at the close of a Commonwealth prime ministers' meeting at which the independence of various Commonwealth countries had been confirmed, Duncan Sandys, then minister for Commonwealth Affairs, concluded by saying, 'We (Britain) are proud of the fact that we have given freedom to 700 million people.' 'Wait a moment,' Kenyatta interrupted:

> I cannot let that pass unchallenged. Several of us around this table are members of a very select club, the PG (Prison Graduates) Club; the man with the longest record is Nehru, with 11 years, then I with 9. Most of those sitting around this table are members, a comparative new boy is Makarios (Cyprus). The freedom you gave us was bought with a price.

Had a similar meeting been held after Mandela's release from prison, he would have had the longest record, 27 years. The road to independence and freedom was paved with mission schools and prison cells.

To continue our story, the natives at Kasenga and Maua who wanted to become Christians joined catechumen classes where they learnt the Bible stories that are part of our heritage and are now part of theirs. After completing their catechumen or instruction classes, they were enrolled as provisional members of the church. If, after two years, they had remained faithful to their tenets, and had done their best to follow the teachings of

Jesus, they were baptized, their heads were sprinkled with water and each one was given his or her new 'Christian' name — Stephano, Joshua, Cornelius, Maria and so forth. Africans who worked for white men were also given English names like Harry, Bill, or Jacko. At Kasenga those who had been baptized were immediately allowed to take Holy Communion; at Maua they had to wait a further six months to partake of the bread and wine. My father nearly caused an uproar by allowing an African in Maua, who had just been baptized, to take Holy Communion.

Some of the converts became preachers and, like the apostles before them, often went from village to village preaching the Gospel. Their message was hammered home, as was my father's, by illustrations taken from the Old and New Testaments. A popular preacher from the Kaga, the mission headquarters at Meru, was Philip M. Inoti. One Sunday, when taking the service in Maua, he used as his text, 'And of his fullness have we all received.' He listed some of their many blessings, finishing by getting his congregation to sing 'Count your many blessings'. On another occasion, when addressing a vast crowd in the open, he illustrated his address with two glass jars, each containing a little dust. One represented Adam and the other Eve. At first Adam and Eve were just 'dust'. The preacher then poured water, representing 'life', into the jars. Satan was represented by a jar of dirty water, some of which was poured into Eve's jar, making her a sinner. Pouring out the dirty water represented confession, and replacing it with water that was pure and clean represented salvation. His audience understood his message.

When my parents first reached Maua, they found a hospital but no church. From that time on they dreamed of building a church of stone that would last and take its rightful place by the hospital, also made of stone. They never expected to live to see their dream come true, but they did. This is how my mother described it.

A couple of years ago Bert felt that though the prospect of building the Church was a remote one, he could at least try getting the stones together gradually. So he bought tools in Nairobi, and arranged for a stone mason from a neighbouring tribe to teach some of our local men. He also asked his brother, Clement, to ask an architect, Mr Adams, to draw a plan for us. From the moment we first saw it, as did everyone else in the district, we felt it was the perfect plan for the setting. So much so, that Meru is having a similar and larger Church built from practically the same plan, and they'd previously tried plans from two other architects and not been satisfied.

Just about the time that Bert had definitely decided that we could begin to build, a letter from Clement came suggesting that the Church should be built as a memorial to father and mother [Thomas and Emily Gerrard], and telling us the family were all willing to help with the cost. This was ideal, and we were thankful. Considering father's and mother's lives and interests, they couldn't have had a more fitting memorial.

In Kenya, Indians do most of the building. Even in this remote place, when it was known there was a job going, there were three or four applicants. It was decided to let a man named Ghulam Mohammed have the contract, and the choice was never regretted. Though he couldn't read a plan, and would have been sadly nonplussed by anything that wasn't absolutely straight forward, like fitting in the coping stones, he was a man who took a pride in his work, and liked a job well done; and under Bert's supervision he built well and truly. The church walls are 16 inches thick; there are lovely roof timbers covered with shingles; the timber is all local — it came from the Meru forest. There is a mill there. Though Meru is 90 kilometres from the railhead, we hear that the mill has orders from South Africa, enough to keep it busy for a year. But, because of the war [this was in 1940], Kenya needs all the timber now.

We were fortunate in having bought most of the timber before timber restrictions came into force here in Kenya. There was some difficulty in obtaining the last lot for doors and screens, but it came just in time.

The foundations of the Church were laid in March 1940. It was finished at the end of July except for doors and screens and grilles for the open window spaces. The glass for the circular windows at each end and for the long narrow windows at the East end, only came the day before the opening, though it had been ordered weeks previously. The yellow of these windows tones in beautifully with the stone work, and gives a lovely light at the East end. The side windows are open, and are to be fitted with wrought iron grilles of lovely design. These are being made by the Meru Indian blacksmith.

This letter is an account of the Church opening yesterday, and is for general consumption.

My father, in a letter to his brother Clement, described the preparations for and the opening ceremony in the following letter.

A little time ago, Mr Hopkins, the superintendent of our District, sent out invitations on our behalf to all Europeans in Meru, and to a few interested people in Nairobi, though it was not to be expected that any of the latter would come as far as Maua. Most of the former accepted, and Doris had to prepare lunch for twenty people. She had the garage cleared out, and the foreman, Kaanake, and his men built a shelter of poles and palm leaves as an extension to the garage. The garage was to have tables round three sides, set out with all kinds of food, from which the guests were to help themselves, and then sit at small tables in the shelter.

Doris and her staff had a busy time preparing meats, salads, trifles, apple pie, fruit salad etc. Dr Hale, the Meru Medical Officer, in accepting the invitation, said Doris's cuisine was up to Ritz standard.

Besides Europeans we had many Native guests. Mr Lambert, the District Commissioner, was to send a lorry load of Chiefs and Elders, and a load of teachers was to come from the mission. We arranged for the former to go to the native café near the market and have cups of tea and plates of food, and two of our local Christians were given a few shillings to see that the teachers were properly entertained.

Yesterday, the day on which we held the opening ceremonies, was dull, but pleasant. The first car load arrived at 9.30 and others followed at intervals till 11.00 o'clock, when the service was due to start. It is a dusty journey of over 60 kilometres from Meru to Maua, and all the guests had to wash and change, the men in our bedroom and the women in the nurse's house. They were all given tea and biscuits. By 11 o'clock there was a great crowd in front of the Church, when we Europeans walked onto the scene. Mr Hopkins and Philip, the Native Minister, wore Geneva gowns, while I wore Mr Laughton's M.Sc. gown. Mr Hopkins, Mrs Lambert and I took our stand on the steps of the church, and the service opened with, 'We love the place, O God,' to the tune Quam Dilecta. I was the presenter, and for this and the other hymns I managed the right pitch and speed, and the singing went very well. A Native probationer prayed, then Mrs Lambert spoke a few words in English, interpreted by Laughton, and then she opened the doors.

It took a little time to get the folk seated. The seats had been put close together. Extra forms were put in at the back, but even then there wasn't room for all, and many stood in the doorway. There were the Chiefs and Headmen in their regalia, hospital dressers, school children,

OPENING AND DEDICATION OF THE CHURCH AT
MAUA
October 8th 1940

ORDER OF SERVICE

AT THE DOOR

Hymn No 6.   We love the place, O Lord.
Prayer   Korinklio Mukira.
Introduction of Mrs Lambert Rev. A. J. Hopkins
Opening of the Church doors Mrs Lambert

IN THE CHURCH

Dr H. S. Gerrard conducting the service.
Hymn No 2. All people that on earth do dwell
Scripture reading. Psalm 84. How lovely is Thy dwelling place,
    O Lord of hosts. From 2 Chronicles Chap 5 & 6. The
    dedication of Solomon's Temple.
Address. Filipu M. Inoti.
Hymn 81

WORDS OF GREETING FROM CHURCH OF SCOTLAND
MISSION — DR IRVINE

Acceptance of the gift of the Church by representatives of the
Maua Christian community.
Acceptance of the gift of the Church on behalf of the
Circuit — Rev W H Laughton.
Acceptance of the gift of the Church on behalf of the
Methodist Missionary Society. Rev A J Hopkins.

Prayer of Dedication. Rev. A. J. Hopkins.

Hymn No 4. O worship the King.

BENEDICTION.

mission men and women in their suits and dresses, as well as crowds of village folk in their calico etc. When all were settled, we stood and sang, 'All people that on earth do dwell' to the old 100th. Rarely, if ever, have the Meru heard a hymn sung so well and so heartily. The lesson, addresses, and two other hymns followed. One hymn was a native air set to words by Philip, and he was shantyman for it. The last hymn was sung to Hanover. The speakers found the building a very easy one to speak in, and all doubts about the lighting were set at rest, for there was ample light from the small, high windows.

The first address was by the Native Minister, Philip, who said that when a man traded with his money, he expected to make a profit. The doctor and his family had given them this Church, and they expected a return, not in money, but in a growing Christian community. Dr Irvine, from the Church of Scotland mission, spoke to them about worship, speaking in Kikuyu, near enough to Kimeru for many of the natives to understand.

After the service, we Europeans came to the shelter in our garden, and ate of the good things Doris had prepared. Besides the mission folk, there were Mr and Mrs Lambert, Dr and Mrs Irvine, an Agricultural Officer, a man and his wife from the Public Works Department, and two women from the Meru Saw Mills, and Davey, the proprietor of 'The Pig and Whistle' at Meru. This was the Irvines' first visit to Maua, and they spoke in high appreciation of our lovely country. I showed Dr Irvine round the hospital. As it happens it has rarely had so few patients, one suggested reason being that the folk are scared of air raids. By tea time, all had departed, and our house staff set to work to restore order. Doris organized her staff work well, and everything went smoothly.

In describing my parents' work in Maua I omitted to mention a happy interlude or escapade: their attack on Mount

Kenya. When they first reached Maua they were actually due for a year's furlough, but they obviously could not abandon Maua for my father had come specifically to man the hospital. But a year later, after five years on the mission field, on 16 August they once more left for home where my grandfather had rented a house, Tamlacht, across the road from their own home, Norfield. Our family, once more united, had a very happy year, though my parents only saw their children during the holidays, for my sisters were at a boarding school in North Wales and I was at Oxford. My parents returned to Maua in May 1936.

Though Mount Kenya cannot be seen from Maua, it nevertheless dominates the area, for with the loss of Kilimanjaro, at 5199 metres (17,058 feet) it is Kenya's highest mountain. Although it is almost on the equator, its summit is always covered with snow. As soon as my parents saw it, they wanted to climb it. So, with a well-worn track to the summit and guides available, when a suitable moment arrived they decided to tackle it. They are not the only members of the family who have tried to climb it. Lewis and Margaret later attempted to climb it, but had to retreat when Lewis developed mountain sickness; John Armitstead, Margaret's son and Christine Budd also tried unsuccessfully to reach the summit. Father's description of their ascent is as follows.

> We got back safely last night from our mountain trip, having thoroughly enjoyed the experience. It is a week today since we left. We called that afternoon at the post office for our mail and for that of the Scottish mission at Chagoria, so that it was dark when we arrived there. As we drove to the Macphersons' house, we passed a noisy crowd of men whom we judged were all eagerly waiting for jobs as porters. They were selected and given loads that evening, and sent off to a camp two miles away where we were to sleep that night. The Macphersons gave us dinner and we listened to tales of their experi-

ences on the mountain, and about 9 p.m. went off to our camp. There was a small two roomed brick house, and huts for porters. We made our beds and settled for the night.

Next morning, after breakfast cooked by Naaman, who was to serve us well throughout the trip, the guide, Nashon, distributed the loads. Then he went with me to Chagoria, to collect hired blankets for them — he got forty, not a whole one among them. Some of the porters used them to tie up loads. I think most of them had their own good ones, otherwise they would have been very cold at night. When all was ready, a line of thirty porters streamed out of the camp, and we went off. That day we walked through forest, climbing easily all the time. Evidence of elephant were plentiful, but we saw none. Towards the end of the walk there were two clearings from which we got views of the peak, away in the distance. Here also there was a fine show of everlasting flowers. When we reached the camp site, the men quickly put up the tents, and made good, roaring fires. We were now 8,000 feet up, and the night was cold.

On Thursday the path went through bamboo forest for about six miles, still climbing easily, and then we came into open country. Our goal was 'the lower hut', a wooden building fitted up with cupboards, tables and chairs, frames for bunks, with a small back room for personal boys. Altitude 10,000 feet. We had time for a stroll, and investigated a stream nearby, which ran at the bottom of a very deep gully; there we found watercress. That night I felt the first effects of the altitude, slept badly; not till I got back here again did I sleep well. Friday's walk was through open country with fine views of the mountains. The path became much steeper, and, owing to the altitude, we soon got out of breath, so we had frequent stops. The hills were covered with little tufts of grass, there were many white everlasting flowers, like a small variety of a rock plant. Further on there were giant lobelia, and groudsell in great numbers. That afternoon we reached Hall Tarn at 14,000 feet. The country was bare and stony; the wind was cold. The porters were in first, and put their tents up on the best site, in the shelter of a rock. There were several pools near by, and also a steep cliff which fell 1,000 feet down to a lake at the bottom. It was a dizzying experience to look down. After supper the cold wind soon drove us into our beds. We had an abundance of blankets and eiderdowns, and were always cosy and warm.

Saturday was the last stage of our climb. It was clear and sunny, and the main peak now looked quite near, its crevasses filled with white, gleaming snow. There were numerous other peaks, bare rugged columns of rock jutting up from the main mass. We had only 3½ miles to go, but we had to climb 2,000 feet. It was steeper than anything we had tackled, and breathing was more difficult. We crossed a ridge by a jagged rock called 'The Tooth', then had a hard scramble along the mountain side over loose rocks and scree, and then over another rise, and there was the 'Top Hut' in a hollow at the base of the main peak, towering 1,000 feet above us. The porters had deposited their loads and gone back to Hall Tarn. Naaman and the guide stayed with us while we had a meal, and fixed up the hut. Mr Matthews was not feeling well, and went to bed immediately, and did not get up again till the men came for his bed on the following morning. During the afternoon Mother and I wandered round taking a few photographs. The air was wonderfully clear, but there was a keen wind blowing. Thinking we were to spend the next day on the top, I did not attempt as much as I otherwise would have done. There was a strong wind all night, rising at times to a gale, but we lay snug and warm in bed. There was a little snow, and next morning the mountain was all in mist. During the night I had decided we had better get down the mountain owing to Matthews' indisposition — at 4.30 I set off to fetch the porters. During the first hour I lost my way crossing some rough scree, but after that it was plain sailing, and by 8.30 I was at Hall Tarn. The porters, taught by the Scotch mission, demurred at first at working on a Sunday, but in a few minutes they went off; some were so quick they seemed almost to run to the top and back again. By noon everyone was down, and we were on our way to the lower hut. We found that occupied by Major and Mrs Dutton, so went on a mile further, and put up tents for the night in a coppice not far from a stream. It rained all night, and it was late when we got away next morning. We travelled at a good speed, Mother leading the way with one of the porters. Mr Matthews collected flowers for his wife who is very interested in Botany. At Chagoria we had tea with the Macphersons, paid off the porters, and by 2 o'clock were off in the car to Meru. Rain had made the road very soft, and we soon had to stop to put on chains. We stuck in some ruts; this delayed us further; darkness came on, and the road was so winding and difficult that progress was necessarily slow, so that it was 10 p.m. before we at last reached the mission. We were fortunate to be back, for the weather continued foul for the next day or two.

My parents hoped, while they were at Maua, that Margaret, Auntie Win and Uncle Tom, who were in *loco parentis*, would be able to visit them. They had actually made arrangements for the trip when Mother discovered a lump in her right breast. The trip was cancelled and three weeks later, on 22 May, Dr Anderson, a surgeon, saw my mother in his office in Nairobi. A biopsy was taken and reported on the following afternoon. Dr Anderson telephoned my father with the news that it was malignant and recommended an immediate mastectomy. That evening, after a pleasant but sombre dinner with the Bisses, with whom they were staying, she was admitted to a nursing home and, on the following day, her right breast was amputated. She took the operation well, but in view of the malignant nature of the tumour Dr Anderson recommended she return to England to the Christie Hospital in Manchester for deep X-ray treatment. Thus it was, having hardly recovered from the operation, she found herself on a Sunderland flying boat bound for England. The plane took off from Lake Victoria and landed at Khartoum, Alexandria, Athens and Marseilles for refuelling, and at night for the passengers to sleep in airport hotels. For my mother, in her weakened state, the flight was the worst she was ever to undertake. It ended when the aeroplane landed on Southampton water where my sister Kathleen, our cousin Catherine Bennett and I met her. Then followed a course of deep X-ray therapy, as it was called in those days, and a gradual recovery.

That summer, as Margaret, Uncle Tom and Auntie Win had been robbed of their trip to Maua, we were all treated to a delightful holiday in Norway, staying at Ulvik at the head of the beautiful Hardanger Fjord. The scene itself could not have seemed more idyllic or peaceful, but the news from the continent was ominous. Germany was poised for war. A German submarine surfaced in the middle of our peaceful fjord. Englishmen of military age were asked to return to England, so I left early and returned to Birmingham, where I was a medical student, to fill sandbags to protect the hospital in the event of air raids. Among the many folk who were helping us was a stalwart labourer who had only one eye; he also had an aortic aneurysm. We called him the One Eyed Bugger because whenever we asked him about his disability, he would reply, 'I, with my one eye can see you with your two eyes, but you with your two eyes can only see me with my one eye. Who's the one eyed bugger now?' I also joined the Home Guard, and found myself in the same company as an elderly man, Dr Auden, the father of the poet, W. H. Auden.

On 3 September war was declared. Not long after, my mother, feeling stronger, decided to rejoin my father in Kenya and, as in 1915, she again set sail for Africa in a convoy of blacked out ships. Her own ship was packed with mothers and children returning to East Africa. The convoy zigzagged its way across the Atlantic, and then zigzagged its way back to the Mediterranean through which it passed safely. Mussolini was neutral at the time, the jackal waited till 10 June of the following year when France was on her knees before joining forces with Hitler and claiming some of the spoils. My father, in Maua, knew my mother had left England but did not know when she was due to reach Mombasa. The days slipped by. He still had no news, so he got into his car and drove to Mombasa. As he walked onto the quay the ship carrying my mother steamed slowly into the harbour. Coincidences like this make one wonder if there is not at times a hand guiding our footsteps.

As they drove to Nairobi and then on to Maua, they had before them the excitement of watching the new Methodist Church in Maua being built, and then the satisfaction of seeing it opened and dedicated. They would then have spent 26 years serving their African brothers and sisters, and with my mother's future hanging in the balance, they felt the time had come for them to think of returning home, this time for good. I once heard my father give a sermon on the text, 'No man putting his hand to the plough and looking back is fit for the Kingdom of Heaven.' He had put his hand to the plough and completed his furrow. The time had come for him to hand it on to a younger man.

Six weeks before they were due to leave Maua, two young and enthusiastic missionaries, Stanley and Margaret Bell, joined my parents. They were replicas of Father and Mother when they first went out to Africa, young, enthusiastic and full of energy and enterprise. Stanley was just out of medical school and both were looking forward to spending their lives on the mission field. As my parents took the Bells round the village and hospital and introduced them to the Africans, they were amazed at the ease with which my parents talked to the Ameru in their own language, using their idioms and sprinkling their conversation with colloquial phrases. As my mother and Margaret Bell set off for the village, my mother would say to Margaret, 'You can get a long way with a *muga* and a smile.' A *muga* is a friendly 'hi' or 'hello'! And Margaret Bell found this was true.

The voyage home was hazardous. When my parents first went out to Africa they had left Britain fighting, but this time she was fighting for her life, and the seas were more dangerous; their convoy had lost at least one ship, but the ship that carried my parents home docked unscathed at Greenock in Scotland. It was Easter weekend. The whole country was blacked out, and there was no one to welcome them home.

9

Growing up in England

M y parents left Kathleen and me in the care of Auntie Winifred, my father's eldest sister, when they returned to Kasenga in 1922 at the end of their first furlough in England. Auntie Winifred, Win for short, was a graduate of Somerville College, Oxford and, though she had attended all her classes and passed her exams, she had not been granted a degree because women were not given degrees at that time. She was single and a teacher. Languages were her specialty; she was fluent in French, having lived with a family in Clermont Ferrand.

My first school was a small elementary one in Cromwell Road, Swinton. I went there with my cousin Raymond. When my parents left for Kasenga, Auntie Win took Kathleen and me to a small private school called Little Felcourt in Kent where she was teaching. My memories are of trying unsuccessfully to play the piano and of spending many happy hours with a pet magpie. I housed him in a shed, clipped his wings, but not so severely that he could not fly, though he could only fly to the nearest beech tree. When I released him, this is where he always flew and I would go after him, quickly becoming almost as agile as a monkey. Towards the end of term his wings were allowed to grow and he flew away.

I only remember one boy, the headmistress's son Pat, a spoilt bully who sometimes made life unpleasant for me. When I tried to find comfort and support from Auntie Win, she told me to stand on my own feet and retaliate.

1. ABOVE. Jonathan and Jane Gerrard.

2. TOP RIGHT. Thomas Lee and Emily Gerrard.

3. ABOVE RIGHT. Bert (Herbert Shaw) and Doris Gerrard, Kasenga, 1932.

4. RIGHT. Stanley and Margaret Bell with their two sons, David, aged nine, and John, aged four.

5. Hospital at Kasenga (inset, the ward), 1920.

6. ABOVE. Hospital at Maua (inset, the male ward), 1934.

7. BELOW. The stone church at Maua on the day of its dedication, 8th October, 1940.

8. ABOVE. How the men spend their days – herding.

9. LEFT. How the men spend their days – relaxing with a smoke.

Raymond continued at Cromwell Road until he was seven. Then his parents decided he deserved a better school and sent him to a Quaker preparatory school, the Downs, nestled on the western flank of the Malvern Hills. Auntie Win thought that I, too, should go there, but it was only when Grandpa Gerrard said he would foot the bill that I went. At the time I was still prone to spells of malaria. One such spell delayed my start at the Downs, so Raymond preceded me. I arrived several days after the start of term and was taken to the Downs by Auntie Dorothy, my father's youngest sister. She introduced me to the headmaster's wife, Dorothea Hoyland, who was as kind and welcoming as any mother could be. No tears were shed when Auntie Dorothy left, leaving me in my strange new surroundings. I was taken almost immediately to my first class. It was a geometry lesson.

The teacher was a big, burly man called Coxwell, whom we called the Booge. He walked with a limp, the result of wounds received in the Boer War. 'What's your name?' he asked me. 'John Gerrard,' I answered. 'We'll call you John Gee,' he said and, turning to Raymond who was in the same class, he added, 'And we'll call you Bun Gee.' And John Gee and Bun Gee we remained as long as we were together, until Raymond went to Cambridge and I went to Oxford.

The boys at the Downs were allocated to packs, or groups of about eight boys. I, like the other new boys, was allocated to the Pics. A year later I was transferred to the Pagans, and remained with them thereafter. Each pack had a leader; I became the leader of the Pagans in my last year. The leaders of the packs were responsible for discipline in the school.

Lessons were important and we were expected to do our best. At the end of each week the marks earned by each class and each pack were read out. If we worked hard and repeatedly gained sufficient marks, we earned a holiday called a 'ninepenny'. It was called a ninepenny because we were each given ninepence to cover the cost of our food for the rest of the day. We would form groups of six to nine boys, pool our resources and go for a long hike or bicycle ride, buying sausages, bread, jam and fruit; strawberries were popular in the summer. On reaching our destination, a hill, barn or wood, after finding a nice dry spot and some logs to sit on, we would build a fire. When it was blazing merrily we would spear our sausages on sticks and hold them over the fire until they were well cooked. They were scrumptious. Then came bread and jam and fresh water to drink. A farmer's wife once gave us our first taste of home brewed Herefordshire cider; I still remember its warm delicious taste. We felt it was good to be alive and better still to be at a school like ours. We felt like Tom Sawyer and Huckleberry Finn rolled into one. We used to earn two to three ninepennies a term.

Days at the Downs started with a quick dip in a bath full of cold water, icy cold in wintertime, followed by breakfast — porridge or cereal, then bacon, sausage, kipper or egg, and toast with either butter or marmalade, but never with both, and tea, coffee or milk. We then gathered in the playground for 20 minutes of exercise followed by classes for the rest of the morning. Then came dinner, meat and vegetables followed by a filling pudding, often rice.

Everyone played games in the afternoon — rugby football in autumn, athletics in spring and cricket and swimming in an open-air pool in summer. We also had 50 minutes of gymnastics once a week. In the summer term cricket lasted for most of the afternoon. In the winter, classes filled the gap between games and a high tea of bread, butter and jam and sometimes a plain cake. Free time for games and reading followed, and then an evening hymn after which, when we were very young, we went to Dorothea's sitting room for a story and private prayers before going to bed. When we were older we had more free time before we brushed our teeth, bathed, said our prayers by our bedsides, climbed into bed and fell asleep.

Not all weekdays were the same, for one afternoon each week was devoted to hobbies. These included collecting snails, flowers, butterflies, rocks and fossils, sketching and painting, and building and running a model railway. My first hobby was collecting snails; I did not know then that there were so many different kinds. After we had collected them, we boiled them, then extracted the snails and mounted and named the shells. An unpopular member of the group was sometimes made to eat the snails; we did not know then that the French considered them a delicacy.

While astronomy was not considered a hobby, sometimes the headmaster, Geoffrey Hoyland, we called him GH, would take a few senior boys onto the roof where there was a telescope and show them the moon, planets, stars and a galaxy, I think in Andromeda. Some might have considered music, playing the piano, violin or other instruments, and singing as hobbies, but they were included in the ordinary curriculum. We all sang and, though I was often out of tune, I enjoyed it. We also had to act at least once, for the senior boys put on a Shakespearian play at the end of the summer term for their own and their parents' entertainment.

GH was a tall, imposing but not intimidating man who was usually cheerful and friendly, though he could be stern if the need arose. I think he wanted us all to be the best we had it in us to be, to exploit to the full whatever talents we might have, and to enjoy the wonders that surrounded us. When I became a leader, he seemed to share the responsibility for running the school with us leaders. In the summer holidays preceding our year as leaders, he would invite us to his home in the Cotswolds, where, with Dorothea, he made us feel as if we were one big family. He took us to Avebury Rings, bigger but not as impressive as Stonehenge, to explore old Roman roads now covered with grass, and to Corfe Castle and Lulworth Cove on the Dorset coast. At Lulworth we met J. G. Jeffreys, who would be my headmaster when I went to Bryanston the following year. GH and Dorothea were like parents would be if they could spend all their time with their children and did not have to go to work. When we returned to our homes we felt that when the new term started we would be helping GH and Dorothea turn the Downs into the best school of its kind in the land.

The Downs was a Quaker school. GH and Dorothea were both Quakers, members of the Society of Friends. Dorothea's mother was Dame Elizabeth Cadbury, an important member of the Society. The Society believes that everyone has equal access to God and vice versa. Popes, bishops and priests are unnecessary encumbrances and may sometimes come between the Almighty and us. They also believe, as we all do, that religion should be part of one's day-to-day living and not something reserved for Sundays. Dame Elizabeth's sons were the well-know makers of Cadbury's chocolate.

Sundays, however, were different, for after breakfast we all wrote letters home. I wrote to my parents in Africa every week and they wrote to me as frequently; my father would write one week and my mother the next. It never once crossed my mind that I was missing anything by staying in England in a boarding school. After letter writing came a Quaker meeting or service. It was held in the gymnasium, a plain, simple and appropriate setting for such a meeting. We sat in three or four long rows, perfectly quiet and still for about 40 minutes, facing one or two shorter rows where GH, Dorothea and a few guests sat, with heads bowed, deep in thought or private prayer.

After about ten minutes, GH or one of the guests would stand up and tell us a short story with a message. One I remember particularly vividly because it concerned me personally. 'A little while ago,' GH began, 'I was walking across the garden at school when I met a boy whom I thought had recently broken one of the school rules — I forget which. We had a word together and, just as he was passing on, I said, "By the way, Bob" — he should have said John Gee — "was it you who did so and so yesterday?" "No, Sir," he answered promptly. He was a very truthful boy and ordinarily I would have taken his word for it, but on this occasion something prompted me to add just as I was turning away, "Honour

Bright?" Immediately a cloud seemed to come over his face, he stopped dead, frowned, and then said slowly, "Oh — no, Sir. Not honour bright." We had a few more words about the matter, settled it satisfactorily and parted, but the incident, small as it was, has remained with me ever since.' It has also remained with me. One or two of the guests then spoke on the same theme. After 40 minutes, GH shuffled his feet, stood up and then he and his guests left; we followed.

The rest of the day was free until after a high tea when we attended our second service. This was along more traditional lines, with hymns, a prayer, a reading from the Bible and a short sermon, usually by GH, based on stories from the New, and occasionally Old Testaments. Then came a quiet hour in GH's study, sometimes listening to classical music on the gramophone but more often listening to GH reading an exciting story, *White Fang* or *The Lost World*, which held us spellbound and longing for the next instalment. GH would then read a short passage from his Greek New Testament, which he translated extempore; then came private prayers on our knees, brushing of teeth, washing of faces, baths and bed.

When I left the Downs I had learnt my lessons well enough to earn a bursary to Bryanston. I had learnt to play and enjoy team games, to swim and run, to appreciate the need for rules and regulations. I had also learnt that Methodists were not the only people who had a handle on God, Quakers had a handle on Him too.

After the Downs came Bryanston. Bryanston was a new school founded by an Australian, J. G. Jeffreys, a remarkably likeable and vital man who gathered friends wherever he went. He was also an accomplished pianist and organist and a good tennis player. GH had met him and had been so captivated by him that when Raymond's parents and Auntie Win asked him which public school he would recommend, he had no hesitation in saying Bryanston.

Jeffreys was born in Adelaide, Australia in 1893. After school he went to Adelaide University, obtained a B.Sc., worked in a laboratory, and then turned to teaching, first in an elementary and then in a high school, Melbourne Grammar. With the outbreak of the First World War he joined the Australian army (artillery) and went to France. He then switched services, joined the Australian Air Force and trained as a pilot. His training took him to Oxford and his love of the organ took him to Westminster Abbey, where he met Sir Frederick Bridges, the dean and a well-known organist, and to Christ Church, Oxford. In both he played the organ and in both he charmed his host.

When the war ended he returned to Australia and was demobilized. Wanting to return both to teaching and to England, he asked the Dean of Westminster if he knew of any openings for a teacher. The dean replied that the headmaster of Westminster had an opening for a science master and would take him if he came straight away, which he did. While at Westminster he put in for a Rhodes scholarship, which he was awarded, and he went up to Christ Church, Oxford, where he studied physiology for two years. He then obtained a teaching position at Radley, a traditional English public school. Public schools had a tradition of putting their imprint on their pupils. Eton turned out one model, Harrow another and so on. Jeffreys thought this was wrong. He thought schools should try to develop the individual skills of every student to the maximum potential. 'Let us,' he would say, 'develop every conceivable interest as fully as possible — literature, music, orchestral and vocal, arts and crafts, mechanical, electrical, natural history, athletics and a host of others. And let us be enthusiastic in everything we do.'

Jeffreys set about implementing his dream and, before long, had bought a magnificent building, Portman House in Dorset, for £35,000, had collected a group of young and enthusiastic teachers and, with the Earl of Shaftesbury as chairman of the board of governors, was able to open the school with 23 boys in 1928. When I arrived in 1930 there were more than 100. The numbers have since increased greatly and now include girls. The school has been so successful that its fees are now among the highest in England. I hope it keeps a few places for those who deserve but cannot afford so outstanding an education.

The school was unusual in that we all wore shorts, blue-grey in colour, summer and winter, with shirts of the same hue. The day started with a cold bath, then came breakfast, prayers and classes. The latter were on the Dalton plan. This meant that we had a few traditional classes, but did most of our studying on our own, guided by assignments given us by our teachers. We did history in the history room, English in the English room, and so on. Laboratory work was carried out under supervision. After lunch there were games, rugby football in the autumn, hockey in the spring, cricket, tennis, swimming and sunbathing by the river in the summer, rowing all the year round, and squash rackets and fives when courts were available. Add to these hobbies painting, music, acting, play reading and photography and the day was full. I learnt to play the oboe and played in the orchestra, learning to appreciate individual instruments and classical music. At weekends, we often went roaming over the Dorset countryside with friends or canoeing on the river.

The holidays were always fun. At Easter some of us, boys and masters, would spend a week in the Lake District walking the fells and climbing the peaks. On one occasion, Bob Graham joined us; he was the first to cover 100 miles in 24 hours, leaping almost literally from peak to peak. One summer we climbed the Cuillin mountains in the magical island of Skye. Another holiday was spent in South Wales where, during the Depression, most of the coalminers were unemployed. We learnt what it was like to live on the 'dole' as we worked side by side with the miners on their allotments.

One summer, my Uncle Tom and Auntie Win took me to a church retreat where an American lady gave a series of lectures on the power of the mind over the body. She introduced her first lecture by telling us that, as a young girl in Chicago, when walking home from church with her parents one day she had seen a man stagger out of a doorway with a knife in his throat. Her parents had covered her eyes and hurried her away, but the episode had so impressed her that she developed a red swelling in the front of her throat. When the inflammation subsided it left her with a scar, which had remained for all to see. When I returned from the retreat I buried my head in books by Freud, Jung and Adler. Having been influenced by teachers and three outstanding headmasters who were as dedicated to their work as my parents were to theirs, I decided to become a teacher, hoping to help other youngsters reach their maximum potential.

Two years after entering Bryanston Jeffreys mysteriously left to start another school, Ottershaw College,[1] and a new headmaster, Thorald Coade, replaced him. Coade came straight from Harrow, one of the oldest traditional public schools, but he, like Jeffreys, believed schools should provide the young with every opportunity to develop their talents to the maximum potential. The best servant of the community, he would say, is the most fully developed individual. He wanted these skills to be used, not for personal ends, but for the benefit of society as a whole. During my last year at Bryanston some of us read and discussed with Coade books such as *Freedom in the Modern World* and *Reason and Emotion* by John Macmurray. We learnt that freedom does not mean giving free vent to the emotions. Freedom carries responsibility and is probably best expressed in the service of others.

Having decided to be a teacher, I talked the matter over with one of the masters who, because I was also interested in the

---

1. The Ministry of Mines took over Ottershaw College during the Second World War. Jeffreys took Holy Orders, served as a priest in London during the blitz, and then in various parishes. He retired to Bournemouth. From there he was able to visit Bryanston from time to time where he loved taking Holy Communion in St Anthony's Chapel. He died in 1977 at the age of 84. He was a great man, without him there would have been no Bryanston.

mind, said I should first see his father, a well-known London psychiatrist. His father said that if I really were interested in the workings of the mind, which I was, I should first become a medical doctor. I pondered this over in my mind and, on the day I left Bryanston, decided to study medicine. Instead of going up to Oxford as planned, I went to a crammer in Manchester to bone up on botany, chemistry and physiology, going up to Oxford the following year, the year that Betty too went to Oxford.

The autumn of 1935 saw Betty installed in Lady Margaret Hall and me in Oriel College. Betty was reading history with an emphasis on the Renaissance, while I was dissecting the human body and learning how it worked. We first met in a café. Betty was petite, had a sparkle in her eyes and was carrying a hockey stick; she was on her way to play hockey. I was on my way to a lab. Betty invited me to a dance at her college. I accepted. We soon found that we enjoyed the same things, mainly games. At Oxford, Betty played cricket and field hockey — she captained both Oxford teams before she graduated — as well as lacrosse and tennis. I liked rugby football and tennis. We both liked music, the visual arts and plays. We were also interested in our work and concerned about the political situation, though in 1935 Hitler appeared to be more of a demagogue than a danger. We joined the New Commonwealth Society, which aimed to provide the League of Nations with teeth in the form of an international police force so that it could enforce its recommendations. In this way we hoped that it might be possible to prevent wars. We had two German friends, one of whom was a Rhodes scholar with whom we had long discussions about how to prevent wars. I went with a group of friends to Germany, first to work on the fields with a saintly group who shared everything except their wives, but left Germany before the outbreak of war. I then spent a month with a group of *Hitlerjugend*, discussing the political situation, singing songs and marching, and in the winter I skied with a second group of young Germans. Baldur von Shirach, who was a member of Hitler's entourage, came to talk to us, but neither the English, the Germans, nor we took him seriously. Betty took an English hockey team to Bremen in 1938, but by this time it was obvious that war was imminent and friendships would get us nowhere.

Looking back, I am profoundly grateful to my parents and to Auntie Win for sending me to the Downs and Bryanston, and to my grandfather for making this possible, but I am especially grateful to Auntie Win. Even though she was only a substitute parent, she and Uncle Tom, whom she had married in 1926, could not have provided a more loving home. Apart from being a professor of mechanical engineering at the Manchester Technical Institute, Uncle Tom was also an ardent Methodist and taught Sunday school for many years. Because they never had any children, they were substitute parents for me, and for Kathleen and Margaret when they were in England, and we were substitute children for them.

During holidays we walked in the Lake District and Switzerland, camped in Somerset, and spent sunny days by the seaside in Cornwall and Brittany. At home in Manchester, we regularly went to the city's excellent repertory theatre and, on Sundays, would go twice to the Methodist church in Great Western Street. Uncle Tom would also go in the afternoon because he was in charge of the Sunday school. These were the days when Sundays were considered to be 'holy' days and days of rest. Our principal minister, Mr G. W. Meadley, would give a meaty address in the morning for the students from Hartley College, sprinkling his sermon with quotes from Karl Barth and Søren Kierkegaard, and a rousing sermon in the evening for those who had slept in the morning. The assistant minister was a little stocky man who had been a padre in the First World War. He had won a Military Cross for bravery when rescuing the wounded from no-man's-land. He was inspirational, and introduced me to the war poets and to Toc H, veterans who met each week to plan for the future and to remember their fallen colleagues.

Growing up in England

My upbringing was rich and varied, spent in three of the most beautiful counties in England, Herefordshire, Dorset and Oxfordshire. Each step of the way I learnt to appreciate beauty in nature, art and music, and in school, university and home life I learnt that one so privileged should aim to serve others and especially the less fortunate.

10

Kasenga and Maua
27 Years Later

My father, when he returned to England in 1941 at the end of his last tour in Kenya, became a family physician. He did a number of locums to learn how to run a practice and then worked for a few years with a partner in Stretford before setting up his own practice in Hazel Grove on the outskirts of Stockport. He made the change from Africa to England without much trouble, but, according to my mother, tended to treat patients with minor maladies rather brusquely.

Our family was scattered. Margaret was at boarding school in North Wales and only came home for the holidays. Kathleen was a fully qualified nurse; she graduated in 1941 and was nursing at Hill End Hospital, a satellite of Barts (St Bartholomew's Hospital), in London treating air raid casualties. I was in Birmingham completing my medical studies. I graduated in May 1941 and was planning to marry Betty that summer — medical students did not marry before qualifying in those days.

Betty and I both came from Swinton, but though we had met once before going to Oxford in 1935 we did not get to know and fall in love with one another until we were both at Oxford. There I did my preclinical training, and then went on to Birmingham, to the Queen Elizabeth Hospital, for my clinical training. Betty in the meantime, having obtained her BA honours in history in 1938, was teaching at a residential school for girls, St James's in West Malvern, a two-hour ride from Birmingham on the Midland Red bus. We became engaged after Betty had obtained her first teaching position; women who were engaged or married had little chance of landing the plum teaching jobs at that time. Before we announced our engagement I had to ask Betty's father for permission to marry his daughter. 'You had better ask her mother,' he had replied, 'She wears the trousers in this house.' The diamond engagement ring cost £20. Two years later, my parents having returned from Kenya and I having obtained my medical degree, we were married. My parents had first met Betty on furlough and had immediately taken to her, so were delighted to be back in England for our wedding. We were married in St John's parish church, Pendlebury near Manchester. Mr Steele, the vicar, took the service and gave the address along the lines of 'In Christ and thee my comfort be' and my father tied the knot. As soon as the reception was over we set off on our honeymoon. Petrol was rationed on account of the war, but we had saved enough coupons to take us in our little second-hand 'Baby Austin' (which cost £20) to the Lake District and Dumfriesshire in Scotland.

My sister Kathleen was accepted into the nursing programme at Barts while she was still at school in North Wales, but being only 17 was told that she would have to wait a year. She spent the year looking after English girls at a 'finishing school' for young ladies in Château d'Oex, Switzerland. She invited Margaret and me out for Christmas 1935 and it was there that we learnt to ski. Kathleen started her training at Barts in 1936 and graduated in 1941. At Barts she fell in love with John Potter, a medical student who graduated in 1943 and whom she married the same year. John wanted to be a neurosurgeon. He spent his first 12 months in medical and surgical wards and when he joined the Royal Army Medical Corps (RAMC), Hugh Cairns, later Sir Hugh, an outstanding Australian neurosurgeon and the first Nuffield Professor of Surgery at Oxford, appropriated him. Sir Hugh had just established a centre, literally his brainchild, for the treatment of head injuries in St Hugh's, a lady's college in Oxford. St Hugh's, under the auspices of Sir Hugh, became the special centre for the treatment of head injuries, at this time caused mainly by air raids in England and battles on the Continent. The unit initially had a complement of 50 beds, but this rose to 430 after the D-Day landings. John Potter gained invaluable experience in the unit, and then spent nine months in Italy and two years in India before being demobilized. He was then an accomplished and experienced neurosurgeon, but on account of the war had been unable to take the necessary exams to climb the academic ladder. To take and pass these he had to return to Barts as a junior lecturer so that he could learn the detailed anatomy that surgeons have to know to ply their trade. He then had to pass the formidable fellowship exams, which he did. He was then free to return to his beloved Oxford, a not uncommon wish of many who, like him, were graduates of Cambridge.

Margaret, while still at Howells, and Lewis Armitstead, then a third-year medical student at Manchester University, had been introduced by their mothers who attended the same Methodist church. Margaret found Lewis attractive and when she went to Manchester University the following year, 1944, she had already decided to study medicine. Lewis qualified in 1946 and he and Margaret married in July that year. He joined the RAMC and concentrated on ophthalmology. Margaret continued to study and to live at home with my parents, but took nine months off to have her first child (Ruth, in 1947) and qualified in 1948. Lewis was demobilized in 1950 and joined a family practice in Haslingdon in Lancashire where he and Margaret made their first home. Nine years later they moved to Leominster where he continued in practice for many years.

My parents did not see as much of their children when they were growing up as they might have wished, but they saw more of their ten grandchildren, and most of their eldest grandson, Jim Potter. Jim lived very happily with them for about 18 months when he was in his last two years at Manchester Grammar School, 1961–62. There he played rugby football and the French horn in the school orchestra; at home he learnt to play and enjoy bridge with his grandparents, and to spend Sunday mornings sleeping, not in the pew but in bed. He also learnt to drive, but only put one bump in his grandfather's car. He went up to Cambridge in 1963, studying natural sciences for two years and economics for a further two. While studying economics he became interested in and decided to specialize in development economics, the economics of developing countries. He got a first at the end of his third-year exams and, in June of the same year, 1966, he married Judith Chippendale.

The Overseas Development Institute and the Nuffield Foundation had recently acquired the funding necessary to offer ten graduates attachments to newly independent countries in Anglophone Africa. Jim applied for a position and by an extraordinary piece of luck, some would say divine intervention, was assigned to the government of Zambia's finance department. So, on leaving Cambridge in 1967, he went straight to Zambia. He had been promised government accommodation, but after three months Jim and Judy were still in a hostel. They would have packed up their belongings had Judy not obtained the position of lecturer in the chemistry department of the University of Zambia. He therefore decided to buy a house. With a little help from Auntie Win he was able to produce the down payment for one of the few available and affordable houses. It was on a ten-acre plot and came with 1000 chickens that were producing 600 eggs a day. This was bought from a white Rhodesian who was in a hurry to move to South Africa. Before he left he taught Jim and Judy, in the course of two evenings, all they needed to know, with a little help from the Ministry of Agriculture, about chicken farming.

As soon as they had bought the chicken farm Jim sent a telegram to my parents telling them that they must come out to Zambia to visit them. The telegram that he received in return said they were making immediate preparations to come out, but Jim and Judy were to make no special plans for their accommodation for they would be happy to sleep on rugs on the floor and use a sack stuffed with leaves for a pillow. This was even though my father was 81 and my mother 73. They were both physically fit, though my mother had had a fractured arm associated with osteoporosis, and both were mentally very alert. Before leaving England, they made arrangements to visit Nairobi and Maua on their way home, though not Kasenga.

So, on 3 April 1968, Kathleen and John drove my parents to Gatwick airport where they boarded their plane for Lusaka. The journey that had taken six weeks almost 50 years before now took less than 24 hours. When they landed at Lusaka, Jim and Judy were there with their Volkswagen bus to welcome them. Jim and Judy's home, a two-bedroomed bungalow three miles south of Lusaka off the Kafue road, was surrounded by a spacious garden and the attached chicken farm, which a fearsome dog defended. My parents would watch fascinated as Jim and Judy cleaned, weighed and graded 600, plus or minus a few hundred, eggs each day before taking them to the market. In the short time he had been in the poultry business Jim had almost paid off the capital costs and was about to start making a profit.

When my parents had recovered from their long flight, Judy took them into Lusaka where they cashed cheques at Barclay's Bank, queued and bought stamps at the post office, took four books, using Jim and Judy's cards, out of a well-stocked library and then visited the cathedral. When they returned to the farm, they, with Jim and Judy, made their plans for the Zambian part of their odyssey. They decided to spend the best part of the first two weeks in Lusaka visiting friends and a school in Kafue, six days visiting Kasenga, Namwala and their old missionary haunts, three days in the Zambezi valley, near where Kanchindu used to be, and a final three days in Lusaka, during which Jim and Judy would drive them to the Kariba Dam. They were due to catch the plane for Nairobi on 2 May.

Simon Munyana, of the United Church of Zambia and the pastor of St Paul's church, was the first Zambian minister to whom they were introduced. They went to his church on Easter Sunday, but on their first Sunday in Zambia, Palm Sunday, they attended the service at Trinity church, where the Reverend Cross, the son of a missionary known to my father, was the preacher. He spoke on the 'Four Faces of the Cross'. At St Paul's the order of service was the same but the seating was different, the men sat on the right of the central aisle and the women on the left, and at the end of the service the women left first. During the service many children from surrounding churches that did not have baptismal services were baptized. At the end of the service Simon introduced my father and mother and asked them to stand up. They were given a standing ovation. The warmth of their reception and the appreciation shown for the work they had done in Zambia must have moved them.

My parents also attended the wedding in Trinity church of one of Jim's colleagues in the department of finance. The ceremony was followed by a reception with a three-tiered wedding cake at which Minister of Finance Elijah Mudenda toasted the bride and groom in both English and Tonga.

Harry Nkumbula, the parliamentary leader of the opposition, was one person in Lusaka who very much wanted to see my parents. He was born in Maala, a village near Kasenga, and had been the first boy from there to attend the mission school in Kasenga. He had also been my father's houseboy while my mother was in England in the late 1920s, so they had known each other well. Some 20 years after my father left Zambia, Harry, by then a well-known politician, had criticized missionaries in general, saying they were 'the biggest hypocrites in the land'. Mr Shaw, an erstwhile missionary colleague of my father's who was in Zambia at the time, was so incensed by Harry's assertion that he wrote to the press as follows.

As the only surviving missionary in Northern Rhodesia

of those who had anything to do with Mr Nkumbula when he was a boy and a youth, I wish to state:

1. I do not quarrel with his words if they refer to me. One is conscious of one's failure to be a perfect Christian. Yet one does try to be faithful as a servant of God and of God's children in this land.
2. In so far as the words refer to the missionary into whose hands Mr Nkumbula placed himself as a young boy — they are not true.

I give the following details: The missionary in the area where Mr Nkumbula was born and into whose hands he placed himself as one eager to learn was a medical missionary. He was the eldest son of a wealthy business-man in Manchester. After a short period of business life he turned aside and started work as a medical student. His desire was to qualify as a doctor and then come to Northern Rhodesia to serve the Baila people, i.e. Mr Nkumbula's home people.

As a qualified doctor this young man came to the Namwala district and set about his practice. In those days the Government had neither the money nor the men to attend to the diseases of the Baila. For eighteen years this missionary devoted his services to the Baila people. His mission salary at first was less than £20 a month — and he sent no bills to his patients.

At that time the Baila were a dying tribe. Owing to disease few of the women could give birth to healthy children. Many large villages had practically no children. This missionary tried to save these people. By day and by night he was their servant. The floods of the Kafue Plain were never allowed to prevent his answering a call for help. Walking, cycling, wading and in dug-out canoes he moved about the land to serve in the name of His Lord.

It is very possible that Mr Nkumbula owes his own

birth to the services of this doctor. The name the Africans gave to this missionary was *Ushibalwazhi*, meaning Father of the Sick.

In addition to his medical work the doctor gathered the boys of the area into a school, and taught them the three Rs and the Word of God. After eighteen years of selfless service the authorities of the mission wished to move this doctor to a hospital in Kenya. At once the chiefs and people of the area served by the doctor put forward a moving appeal that he should be allowed to stay amongst them. 'How can we live without our father?' they asked. I think Mr Nkumbula will remember all this. Perhaps he also remembers how this same doctor and his wife took into their home the black infants whose mothers had died in childbirth, and how they cared for them until the babes were old enough to return to their relatives and live on their village food.

Remembering these things, I ask Mr Nkumbula, as an honourable man, to write to the *Central African Post* and state that the word Hypocrite did not apply to Dr Gerrard — who gave the best years of his life to the service of the Baila tribe and to the service of Mr Nkumbula himself.

Yours ever.

John H. Shaw.
Lusaka. May 1955.

Mr Shaw's letter was written 13 years before Harry arranged to see my father and I am sure that no mention was made of it at this time, they had more interesting things to talk about. Harry came at 9.00 one evening, arriving with Simon Munyana, the minister. My mother thought he had obviously had a drink before he came and while he was with them he continued to fortify himself with beer; he also chain smoked cigars. Simon had only lemonade. Harry first told my father the latest news of mutual, surviving friends in Maala and then went on to ask about my sister Kathleen and about me. As for himself, after leaving school he had persuaded his father to sell two of his cattle and to give him the money. With this he had paid his way to Dar es Salaam, where he had bought 100 pink seashells at 6*d*. each. For these, when he returned to Zambia, he received 100 cattle. He repeated the journey twice. He married and from his first wife he said, 'I got three children, all of whom were doing well.'

With independence approaching he entered the political arena. His rival for the presidency was Kenneth Kaunda. Kaunda had graduated from a Scottish mission school. He first met Mr and Mrs Stamp when the latter were stationed in the Copper Belt where he was a teacher. Muriel and Ernest Stamp used to meet him at monthly interracial tea parties and Muriel used to talk with him when most of the guests had departed. She mentioned her conversations to Ernest who said, 'That man will go a long way.' And he did.

Jim worked closely with Kaunda when negotiations were underway for the government's purchase of the copper mines. At the time it was thought that nationalizing an industry would divert much needed money from the pockets of the shareholders to the coffers of the country. Kaunda did not want to strike a hard bargain that might antagonize the mineowners; after all he was a Christian and an honest one. Sadly, he bought the mines when the price of copper was high. Soon afterwards the demand for and the price of copper fell, and for the next 15 years Zambia, and not the original mine-owners, were the losers. Zambia's difficulties were compounded by the fact that the government had, in Jim's words,

completely neglected the agricultural sector, and had artificially subsidized the price of food thereby destroy-ing the normal market economy which is so vital in less developed countries. Zambia had a good climate and plenty of underground water — it could have been the

Kansas of Africa. Kaunda [Jim felt,] did not have a hard enough streak — the strength — to run his country firmly as well as fairly.

As a matter of interest, Kaunda, and most if not all the members of the government had, like Nelson Mandela, started their education in mission schools and had completed it at what was then, 1960, the only residential college for blacks, the University College of Fort Hare in South Africa. Fort Hare, Nelson Mandela declared, was 'Oxford and Cambridge, Harvard and Yale all rolled into one'.

When Kenneth Kaunda became the president of an independent Zambia in 1964, Zambia's wealth depended on the copper mined in the Copper Belt; copper at the time was in great demand worldwide. The war in Angola and apartheid in South Africa cut Zambia off from its markets and, by the time the Chinese had built a railway to Dar es Salaam, the demand for copper had fallen and Zambia was penniless, having spent all its assets on schools, airport, parliament and other government buildings and a new university. Before my parents left Lusaka, Jim and Judy took them to see the parliament buildings. They had hoped to sit in on the parliament, which was in session at the time, but because Jim and my father were not wearing jackets and ties only Judy and my mother were allowed in.

While my parents were staying, as they called it, at Jim's farm, Jim and Joan McCormack arrived to arrange to take them to Kasenga, where Jim McCormack was stationed, and where Joan, his wife, was the doctor in charge of the hospital. Jim McCormack, I suspect, was a little downhearted, for six months before my parents' visit, he had written to the Mission House in London, saying:

The Methodist Church came to this country over 70 years ago, to an area West of Kasenga. After 20 years in the area it met with some response, for when I visit that area, as I did 10 days ago, I find some grand old Christians there. But even though the Church has been in the Kasenga area for 60 years, there has been very little response. The few Christians stationed around Kasenga are from the area of our first 'station'. I cover 300 square miles. In an area where there once were 5 missionaries, there are now two.

My parents spent the night at the mission in Kasenga. After they had left, it had been moved away from the river, where it had been marooned every year by floods, to the village on higher, drier ground. Next morning, soon after breakfast, a group of African visitors, old friends of my parents, came to see them and after giving them a very warm welcome, chatted happily about old times. My parents then went to see Solomon, one of the two original Christians, now an old man and almost blind, but my father still recognized him as the person he had inherited from Edwin Smith. He was living, not in a round, but in an oblong, house with a thatched roof.

My parents were up early the next morning, intending to go to the school for prayers, when Jim and Judy appeared. Having arrived back late the previous evening they had spent the night in their van, for Jim was anxious not to miss out on being with my father when he returned to the site of his original mission station. On their way there they called at the school at Kaabulamwanda, where my father spoke to the children. My father had not spoken Baila for more than a quarter of a century, but in the short time at his disposal he had honed his linguistic skills and, though Jim Potter had no idea what he was saying, the children seemed to listen almost spellbound to his every word. After he had visited the school, many old friends came to welcome and speak to him and my mother. They then went on to Maala, visiting Jones's store. This had been greatly enlarged and boasted a petrol pump. From there they borrowed a Land Rover to take them to the original site of the Kasenga station.

There was little to see apart from scattered piles of old

bricks. My parents had difficulty identifying the site of their old home, hospital and school, made more difficult because when Mr Price moved the station to higher ground he had planted a new avenue of blue gum trees. Luckily, an African who was able to tell them where the original buildings had stood appeared on the scene. A short service and prayers were held at the grave of Kathleen Delaney, a missionary who had died, aged 35, after only a year at the Kasenga station.

Escorted by Matthew, whom I think was an African preacher, my parents visited many of their old friends in the surrounding villages, among them Chief Job Nunkabela, who, together with his eight wives, gave my parents the warmest of welcomes. He had been a pupil of my father's at Kasenga and had then graduated from the Kafue high school. He was now the very successful chief of a large village with a government-run primary school. The brick houses of his wives, each of whom had her own separate home, surrounded his own brick house. They were delighted to see my parents and sat down and talked animatedly with them about the old days.

In the same village they also chatted with Moosmoke, whom my parents originally called Moses. He was now married, and had two wives and five children. Another old friend they met was Priscilla, the wife of Sianga, the cook who had caught the milkman diluting the milk with water.

Matthew then drove them to Namwala, where the district commissioner had lived in colonial days and where now prisoners and the emergency ambulance service they provided were housed. Today it boasts a secondary residential school for 730 boys and girls, with dormitories, beds on which to sleep, showers, washrooms, a dining room in which the children learn to eat with knives, forks and spoons, classrooms and laboratories. The next day was Sunday. Services were held in the dining room, the first being Mass for the Catholics, the next being a service for the United Church of Zambia. After the service my parents were introduced and welcomed and my father replied. My mother was presented with a beautiful mahogany bowl. The head of the school, Mr Mawunda, was a Zambian who had had two and half years' training in the UK.

From Namwala they were driven to Choma on the main railway line 150 kilometres south-southwest as the crow flies. This took them only a few hours; it used to take them a week when trekking or with an ox cart. In Choma they did some shopping and my father bought a pair of shorts. Then, instead of trekking through the jungle with 100 porters, they drove south for 50 kilometres on a tarmac road to Sinazongwe on Lake Kariba near to where the original Kanchindu mission station was resting peacefully below the placid waters of the lake. When the Kariba Dam was built, the Batonga were moved and had to leave their homes, schools and churches. The government gave the villagers £2000 for each new school that had to be built, and the missions £3000 for each new church and manse. Their huts, I presume, were thought to be disposable.

Jim McCormack also took my parents to Maamba, 20 miles upriver, to see a huge opencast coalfield where trucks were being loaded and taken by a new line up to Choma. They spent the night at the mission station near Sinazongwe.

On the following day, Jim McCormack drove them up out of the valley, past more coalmines to Batoka where Jim and Judy met them in their Volkswagen bus. Judy drove them home, averaging 60 miles an hour. Three days later, Jim and Judy took them on their last Zambian excursion into the Zambezi valley to see the Kariba Dam. After a good view of the dam and the lake, they drove to Gonda, a pleasant little resort where there were chalets and boats. Not far away they found a quiet bay where they picnicked and Jim and Judy had a swim with no fear of being attacked by crocodiles. On Wednesday 1 May they had a final supper at Simon Munyana's home. The following morning, Judy drove them to the airport to catch their flight to Nairobi via Ndola and Dar es Salaam, at both of which the passengers had to disembark for customs and immigration. They reached Nairobi that evening where their old friends the Mortimers met them.

My parents spent their first two days in Nairobi looking round the city and confirming their flights home. The next ten days are, I think, best described through extracts from my father's diary.

Sunday 5 May
Service at Larington Church. Taken by Rev. Myer. Two baptisms, one black, one white. Sermon on importance of little things. Tea served afterwards outside. After morning service called on Rev. Ronald S. Muzonqua. In the afternoon went to the Game Park where a warden friend of the Mortimers drove us round for over two hours. Park is 44 square miles. Good wildebeest, zebra, Kangoni, Thomsons gazelle, ostriches, two cheetahs watching a herd of antelopes, and as we neared the exit we had a very close view of a giraffe lit up by our car headlights.

Mortimer's house is 3 miles from the centre of the city in a suburb with houses of ambassadors, millionaires etc. We occupy a downstairs bedroom, and have our own bath and WC. Mr Mortimer, being crippled with rheumatoid arthritis, needs help in dressing, shaving, etc., but manages to drive his car. He can only hobble as he walks. The house has a fine garden, grass surrounded with shrubs and trees. Meals. Breakfast at 8, bacon and egg, pawpaws to start. Lunch at one o'clock, meat, salads, fruit, biscuits and cheese. Dinner about 8, soup, joint, sweet, coffee.

Monday 6 May
Into Nairobi. Visited The National Assembly. Beautiful 1961 modern building, older parts not now used for sittings. House — as British Parliament. Speaker's chair, Government and Opposition, speakers and public and Press galleries. Called at Bible House; drove around Indian quarters and market of second hand goods. Lawi called at 2.30.

171

Wednesday 8 May

Lawi[1] came about 10.30 to take us to Meru. Lunch at the Thika Hotel. Thika Falls. Took on a passenger, the manager of the bookshop in Meru. He sat with Lawi. Doris and I sat in the back of car. Road misses Nyeri. Arrived Nanyuki about 3.30. Introduced to Meru doctor. Educated by B. Jones, (a very well known English orthopaedic surgeon), trained Makerere and Edinburgh, Lawi says he is a clever doctor. Has surgery in Maua street. After some difficulty found Mrs Brown, widow of a Scottish missionary. Big Alsatian gave us a boisterous welcome. Lawi left us there to have tea. Dark before we reached Meru. Lawi occupied Laughton's old house, with his wife Florence and several children.

Thursday 9 May

Visited Meru township school, Rural Agricultural Farm Training School, Meru Bookshop, Githongi School and St Paul's Church — English service. Lunch with Mrs MacKenzie. Evening Lawi's father and mother came to see us. MacKenzie's for dinner. Joined by Mr Carling from Agricultural Farm Training School.

Friday 10 May

Visited market etc in Meru, while waiting for repair (broken spring) to Land Rover. Walked round town and waited in Book Room. Left at 10.30. Our driver, Tharunya, drove well. When road good 50–60 mph. Often rough and rutted. In one place, between hills (Togania), we encountered very wet patches. First, one lorry stuck, and waited till it was towed and pushed out, lorry in front and men behind. Later another lorry badly

---

1. Lawi I'Mathi was a Methodist minister who had a special interest in Maua as his father had been one of the first nurses in the hospital, and his mother had been a patient in it.

stuck but Tharunya managed to drive round it as Land Rover bumped and slid in the ruts. Passed Kianyai, Kangeta, arrived Maua at noon. Approach along causeway. At entrance to mission there was a large sign, and on it, in bold letters:

WELCOME TO OUR FRIEND
DR AND MRS GERRARD

Coloured flags between trees. Drove up to Dr Bastin's house, and Jinkew joined us for coffee served by Mrs Bastin. Good double bedded room for us. Lawi goes back to Meru. People sent lots of food for us, meats, eggs, vegetables.

Kaaga, the headquarters of the mission, has 55 preaching places, 376 Local Preachers, five named Gerrard.

Friday evening. Guests for supper Dr and Mrs Sewell, Sister Latchen, Sister Tutor J. Walker, Henry and his wife — Jinkew.

Saturday 11 May
After breakfast walked to market. Many gathered round to greet us. 10.30 Jinkew took us to village down hills road to Game Park. Expected to have baptismal service, but owing to misunderstanding no people there. Simple church. On our return visited market. Now full of people, charge of 20 cents. Lots of people gathered round and greeted us. Had to walk round outside to avoid crush. Saw men of old labour gang — M. Ndaulo and M. Mwanbia.

Afternoon. Welcoming ceremony in the Kieni. A great crowd of men, women and children — a colourful crowd. Children sang songs, some made up in our praise. Letter read in English and then in Kimeru. The letter read:

Maua church,
Maua Meru.
9 March 1968.

Dr and Mrs Bastin,
Dear Dr and Mrs Gerrard.

We have found it good that you and ourselves should entertain Dr and Mrs Gerrard. Therefore on behalf of Maua Church we have sent to you this little food[2] to make some food for them.

Yours sincerely,

Henry Murungu,
For Maua Church.

The following is a second, rather longer address given to my parents on the same occasion.

We are very grateful to welcome you here today on your momentous visit to us. This also makes us happy.

We have always been remembering the works of love which you did to us. You have been manifesting your love towards us in the way you have been sending greetings to us from your home.

We shall never forget you, Dr and Mrs Gerrard, neither in this generation or in the future one, for your most generous gift to us. The church here and the school are perpetual symbols to Christians and the children who attend them.

Due to the cost of living today, and the financial stringency in many spheres, the church being no exception, this church by itself denotes the greatness of our appreciation and fortune that we had missionaries filled with the Holy Spirit like you. Nowadays, in an autonomy

---

2. Two chickens, piece of pork, eggs, milk, butter, tea, flour, beans, potatoes, carrots and bananas.

status, (Kenya gained her independence in 1963) it is not possible to erect a church of this size and magnitude. The schools, the same Maua primary school, is of the same standard even today.

We remember your devotion to the work of God, the tedious walk to remote places to preach the Word of God, and heal the sick, like Athimi, Gaiti, Kaurine, Kiegoi and Njia. We cannot in the least neglect the work done by Mrs Gerrard in teaching our women domestic classes.

Your work on the soils cannot be forgotten. The way you taught us to plant trees is highly appreciated. The trees you planted for demonstration have been very helpful. Some of the trees were cut and helped to build Njia Church and school.

All that we have mentioned is but a few of the many benefits, and we cannot count all, including the spiritual food from the Lamb of God. Your work and influence among the people of this area have been demonstrated by the way some of the parents have named their children after your name. So, Dr and Mrs Gerrard, many are the children named after you because of your deeds and kindness.

Lastly but not least the work that you started has been blessed a hundredfold. We thank God that He has sustained you to a rich age, and brought you back to see us in this appropriate time. To answer to our children the questions they have been asking, 'Who built this church? Who is the person appearing in the plaque?' They can now see you and get settled. Thanks to God for bringing you. May He keep you longer.

We are constrained to mention that our welcome to you would have been more rousing if we had been properly informed of your coming. Somehow someone, for reasons beyond our understanding, was keeping it to himself. We feel, as do the church leaders, that we should have been informed as soon as it was confirmed that you were coming, for we owe you in particular so much more than we owe anyone else, here or anywhere.

An old schoolboy of Doris' spoke in her praise, and told of the success of some pupils. Presentation by children of gifts to us — for Doris a calabash, 4 lb of coffee, and flowers, for me a circlet for my head, and a switch in a case. More singing by the children and the women. They seemed prepared to go on indefinitely, and we left our seats at 4 o'clock, when men came to greet us. Had to ask their names, for some we didn't remember, others were only young in our time. Kaanake came to greet us, still strong and active. Another gave me a present of ten shillings. Mrs Bastin had lots of food brought for us — meat, beans, potatoes, butter, eggs etc.

Sunday 12 May 1968
We attended service in the Maua church. Part filled at the beginning, but filled up during the service. Form of morning service: Lesson from NT, Matthew chapter 25, Luke — Dives and Lazarus. Preacher eloquent. Collection after lesson. But late arrivals went up and put money in box. Lunch with the Sewells. Left about 3.30 in borrowed Land Rover. Jinkew drove and got us safely through a very bad patch in Tigama, but puncture 2 miles from Meru. Spare also leaked a little, but when blown up got us safely to Kaaga. African minister, Francis, arrived, and Ibrahim and Peter. Next morning also picked up Jonathan and Joseph. Florence provided supper of cottage pie, rice and fruit salad.

Monday 13 May
Roused at 5.30, dressed, cup of tea, and ready by 6 o'clock. Book room, bus ready to take us. Loaded up — 5 parsons and ourselves. Parsons going to Mombasa for a 3-day retreat. Did the round of garages, as the tyres

needed more air in view of the load. Off by 7 o'clock. Nanyuki at 8.30. Snack breakfast at Marina. Now tarmac road all the way. Lawi drove from Meru to Saganwe. There Jinkins took over. Road hilly and more winding, and speed therefore slow. Good view of Mount Kenya as we approached Nanyuki. Arrived Mortimer's about 12 o'clock. Men had drinks of Coca Cola and then pushed off.

Tuesday 14 May
Went into Nairobi. Doris bought fruit etc. Visit Government House and went up tower by lift. Notice NOT IN USE, but Charlie Mortimer found a mechanic who put it in order. Fine view from top. Charlie not well at lunch, pain in left groin and nausea. Examined him after tea. Swelling in groin, tried gentle pressure to reduce it, without avail. After some trouble Win got physician to come and see him. He reduced the hernia.

Charlie got a friend, manager of Express Delivery Service, to send a car to take us to the air port. Large van turned up at 8 o'clock. Win and Doris sat with driver. Charlie and I in van with luggage. Charlie and Win saw us fixed up before they left. Plane left on time at 9.40. Doris took two soneryl and slept soundly till we reached Frankfurt – 3.40 local time (5.40 Nairobi time). Taken by bus to airport buildings to stretch our legs. Left about 4.30, and reached Heathrow at 5.50. Soon through customs, and found Kathleen already there, having had a quick run from Oxford. She had risen at 4.30.

I do not know what my parents said to Kathleen and John on their way to Oxford, but I am sure that when they reached their own home in Hazel Grove, they looked back over their years together and thanked God that they had been able to work for so many years together and that they had been able to save motherless babies, help mothers safely through childbirth, and give men mauled by lions a chance to fight again. They had shown them that the modern medical doctor had more to offer them than had their own *muga*s, that no harm came to those who cared for the dying or buried the dead and that a whole new world lay before them. Whether it was good or bad depended in large measure on them. They were also grateful to my father's brother, Clement, and to his three sisters and other relatives who had borne the cost of the church they had built at Maua. And, last but not least, they were grateful to their grandson Jim Potter for having invited them to see for themselves the transformation that had taken place in the lives of many Africans, and their gratitude to those who, like my parents, had helped to engineer the change.

My father died the following year. My mother moved to Oxford where Kathleen kept a motherly eye on her and she spent several happy years. Chris, when he was at Oxford, had lunch with her nearly every week and remembers taking her to the University Parks in her wheelchair. She died eight years later.

10. How the women spend their days – child-bearing; carrying wood, water and straw for roofing; grinding corn and looking after the crops (not shown).

11. ABOVE. Men in war-paint at a Baila funeral.

12. LEFT. Young women dressed for a dance. The sexes dance separately.

13. ABOVE. Baila chiefs
dressed to see the Prince
of Wales at Broken Hill,
Kasenga, in the 1920s.

14. RIGHT. A young girl
waiting to be
circumcised, Maua, late
1930s.

15. ABOVE. Homes in Kasenga in the 1930s.

16. BELOW. A home in the Zambezi valley, subject to floods, 1932.

11

Maua after Independence: The Price of Freedom

I cannot leave Maua where my parents left it, for it too has a story to tell. Six weeks before my parents were due to leave, two young and enthusiastic missionaries joined them, Stanley and Margaret Bell. Like my own parents, the Bells had come out to Africa with a view to dedicating their lives to a combination of missionary and medical work. Fired with youthful enthusiasm and zeal, the young couple were determined to follow on from where my parents left off and to devote their skills to the needs of the Ameru people. Witnessing the ease with which my parents conversed with the local people, they resolved to follow their example.

So the Bells quickly settled down to learn the local language, Kimeru, and to earn the affection and trust of the Ameru people, for some still distrusted the white man, especially if he was a stranger. Dr Bell's first need was for a nurse to stand by his side when he was examining women and children. Dr Brassington's sister, who was a trained nurse, had filled that role for him. My father had persuaded the Missionary Society to provide him with a nurse and Joy Bannister had been sent to Maua to help him. She was a tremendous asset. However, when the Second World War broke out, she left Maua and joined the East African services. So Stanley found himself without a nurse and remained so for three years until May Poulson joined him. When Joy returned at the end of the war, she was

179

able to help with a programme to train nurses, which Stanley had already started. He was providing a supply of nurses not only to Maua but also to other hospitals.

There were other problems that needed attention. My father had piped in running water to the hospital from a nearby stream, but sewage disposal remained a problem. Since the area was volcanic and the hospital had been built on lava, deep latrines were out of the question. Sewage had therefore to be collected in buckets and carried out by hand. Handling excreta was taboo for the Ameru, but Stanley managed to find some Africans who were prepared to carry sewage-filled buckets and to dispose of their contents elsewhere — at a price.

My father had added a six-bed maternity ward and laundry to the buildings. Stanley wanted to add power and toyed with the idea of utilizing power from the stream to generate electricity, but in the end this remained a pipe dream. A later medical superintendent, Dr Bastin, was able to obtain an oil-driven generator to provide electricity for the hospital, which also made it possible for them to install X-ray equipment.

Both Stanley and Margaret were as happy in their work as my parents had been. Stanley, too, became fluent in Kimeru, he even developed a local accent — Meru is the name of the district, Kimeru the language, Mumeru the name of the individual, and Ameru the name of many.

While at Maua the Bells' two sons were born, David in 1942 and John in 1944. During their second spell at Maua, 1945–50, Margaret taught David to read and write, providing him with home schooling, but both she and Stanley felt the children needed a proper education in England. They also felt that their family should not be divided and, though happy and pleased with the work in Maua, they spent the next ten years, 1950–60, in England. After a short spell in general practice, Stanley went to the London School of Tropical Medicine where he obtained a diploma in tropical medicine and hygiene. Then, after submitting a thesis, he obtained a doctorate of medicine from the University of Durham. The thesis, titled 'Clinical

Epidemiology in Meru, Kenya', contained a masterly description of the customs and taboos of the Ameru in Kenya.

When David and John went to university and were able to look after themselves, Stanley, even though he was well established as a reader in tropical medicine at the University of London, felt free once more to volunteer for service abroad and asked to be sent back to Maua. The Mission House decided he would be more valuable in India, so he spent the next three-and-a-half years in Mysore followed by a second three-and-a-half in the Punjab. Before going to the Punjab he again asked to return to Kenya, and was again refused. But when he returned to England in 1969, the year after my parents had had their moving welcome at Maua, he was asked to return to Maua to put the hospital on a sound financial basis.

The Berresford Memorial Hospital had been taken over by the new independent Methodist Church of Kenya and had been renamed the Maua Methodist Hospital. It was no longer the responsibility of the Methodist Church in Britain, and was in severe financial straits. So, when Stanley and Margaret Bell returned to Maua they were greeted with suspicion rather than the welcoming open arms they had expected.

In the 21 years that had elapsed since they were last at Maua, profound changes had taken place in Kenya. There had first been the Mau Mau rebellion, then independence and self-government. Kenya was now a republic with a black prime minister, Jomo Kenyatta. These changes were associated with the breakdown of the old tribal system. The old hierarchy no longer existed; everyone was his or her own master; everyone was free. The Kenya Methodist Church had also declared its independence from the mother church in the United Kingdom, and the latter, bless her heart, did all she could to help her offspring stand on her own feet. The Kenya Methodist Church was now free to run its own affairs. One of the first things it did, in Maua, was to change the name of the Berresford Memorial Hospital to the Maua Methodist Hospital, but the plaque commemorating the generous gift of Sam Berresford remained intact in the entrance.

Independence did not interfere with the growth of the Methodist or any other church, nor did it interfere with the growth of the Maua Methodist Hospital, but the attitude to missionaries in the eyes of some Africans changed. Where they had once looked upon them as white men who had come to help their less fortunate black brothers, they now looked upon them as penitents trying to redress the harm that had been inflicted on them in the past. The church, however, took on a new life. The little church my father had built was no longer able to accommodate the Sunday congregation, which had swollen from 500 to 1500.

The hospital had also grown. It now had 50 maternity and 50 paediatric beds and cots as well as an increased staff, but its superintendent, Dr D. L. Knight, was in poor health and was about to return home to England. Though a medical student from Birmingham, Paul Crook, was ably supervising the work, the hospital was now competing with government hospitals, which did not charge for their services, and was heavily in debt.

The Mau Mau rebellion, however tragic an interlude it may have been, probably hastened independence. Though in part a rebellion of the Kikuyu against the white settlers and in part a violent attack on British rule, it was also linked to a powerful Kikuyu oath. The oath needs a little explanation. A council of elders usually settled disputes between autonomous groups or *rugongos* of the Kikuyu, but very occasionally they did not. In such cases, the disputants would be told that the oath would be administered. The mere threat of the oath was nearly always sufficient to determine the guilty party, but if not the oath was administered. Each disputant then swore that his statement was true and proclaimed that if it were not, 'may I be killed by this oath'. The power of the oath was so strong that no disputant in the wrong would dare take it. The Mau Mau took the oath to keep the identity of its members secret and, by linking it with their traditional oath, ensured that it would never be broken.

The rebellion started in 1952 and ended after four years of violence and sabotage. The colonial government of Kenya had to step in and wage a military campaign in which more than 11,000 rebels, 100 whites and 2000 African loyalists were killed. The government also put 20,000 Kikuyu in detention camps, where efforts were made to re-educate them. Jomo Kenyatta was imprisoned for nine years, being released at the time of independence to become the country's first prime minister. The Meru community was not unaffected, as the son of a Methodist minister, Harry Laughton, who had gone out to Kaaga, Meru, in 1929 to teach and train African teachers, discovered. Harry worked closely with Arthur Hopkins, the superintendent of the Kaaga mission, became fluent in Kimeru, built the Kaaga boys school and became principal of the Kaaga teachers' training college. He also wrote a thesis, based on his own anthropological studies, for the Centre of Anthropological Studies in London. With the onset of the Mau Mau rebellion, life became hazardous for white men in general and for black Christians in particular. Harry joined the Kenya Police Reserve and acted both as an interpreter and as an interrogator of suspects. The Mau Mau targeted Harry and once, on returning with his wife from a dinner with the district commissioner, he found a dead dog strung up by his home as a reminder of the danger he faced.

Reverend Philip M. Inoti was treated more harshly. Philip was not only the most distinguished of the African preachers, but he was also the paramount chief of the Ameru. He, like his superintendent Arthur Hopkins, was known as a great conciliator, and was looked up to and respected by both Ameru and white members of the church; he bridged the gap between black and white. As paramount chief he had a truck so that he could visit his people. One day, when driving round Meru district, and making a very sharp turn, a young man with a lorry drove ferociously into his truck and knocked it right off the road. Philip was taken to hospital where Reverend Fred Valender saw him. He was so severely injured that he only lived a very short time. His injuries were said to have been caused by an accident, but everyone knew that it was the work of the Mau Mau.

Stanley and Margaret Bell had hoped and expected their return to Maua to be a return to the happy, halcyon days they had enjoyed when they first went there, but it was not. The staff knew that the Bells had returned to Maua to try to put the hospital on a sound financial footing, but merely asked them how a charitable organization could possibly be expected to make ends meet. Moreover, during the nearly 30 years that had elapsed since they were last in Maua, the staff had increased greatly; there were now two doctors, three nursing sisters, three nurses, a minister, a retired bank official on a two-year stint, as well as numerous orderlies and other helpers, but there was no one in overall charge. They were all ordering whatever they thought necessary and no one paid for any medications he or she might need for personal use or for the use of hospital transport for private needs. When Margaret started charging them for these, they were displeased. In addition, Africans working in the hospital were stealing needles, syringes and medicines to sell in the market, making tidy profits. When the Bells introduced strict accounting, the staff was taken aback and complained at the Maua quarterly meeting that the Bells did not love their fellow workers as they should and that, in addition, they were practising poor medicine.

The Bells took these complaints to Nairobi, to Bishop Lawi I'Mathi, the same Lawi who had chauffeured my parents when they had been in Nairobi three years earlier. He supported them and they managed to put the hospital on a sound financial basis before returning to Britain, somewhat disillusioned with the Christian community in Maua but thankful that they had at least completed the task they had been given.

While they were at Maua in the 1970s one happy and quite

unanticipated incident had made them remember their first arrival there. As Margaret recorded it later:

> On January 8th, 1974, a young man turned up on our doorstep saying he was Christopher Gerrard! His amazement was great when I said, 'You must be John's son!' I knew that John had gone to Canada, and I recognized Christopher's accent. I am certain of the date because he and his friend signed our visitor's book! He was also amazed to find someone in Maua who had been there with his grandparents, and it was a great pleasure to show him round the hospital, and to be able to tell him which buildings had been there in their time, and the church they had built as a memorial to their parents. I remember taking a photo of him on the steps of the church. We were able to introduce him to Africans who had remembered his grandparents, and to tell him of the high regard in which they were held.

Before visiting Maua, Chris and his friend Tom, a Californian student studying at Oxford, had toured Kenya, visiting Mombasa and several game reserves before returning to Oxford. Little did he realize that he would be returning to Africa again and again, sometimes three or four times a year. Chris obtained an M.Phil. from Oxford and then spent two years in Addis Ababa working for the United Nations Economic Commission for Africa. He then went to the University of Minnesota where he earned a Ph.D. in agricultural economics. While still studying for his doctorate he was asked to join a team of Americans who were studying ways to improve the storage of grain in Kenya. Much grain was lost because it became damp when stored, permitting moulds to grow. The moulds produced powerful toxins, which caused cancer of the liver in those who ate the grain. After obtaining his Ph.D. he joined the economics department at the University of Saskatchewan, later becoming its head; while there he also worked for CIDA and the World Bank on projects designed to improve agricultural services in Anglophone Africa. He was asked to devote all his time to this when he joined the World Bank. He has continued the work of his grandfather among Africans, teaching them the skills they needed when they became independent. Jim Potter did the same when he spent two years in Zambia.

Nine years after the Bells had retired and left Maua with very mixed feelings, they returned, again with mixed feelings, but as Margaret later wrote:

> I am glad to be able to tell you, that when we went back to Kenya on holiday in 1983, we found a totally different attitude to us. We were welcomed with open arms, and were asked many times, 'Tell us what it was like when you first came to Maua.' They were amazed that we had been there so long ago, and could speak their language. We were delighted to find they were now interested in their past, and had in fact quite a good museum at Meru, and were genuinely interested when we said, 'This is like it was when we first came.' The staff seemed to have grown up and had enough confidence to look their primitive past in the face, and be proud of what they had accomplished. They loved the fact that Stanley could address the congregation in his fluent Kimeru, and we met many of our old friends — our age group — now elderly!! We were very glad we had gone back, as it was very heart-warming after our very difficult last three years working at Maua.

Chris visited Maua a second time. While working for the United Nations in Addis Ababa from 1974 to 1976, he invited Betty and me to meet him in Nairobi from where he drove us to Addis through northern Kenya and southern Ethiopia. We paused on the way at Maua to see the church, talk to children in the church and meet some of the old men who had known my parents.

My son, Peter, and his wife Nikki were the next members of the family to visit Maua. Peter had worked for Price Waterhouse in Nairobi for two years and, while there, he and Nikki had visited Maua briefly and then, in 1979, they invited Margaret and Lewis to stay with them in Nairobi. While they were there, they all drove to Maua where they were welcomed and shown the church and hospital, followed by a lavish luncheon and a demonstration of African dances. Margaret was given a live fowl as a token of gratitude for our parents' work. They were also introduced to a group of old men who had known our parents, one of whom had been my father's gardener. Following their visit to Maua they set out to climb Mount Kenya, taking the fowl, still very much alive, with them, but not wanting it to suffer from mountain sickness, they gave it to some villagers at the foot of the mountain. Unfortunately, it was Lewis who developed mountain sickness — he had not had time to become acclimatized to such great altitudes — and the party had to retreat before reaching the summit.

The next member of the family to visit Maua was my sister Kathleen in 1992. Maua, as Chris observed, had become a Mecca for our family. Her son, Jim Potter who, as mentioned earlier, had invited my parents to visit him in Zambia in 1968, now invited his mother to accompany him, with his second wife Hilary and daughter Caroline, to visit Maua. While at Maua they stayed at the Nambarene Lodge; Maua now had a serviceable modern motel. The church was unchanged apart from the bell, which had been moved from its perch above the front door, where it was thought it might be dangerous, to a little bell tower on the ground in front of the church. Plans were afoot to build a second church to hold 1500, large enough to accommodate the whole congregation, the majority of which had to stand outside and listen to the service relayed by loudspeakers. If and when this new church is built, the church my father built will become the hospital chapel. There were at the time two ministers, the assistant being the hospital chaplain.

The hospital was much larger and more impressive than Kathleen and Jim had expected. There were male and female wards, each with 50 beds, a children's ward with 40 beds, a maternity ward with 50 beds and an isolation unit for those with infectious diseases. There was an operating room, an X-ray unit, an outpatient department, a family planning and childcare unit, a kitchen, pharmaceutical and administrative buildings and a mortuary. There were new dental and eye units, provided by Methodists in Pasadena, California. The dental unit is dedicated to Claudia Turner.

The male and female wards, the isolation unit and the administrative buildings were the only original buildings left; everything else was new. The dental unit, which was particularly impressive, was staffed by an American dentist and had been fitted out by his colleagues in the United States. A well-trained Kenyan dentist was expected to take over the responsibility for it in the near future.

There were five doctors on the hospital staff. First, there was the superintendent, an over-worked young Englishman called John Harbottle. He had been at Maua for six years and he and his wife Sharon had two children aged eleven and six. Second and third were two Americans, Lynn and Sharon Fogelman, who had also been at Maua for six years — each serving two three-year periods and expecting to serve another. Fourth was Clare Smithson from Leeds who had been there for two three-year terms and was starting her third one. And finally, there was John Leucoma who had arrived from Uganda in 1976. He had obtained his medical degree in what was then Czechoslovakia, where he had spent six years before returning to Uganda, and he had been at Maua for 16 years. There were in addition three medical students, two from Britain and one from the United States. They each stayed for eight weeks; for the first two they were a burden, for the last six they were very helpful.

Bob Harland, the dentist, had established and was in charge of the dental clinic. In addition, there was a hospital minister, a matron, four registered nursing sisters and a training school for nurses, which Stanley Bell had started. It was thriving and was training 70 students at a time. Kathleen and Jim inspected the library, classrooms and living quarters and saw many students, who were dressed in green. All in all, the hospital and nursing school employed about 300 people. The increase in the size of the hospital, its staff and its work put a strain on its financial resources and, in 1988, it was threatened with closure. Bishop Lawi I'Mathi, now the head of the Methodist Church of Kenya, was able to persuade the government to come to the hospital's rescue, and it was once more put on a sound financial footing. Bishop Lawi was president of the World Methodist Conference from 1986 to 1991.

The next visitor to Maua, Christine Budd, was a family friend and a friend of John Armitstead, Margaret's eldest son. She was a medical student and had chosen to go to Maua for an elective to broaden her experiences because of her contacts with our family. In her medical training she had been taught the value of cleanliness and sterility, the danger of transmitting diseases by using syringes and needles more than once, and the value of laboratory tests in the investigation and treatment of diseases. She was told to work first on the paediatric ward and was horrified at what she saw. When I read what she had to say, my first reaction was to sanitize it, but on second thoughts I decided to share her reactions with the reader, bearing in mind that she was a young woman who had stepped straight out of a modern London hospital and that after six weeks she said that she felt very comfortable working in the hospital.

The following extracts are from letters written soon after her arrival and later when she had settled down in her new surroundings.

Wednesday 24 February 1993, 8.22 p.m.
Well I've survived the first day here — survival is probably the best word to choose. I was due to work on paediatrics for the next week or so with Dr Claire. This

morning I met her for the first time. She had been on duty all night, and had admitted three children and delivered one baby who never breathed. The first three hours were to be somewhat shocking to me. I hardly know where to start in describing it. There are two paediatric wards, A and B, each with three bays. We spent the morning on A ward. It was stacked full. There were two to three babies in most of the beds, plus the mother (or grandmother if the mother had an even younger baby at home). It smelt — I can't describe the smell — but it was not that pleasant. Many of the babies had drips in their scalps with jars/bottles hanging from pegs on the walls and attached by old cloth straps. Firstly we did an 'abscess' ward round — to assess who would need to go to the theatre later. The first had a large abscess under his scrotum which was already draining; the second, a six month old baby, had an *enormous* swelling on his thigh. We took him to the theatre in the afternoon (more on that later!). Then we went to the neonatal unit; there were six or seven with sepsis or pneumonia with or without malaria. All the translating was done by the nurses.

The second bay was *loaded* with babies with kwashi-orkor or marasmus, many of whom also had malaria. Eight or nine beds with 18–19 babies. They looked awful, some worse than others, and some mothers were told quite frankly that her baby would probably die. All the babies were less than the 3rd percentile for weight. There have been no cases of malnutrition like these since 1984. Last year there were five cases altogether. The reason is the rains. The rains before the last never came, so there was no harvest. The last rain, usually a short rain, didn't stop, so there was again no harvest, so now there is kwashiorkor plus plus. There doesn't seem to be this problem at Chagoria, only 60 kilometres or so away. The babies were usually in their mother's arms, often dangling from a breast, when we examined them. They wore scruffy vests and jumpers. None had nappies, and the diarrhoea just came out into the rags and blankets they were wrapped in. One toddler just stood up (no mother) and peed and poo'd on the floor — just like that.

The kids were on some kind of oral feed and anti-biotics (if pneumonia) plus chloroquine or some other anti-malarial medication, as most also had malaria. It just went on like this all morning. Some were having blood transfusions because of the malaria causing a drastic anaemia. What is so weird is there are no labora-tory investigations. The only investigations that can be done here are blood films for malarial parasites, examin-ation of the cerebrospinal fluid for meningitis and of the stools for ova and parasites, blood sugars and haemo-globins, and X-rays on Tuesdays and Thursdays only.

I had an hour off for lunch. Vibeke, a Danish medical student, took me down town as I'd not bought food as yet — I got onions, potatoes, tomatoes, mung beans, spaghetti, mangoes, milk, eggs, toilet paper, soap pow-der and stamps. A strange mad man, almost completely naked, harassed us in the post office. We were the only *mazungu*s (whites) in town! Then we returned and bumped into Sandy — an American Dental Hygienist — *very* friendly and welcoming — much *more* so than *any* of the Brits here. She showed me where I had to pay for my accommodation.

I went to the theatre, if you can call just a room a theatre, in the afternoon. Some one was cleaning the windows and water was pouring in! The babies were screaming. Anaesthesia was given intravenously. The baby with the thigh abscess, due to an infected DPT [diphtheria, whooping cough and tetanus] shot, screamed blue murder — I should think about 100 ml or so of pus came out. *Everything* in the theatre is re-used, including needles, swabs, syringes, masks, and even fine rubber gloves. It felt very weird. The day passed mercifully without a death — quite unusual I gather.

Vibeke had some mega experiences on her first call. There is a lot of violence with panga knives. She had one man whose hand had been almost chopped off, then his arm and chest had been slashed; he survived. I have been spared this so far, but I'm on call tomorrow night. There is a lot of chewing of *miraa* leaves and drunkenness due to alcohol among the Meru men.

In letters to Margaret and Lewis, Christine painted a happier picture.

The Jacaranda trees that your mother planted are very beautiful, and it seems strange to think of them as tiny seedlings as they are very big now (not in flower at present). Today I was covering the wards, and I have a day off tomorrow. Last week I worked on Maternity. The nursery you'd love to see, so I've taken some pictures. The cots are made out of up-turned cupboards, and there's a tiny electric fire keeping the temperature up, and a kerosene lamp. It's a little disconcerting to see tiny cockroaches crawling over the tiny babies. Today I had great joy in giving both of the two boys, Felix and Gerald, who have fractured femurs, some pencils and crayons and an exercise book, and a post card of London. Their faces lit up like I had *never* seen, as they'd been lying in traction ever since I arrived, doing *nothing* — day in day out.

Monday 1 March
I'm not sleeping terribly well, and this doesn't help. I'm having nightmares about being on call, so it wakes me up! So far I've not worked in male or female wards. The males all have panga wounds, only a few have medical problems.

Tuesday 9 March

Last night there was a *matatu* (a local taxi) accident.[1] Vibeke was called. There were 20 or so injured and one dead. The driver was drunk, drunk and chewing *miraa*. There was a good deal of stitching and referring to do. There is also a case of miliary tuberculosis in an 18 year old. It looks bad. I am on paediatrics again this week. Paediatrics is quieter — either dead or discharged. Have had three tetanus deaths. There are fewer cases now of malnutrition. Tomorrow I'm assisting in the amputation of a finger in an 18 month old with osteomyelitis. It's horrible, the bone is sticking right out through the skin, and everything is distorted. I'm still not sleeping at all well and I'm not sure how to rectify this. We sleep above the boys' dorm and before nine a.m. they are very noisy. I seem to be troubled by nocturia so am trotting for a pee two or three times a night, and have dreams about being on call!!!!

I've been 'running' the male ward this week as Dr L was only there on Monday morning. It's been fun. Today we reduced a dislocated hip (anterior dislocation) on a lovely old farmer. One of the two mute boys that share a bed *spoke* today. We resuscitated a GI [gastrointestinal] bleed, and there's a chap with a large bowel obstruction who may go to the theatre. I also stitched a chest stab wound.

I was on call last night, and it was the first night I felt comfortable and confident. Dr Claire was the doctor on call, and she's the best to have around and we get on pretty well. I admitted quite a few people. Female ward was so packed that nearly *all* beds were being shared, and that made me giggle. If there was a really sick one, then we'd turn one out, and they'd have to get in bed

---

1. *Matatu* accidents were common. There was one when Jim Potter was visiting Maua.

with the next one. There were no complaints, they'd just squeeze in!! It no longer shocks me at all. I'm really enjoying it very much more. I did an I and D [incision and drainage] of a huge abscess all by myself last night while doctors D and C watched. The needles were *blunt*. I sutured a scalp wound and admitted a chain saw laceration of the forearm injuring the *ulnar* nerve; he was only my age, and it was an accident (for once!). My stomach is getting stronger for these things!! I'm really feeling more settled in, so the last three weeks should be good.

Dr John asked me if there was a chance that John Armitstead could bring 5,000 quinine tablets when you come. We've had none in the hospital for 2–3 weeks but I'd understood they were on order.

The men chop each other up with pangas. A man will come in and say, 'It's *only* my hand — just sew it up so I can axe the neighbour that did it to me.'

This morning went to the theatre and sutured a six inch laceration in the arm and deltoid. He had panga wounds including the tip of his right little finger, and the ring finger was hanging on by a tag with the cut going through to the 4th metacarpal in the palm of his hand, plus several on his torso and skull!! All done by a neighbour. The anaesthetic seemed incomplete and he wriggled round the table, and I wasn't sure he had a good airway, and the oxygen wasn't monitored anyway.

It was our day off yesterday — but did a Caesarean Section with Dr John. It was the first time I'd worked with him, and he was very pleasant and helpful. The tetanus baby had two respiratory arrests yesterday and two today. There seems to be a lack of doctors — or just too many patients at present. There are 71 kids in 35 or 40 beds (plus mums sharing beds!).

The church bell has had a new roof now. Pass this on to Jim Potter. The bell is rung whenever there is a major *matatu* accident, and on Sundays!! Fortunately it hasn't been rung while I've been here.

There's a crazy man wandering about Maua, and we have been warned about him. He has AIDS and is mega angry about it. He has weeping leg sores and has got hold of a syringe and needle and tries injecting people as they jostle about in the market. The police have been informed, but so far nothing's been done — so the locals are in an uproar and want gang justice — apparently they will either stone him, or put a tyre round him and set fire to him. I don't know what will happen — but I'll be careful. I'm not as aware of HIV and AIDS as I'd expected to be because we do not test for it. In retrospect I think there was a lot. It is the young men that die from it — the *miraa* dealers who use prostitutes in Nairobi; I guess their wives and kids then get it.

HIV, the virus that causes AIDS, was unknown when my father worked in Africa. It was discovered in 1987, 46 years after he left. Had it existed then he would most certainly have caught it and developed AIDS. The first medical doctor to acquire AIDS through her work, a hazard of her occupation, was a medical missionary, Lucille Teasdale. She was a Catholic and a Canadian. From an early age she had wanted to be a doctor and was one of the first women surgeons in her province. With her husband, Pierre Corti, an Italian doctor, she went to northern Uganda in 1961 and established a clinic among the Furli.

They soon converted the clinic into a 450-bed hospital, St Mary's Lacor. In the 1970s, with Idi Amin in power, civil war broke out and Lucille started to do war surgery. While cleaning wounds and removing bullets from her patients she cut herself repeatedly. In 1982 she started to develop infections, including pneumocystis pneumonia, to which AIDS victims are particularly susceptible, and, in 1985, the diagnosis of AIDS was made. She continued to work, believing that surgery in the hands of a surgeon with AIDS but wearing rubber gloves was preferable to no surgery at all. She continued to operate, even when she fell ill, resting only on Sundays. She died in 1996 in her little hometown of Besana at the foot of the Italian Alps.

When Christine Budd had been working in the hospital for a month, Margaret and Lewis paid a second visit to Maua and John Armitstead a first. John brought with him a large supply of quinine and Fasidar, another antimalarial medication. The hospital had been out of both for several weeks. John also brought kits for testing for HIV infections, as well as other much needed medical supplies. All were confiscated when he arrived at Nairobi airport, but were delivered to the hospital a week later. John also helped in the work of the hospital.

Margaret was again given a warm welcome and met the staff as well as a few old men who remembered our father.

Two years later, in 1995, Margaret and Lewis paid a third visit to Maua, this time at the invitation of their son Martin and his wife Jenny. After touring game reserves in Tanzania and Kenya, they arrived in Maua on a Sunday afternoon and, having checked in at the Nambarene Lòdge, they walked along the avenue of jacaranda trees to attend the evening service at the church. Near the church were the stones marking the foundation of the anticipated new church, now in limbo through lack of funds.

On the Monday morning, the doctors and staff at the hospital gave them their usual warm welcome and then showed them round the facility. Martin, as the manager of a hotel in a large, well-known, expensive, elitist chain, not surprisingly looked with some disdain at the Nambarene Lodge. Its security, he noted, was poor. He also noted the relatively primitive conditions under which the staff at the hospital worked. In the maternity ward there were as many as three mothers to a bed, often with a baby hanging on; in the male ward many of the men had dreadful panga wounds, the result of brawls; on the bushes near the hospital washed sheets and linen were spread out to dry; meals were cooked in large open cauldrons on open wood fires; the bodies in the mortuary were baking under a hot tin roof; and, in the village, men were openly chewing and selling twigs of *miraa*. On the other hand, Martin was impressed by the dedication, cheerfulness and untiring zeal of the whole hospital staff.

On returning to the Nambarene Lodge, Martin noticed that the locks on his suitcase and camera case had been tampered with and that some Kenya shillings, English money and US $320 in traveller's cheques had been stolen. He immediately notified Joel, the manager, who in turn notified the police. By this time it was early evening and, to make matters worse, the spasmodic electricity supply had failed and the hotel was plunged into almost total darkness. The family sat in the court-yard and waited for events to unfold. The security guard silently patrolled the premises, blending fully with the darkness, with a menacing bow and viciously barbed arrows. Clearly, he was not averse to using them on any unauthorized intruder.

Martin was given occasional progress reports ranging from the hotel paying for the petrol for the police car so that it could be driven to the hotel, to the apprehension of the plumber who, that afternoon, had been fixing washbasins. It transpired, two hours later, when Jenny and Martin squeezed into the manager's office along with the police and an inter-preter, still in total darkness except for a small torch emitting a feint sinister glow, that on being apprehended the plumber had thrown down the traveller's cheques and these were duly returned. Martin was then asked if he wanted to press charges. He said he would take guidance from the police. He was then told that pressing charges would cause an administrative problem, would cost the government a lot of money and that there was another way with which the matter could be dealt. The interpreter whispered that the thief would be taken to the police station and discreetly beaten. Martin responded by saying that this was a matter for the police and should be dealt with by them in a manner they and the hotel manager felt appropriate in accordance with normal custom. And that was the last they heard of the plumber.

If Margaret and Lewis were able to return to Maua today, they would be amazed at the transformation that has taken place in the last four years, mainly through the dedication and determination of the Methodist Church of Kenya and the generosity of EZE of Germany, Sonnevanck, a Dutch foundation, and a host of individual donations from the United States and Britain.

In the 1980s, the hospital raised 600,000 Kenya shillings (the equivalent of £50,000 sterling or US$ 85,000) with a view to building a much-needed new maternity unit. The funds were insufficient to meet the cost, so they built a new outpatient facility instead. On 12 February 1996, after many preliminary negotiations with potential donors, the presiding bishop of the Methodist Church of Kenya, Zablon Nthamburi, signed an agreement with EZE of Germany to cover the construction costs of a much larger project than had been visualized initially. The project was to cost 82 million Kenya shillings (£870,000 or $1,410,000) and EZE promised to cover 79 per cent of this provided the Methodist Church of Kenya covered the rest. This, with the aid of Sommevanck and many individual contributions from the United States and Britain, it did.

The foundations for the new block, which had to be strong enough to support two extra floors, were laid in April the following year. And, within a year, on 21 March 1998, the new part was opened. It was composed of two wings. The north wing contained 53 maternity beds in eight wards containing between one and ten beds in each, three delivery rooms, two labour wards, two nurseries, a reception area, a lounge and a kitchen. The building as a whole was dedicated to EZE, but the labour and delivery suites were dedicated to Sister Muriel Chalkley, who had been the inspiration for the maternity unit and who continued to be involved with it even though she had retired and was living in the UK.

The north wing housed three air-conditioned operating

theatres, two major and one minor, a sluice, and recovery and changing rooms. The south wing, which housed 45 surgical beds in nine wards, was dedicated to Drs Judith and Adrian Goede and to Sonnevanck. Additional new features included improved laboratory services, automated haemograms and facilities for measuring drug sensitivities, a laundry with a drier, emergency electric power, and oxygen, compressed air and suction throughout the buildings, all of which were joined by covered walkways. The total bed capacity is now 238. The bed occupancy rate in 1998 was almost 130 per cent, so there are still some beds with more than one patient in them.

Last year there were 8227 admissions to the hospital, 3531 of which were maternity cases. There were 3317 normal deliveries and 363 Caesarean sections. The main causes of death in the patients admitted to the hospital were cerebral malaria, uncomplicated malaria, anaemia and pneumonia.

In addition to admitting and treating in patients, 22,996 were seen as outpatients, and many more at the dental and eye clinics, as well as at the 15 community health clinics the hospital now runs. All this, and the provision of round the clock service, keeps the five doctors very busy. It is a far cry from the day when Dr Brassington wondered if he would ever win the Africans' confidence and trust.

With Kenya now an independent country, Kenyans and the Methodist Church of Kenya know they themselves are responsible for providing good health care for their community. They also know that it is up to them to find a new way of life to replace their old tribal system. These are daunting tasks, but they are being made easier by the help they are receiving from those of us who are more fortunately placed than they are.

The construction was to include the following:

- 64 solar panels to provide heat for hot water, with electricity providing power on cloudy days;
- a stand-by generator to clock in automatically in the event of a power failure;

- a 4800-gallon water-storage tank with water laid on from a stream one and a half miles away.
- a 6840-litre sewage tank;
- centralized oxygen, compressed air suction;
- the installation of fire hydrants, fire-fighting equipment and hoses; and
- upgrading the electricity supply throughout the hospital.

The laboratory facilities were also to be upgraded. Haemograms have been automated and it is now possible to test the sensitivities of bacteria and parasites to the available antibiotics and antimalarial medications.

Construction went ahead remarkably quickly and when cost overruns threatened the project, the Methodist Church mobilized its resources and, with the help of a number of innovative schemes, raised an additional 1.5 million Kenya shillings. Professor Zablon Nthamburi, the presiding bishop of the Methodist Church, inaugurated the new facility, the Maua Methodist Hospital Maternity Project, at a fitting ceremony on 22 March 1999. This was just three years and one month after he and EZE had signed their initial agreement. After the opening ceremony, the National Hospital Insurance Fund, because it was impressed by the great improvement in the standard of care that the upgraded hospital would provide, increased its per diem payment for patients from 2.50 to 4.50 Kenya shillings.

Had Sam Berresford been present at the opening ceremonies he would have been amazed to discover that his original gift of £3000 had grown into a hospital of which the Methodist Church and Maua were justifiably proud.

The 1998 annual report stated that panga wounds accounted for only a small part of the hospital's work; that the hospital's bed capacity was 238; that during the year there had been 8227 admissions in addition to maternity cases, of which there were 3317 normal deliveries, nearly ten a day, and 353 Caesarean sections; and that the bed occupancy was 129 per cent.

Maua after Independence: The Price of Freedom

In the years since my father left Maua in 1941 the world has changed and no more so than in Kenya and the rest of Africa. Doctors who go there to help the Africans face new conditions and new challenges — panga instead of lion wounds, women crowding into maternity wards instead of avoiding them, traffic accidents, drunkenness, and the very serious prevalence of AIDS. Populations have exploded. At independence there were nine million Kenyans, now there are more than 20 million. The developed world has sent much aid to African countries, but not always the right kind of aid. It is a learning experience to know how we can best contribute to the wellbeing of African peoples.

12

Grandsons in the Steps of their Grandfather

I n the last chapter we followed Maua's vicissitudes and progress after independence, culminating in the gradual transformation of the relatively primitive Berresford Memorial Hospital into the new Maua Methodist Hospital with many of the trappings, oxygen, suction and air-conditioned operating theatres of a modern hospital. While these changes were taking place three of my father's grandsons either lived or spent time in Zambia, Kenya and other parts of Africa witnessing the changes that came with independence and helping them, as they were able, to make the changes as painlessly as possible. Jim Potter was the first, in 1967, to fly out to Africa. He had the thrill of taking his grandparents to see Kasenga and the responsibility of helping Kaunda grapple with his economic problems. Chris went out to Ethiopia in 1976 and later to Kenya and most of Anglophone Africa, Zambia included. Peter and Nikki, having visited Chris in Addis Ababa, returned to Nairobi in the following year, and worked there for two years, spending six weeks in Zambia when it was touching rock bottom.

In addition, Jon, my eldest son, christened Jonathan after his great great grandfather, visited Benin, formerly a French colony in West Africa, in November 1995. He was a distinguished physician and medical researcher who turned to politics because he felt that there was a need for scientists to play a more active role in government. From 1993 to 1997 he was in the Canadian cabinet as Minister of Science and Technology. In this capacity he represented Canada at a meeting in Benin of ministers of science from about 40 French-speaking countries. While there he had the pleasure of presenting an ambulance from Canada to the people of that country. In addition a fifth grandson, John Armitstead, as already mentioned, took medical supplies to and worked in the Maua Methodist Hospital for a short time.

The three grandsons who spent the most time in Africa tell their own stories in the following pages.

Jim Potter writes

I went to Zambia in September 1967. During the late 1950s and early 1960s the majority of the British colonial territories became independent, starting with Ghana and Nigeria in the west, with Uganda, Tanzania, Zambia, Malawi and other smaller territories such as Swaziland gaining their independence in the early 1960s. Zambia finally gained a relatively peaceful transition to independence on 24 October 1964. The majority of the senior African politicians, Kaunda included, had spent some time in colonial gaols but there had not been the Mau Mau type of violence that had occurred in Kenya. Both the greatest advantage and disadvantage to Zambia at the time of independence was copper. The price was riding high, Zambia was the third largest producer of copper in the world, and the excess profits could be creamed off in the form of taxes or investments in the education, health and transport infrastructures of the economy. The downside was, of course, that the economy depended totally on copper. The mines were owned by two of the large South African mining conglomerates, Anglo-American and the Roan Selection Trust (RST). The workings of the mines were almost totally dependent on the white expatriate staff and, given that copper accounted for over 95 per cent of Zambia's exports, the economy was extremely vulnerable. The other major problem that Zambia had at independence was a terrible lack of educated man-power. In 1964 there were only 100 Zambian university graduates and two with a Ph.D. On the plus side, the country had a relatively healthy climate, a predictable rainy season, was very sparsely populated and had plenty of good agri-cultural land and underground water. With seven main tribal groupings and languages and more than 300 local tribal dialects, there were relatively few tribal and population stresses and strains. English was accepted as the common national language and, on the whole, politicians from different parts of the country seemed to be able to work adequately together.

The lack of well-educated manpower was a cause of substan-tial concern. The unwillingness of expatriate colonial civil servants to stay on and the equal reluctance of the newly emerging politicians to trust those who did, exacerbated the situation. Throughout the 1960s there was an influx of new expatriate professional staff, normally on two- to three-year contracts to fill the gap until locally educated people were available. In London the Overseas Development Institute, a private charitable foundation whose main objective was to provide research and briefing facilities on the newly-emerging developing countries, principally to MPs in Westminster, entered into a partnership with the Nuffield Foundation, which enabled them to recruit between six and ten newly graduated economists from British universities and place them on two-year contracts as professional civil servants to the East and Central African countries. These ODINs (the ODI Nuffield Fellows) received no specialist training and were, in my day, raw out of university, but were supposed to be of more use than hindrance to the countries to which they were sent. Zambia had been receiving two graduates each year for three or four years (this was to continue after I went) and I was one of two who went out in 1967. I was posted as an economist in the Ministry of Finance and was actually paid as a local Zambian civil servant on Zambian civil servant pay, but with my salary topped up in London through the Nuffield Foundation's grants.

The Ministry of Finance, like the whole of the government, was based in Lusaka. New buildings were arising quickly, the shops were full and there was little crime. At no time in my three years in Zambia did I feel physically at risk. And I was lucky to be in the country when it was stable, safe and quite well administered. In the final resort this was wholly due to the level of the copper price.

During the period of independence there was one country where things went seriously wrong. In Zambia, which had been Northern Rhodesia, a clear black political leadership emerged. Southern Rhodesia's ruling white settlers decided that they were not ready to accept a one man one vote independence and in 1965 Ian Smith, the prime minister, made a Unilateral Declaration of Independence for Southern Rhodesia. This presented a particular problem for landlocked Zambia, which during the colonial period had shared an airline, a railway system and the electricity industry with its southern neighbour.

I therefore found my work in the Ministry of Finance after the first three months or so fell into two categories:

- working with the senior economist in the ministry on general economic planning; and
- dealing with the financial aspects of the air, rail and power infrastructure, and in particular with the complications arising as a result of Southern Rhodesia's UDI.

On the railways I assisted with the purchase and financing of 24 new diesel locomotives, which were to work the rail stretch from the Copper Belt to the Rhodesian border. Copper was still going out through Rhodesia by train on a special United Nations dispensation.

Like many emerging nations Zambia had to have its own airline and I seemed to spend quite a lot of my time trying to prevent Zambia Airways from being fleeced by the major aircraft manufacturers, particularly when it came to spare parts.

Lockheed were appalling in this respect. When we purchased five Hercules aircraft to assist with an airlift of copper out to Dar es Salaam on the African east coast when the Smith regime closed the railroad to Zambia, I discovered that Zambia had been sold spare parts to a value of at least two further aircraft most of which they would and, in fact, never did need.

But the most exciting part of my job in the early days was to do with electricity. Before independence the Kariba Dam had been built on the Zambezi River and the first power station had been located on the south bank in Southern Rhodesia. Nearly all the power from this power station came north to operate the mines in Zambia; indeed without it there would have been immediate flooding and some of the deeper mines would have been irretrievably lost. Despite the difficulties UDI presented, there had been a clear understanding between Britain, Rhodesia and Zambia that nothing would tamper with this power system. I joined the Board of Directors of the Central African Power Company as the Ministry of Finance representative from Zambia and two of my white Zambian colleagues I and met on a regular basis with the three Rhodesian members of the board. To a certain extent the meetings were a farce. A wiley old tea planter chaired the board and a shrewd managing director, who was an engineer at heart and was solely interested in ensuring that the system continued to run properly, ran the day-to-day business. The board itself therefore did relatively little except keep the cap on any political explosion. We were supposed to meet on alternate months in Zambia and Rhodesia. However, since it was impossible for the Rhodesian civil servants to come to Zambia, on alternate months we met at the South Bank Power Station — which for the purpose of the meeting was in Zambian territory — and in the Rhodesian capital of Salisbury, now Harare, on the other alternate months. My passport of this time is covered with VIP stamps for these visits, which provided the Rhodesian border authorities with a bit of an enigma when my wife and I later travelled down through Rhodesia for a holiday in South Africa in our beaten-up old minibus and holiday clothes.

Zambia needed to become independent of Rhodesia for electricity and the obvious thing to do was to build another dam on the Kafue River some 80 miles north of the Zambezi or an additional power station at Kariba, but on the north bank. In the event both were done. I was deeply involved in the Kafue project negotiating the financial terms with the Yugoslavian company, Energoprojekt, which was eventually awarded the contract. In my last few months in Zambia I also negotiated the finance for the Kariba North Bank Power Station from the World Bank. That power station was later opened in 1973.

In late 1968 President Kaunda announced that he was going to nationalize the copper mines but that he would strike a fair deal with the owners. In hindsight, and even at the time, it was clear to me that this was the start of the slippery slope for Zambia and indeed after I returned to Cambridge I wrote a chapter of a book with a colleague on the copper mine nationalization. The problem was not that the mines were to be nationalized but that Kaunda had stipulated that a fair price should be paid and guaranteed. As I was now (at the age of 24) the senior economist in the Ministry of Finance, it fell to me to accompany my permanent secretary to the regular meetings to negotiate the terms of the deal. From the Zambian side, the permanent secretary in the Department of Trade and Industry, a naturalized Zambian of Greek Cypriot origin who was a very good personal friend of Kaunda, led the negotiations. It became clear from a fairly early time that the companies were going to get an excessively good deal. Not only were they going to be paid a full price for the mines based on current profits that were being made at a time of exceptionally high copper prices but also there were, quite naturally, going to be long-term management contracts, which were necessary to keep the mines running to avoid a mass exodus of expatriate personnel. The whole thing was a disaster. Three quarters of the way through the negotiations my personal permanent secretary decided he was better off out of it and went off to a World Bank conference in Washington. I remember well the day when I asked for a personal discussion with Vice-President Simon Kapepwe who was also my finance minister. I told him very clearly that the terms of the copper-mine nationalization deal were a disaster but that there seemed to be little he could do. To this day I believe that this one deal was the single most self-inflicted factor in Zambia's later deterioration and indeed in Kaunda's downfall.

My two-year contract in Zambia was extended by six months, mainly because they did not have a replacement senior economist and the budget for the financial year 1970 had to be prepared. This became almost totally my responsibility to coordinate and I ended up by writing most of the minister's speech to parliament. It was to be the last year of high copper prices. Despite many heated arguments the tendency to use much of the windfall cash gain to subsidize the agricultural sector continued. When the price of copper fell in the 1970s, Zambia had not developed the self-sustaining agricultural industry it had the ability to do given its climate and the availability of water and good labour. By the end of the 1970s Zambia had become a net importer of food.

I have not been back to Zambia since 1970, although a number of my ODIN colleagues have. It seems now to be a sad place though it has certainly not been through the sorts of horrors that have occurred in Ghana, Nigeria, Uganda or Kenya. It has at least seen the first free election in sub-Saharan Africa in which presidential and parliamentary power were transferred peacefully. The copper mines are, however, struggling. The price of copper is low and much of the Zambian copper is deep mined, in contrast with the large opencast mines in the Soviet Union, Chile and Peru, which are cheaper to operate. I believe it is still a net importer of food.

Grandsons in the Steps of their Grandfather

Peter Gerrard now writes

In 1976, my brother Chris, who was working in Addis Ababa, invited my wife Nikki and me to visit him. We jumped at the opportunity because we both had a yen to travel. My grand-parents had been missionaries in Africa and Louis Leakey and Olduvai Gorge, one of the cradles of humankind, fascinated Nikki.

On the trip to Ethiopia we paused in London to visit Richard and Rita Pankhurst. Richard is the grandson of the famous suffragette Emmeline Pankhurst, to whom there is a statue in London to commemorate her contribution to women obtaining the franchise. Richard is an historian and Rita a librarian and their lives had become deeply interwoven into the fabric of Ethiopia. Ours was a symbolic visit, for Nikki had become intensely involved in gender and race studies.

We spent an eye-opening week with Chris exploring Addis and its surrounds, gaining an introduction to a nation at odds with itself. Two years prior to our visit, the military had over-thrown the long-time ruler Haile Selassie. While we were there we were told that the 'people' had been disenchanted with Haile Selassie and now appeared to be in the process of becom-ing even more disenchanted with the military dictatorship. Our sense was that more had been lost than gained in the transi-tion, and that the infrastructure was collapsing. There was a loss of physical capital in that the roads were deteriorating and a loss of intellectual capital in that the educated Ethiopian civil service had been put out to pasture. Their talents had been lost rather than redirected. There was a loss of social capital in that ethnicity was creating strains in the social fabric.

Two years later I was to revisit Addis in my capacity as auditor of the United Nations Desert Locust Control Organiz-ation. This organization was a cooperative effort between Kenya, Tanzania, Uganda, Sudan, Ethiopia, Somalia and Djibouti. Locusts in East Africa seemed to originate in the horn of Africa where Ethiopia borders Djibouti and Somalia. If allowed to gather momentum, they would multiply and destroy the crops throughout the seven countries. The head office was in Addis Ababa; the aeroplanes used to control the locusts were based in Somalia, while most of the funding came from the United Nations, Kenya, Uganda and Tanzania. At the time of my visit, the organization seemed to be paralysed. Its chief executive officer, an Ethiopian, lived in Nairobi, Kenya, because he was *persona non grata* in his own country. Ethiopia and Somalia were at war with each other. This made it all but impossible to spray locusts from the air. Fortunately, the locusts were not a problem that year.

After visiting Chris in Addis Ababa, we flew to Nairobi where we went on safari to many Kenyan and Tanzanian game parks. We drove first to Masai Mara, the Kenyan portion of the Serengeti plains, then continued into northern Tanzania, which includes the Serengeti, Olduvai Gorge, Ngorongoro Crater, Manyara and Mount Kilimanjaro, before returning to Kenya and visiting Tsavo on the way back to Nairobi. We then drove to Maua, on the northeast side of Mount Kenya, where my grandparents had worked. The varied topography of Kenya reminded me of California. It ranges from beautiful ocean beaches to deserts, lush farming country, large tracts of forested highlands and a snow capped mountain. While it lacked California's economic activity, its savannahs were home to vast numbers and a wide range of wildlife. The herds of wildebeest, zebra and other grazers were incredible to behold. I thought I had good eyesight, but that of the guide we hired in Masai Mara was much keener, for he could spot game that I could barely make out, even with binoculars. On one memorable occasion he was the first to spot a pair of cheetah sprawled out on the grassy plain. We drove our car over the savannah to take close-up photographs. Before long, upwards of ten tour vans and cars had joined us. We have photographs of these two cheetahs surrounded by vans and cars, basking in the public eye seemingly unconcerned by the interest they were generating.

While in Nairobi we paid a courtesy call to the Price Water-house office, for I was working at the time for its Winnipeg branch in Manitoba. We also set events in motion that would lead to our return to Nairobi the following year.

We were told, when we returned, that we were expected to hire a servant to help us clean our apartment and that if we did not do so we would be exploiting our situation, even though we could have cleaned it easily ourselves. North Americans were considered the most generous employers, followed by Europeans, Asians and Africans in that order. Anne Marie, the daughter of a neighbour's servant, came and worked for us. We lived in a block of eight flats, at the rear of which were the servants' quarters.

We thought that Nikki would find work quite easily, but ran into difficulties when we discovered that the authorities only allowed one work permit for each expatriate family, presumably to spread the 'wealth' around. Nikki carved out a life for herself by becoming a museum guide, running workshops on communication, joining the American Woman's Society and, through it, participating in a gourmet luncheon club and other groups for which she would never have found time in Canada.

Both poverty and affluence were more readily visible in Nairobi than they were in Canada. Half the population was under 20 and the birth rate was extremely high. Unemployment was a problem. In the year preceding our arrival the government had decreed that every business had to increase its staff complement by 10 per cent. Price Waterhouse did this by hiring its own couriers who used bicycles to deliver and pick up mail in Nairobi, and by having a 'tea lady' and a 'coffee man' bring refreshments to our desks while we worked.

At the top of the hierarchy in the Price Waterhouse office were white males, usually born in Kenya. Then there were the managers and senior staff, like myself, who were mostly expatriates and had been brought in on work permits because there were insufficient skilled locals to fill these positions. One member of my group was an Asian local who went to England to get his accounting certification before returning to Kenya. Several years after we left Kenya he was promoted to partner. We enjoyed his company and he visited us later in Canada. Another colleague was a talented Ugandan who eventually returned to Uganda after Idi Amin had been ousted. Working for the other managers and myself were a large number of Kenyan accountants in training. One of the perversities of the job market was that as the talents of the individuals in this group developed, local businesses snapped them up and so the hierarchy at the top our office remained predominantly white.

When we returned to Kenya in 1977, the border with Tanzania was closed. With Idi Amin in charge, Uganda was not a friendly place to visit. Kenya's other neighbours, Somalia and Ethiopia, were at war with each other. Kenya, Tanzania and Uganda jointly operated an airline. Kenya was the most prosperous of the three countries and, as it felt that it was doing most of the financing without getting its proportion of the benefits, it arbitrarily took over the joint assets in Kenya in lieu of the debts it was owed. This did not sit well with Tanzania, so the latter closed its border with Kenya. This in turn hurt Kenya's tourist industry for the most abundant wildlife was on the Tanzanian side of the border. While we were in Nairobi, Tanzania and Uganda were at war with each other; Tanzania forced Idi Amin out of Uganda.

The English had their War of the Roses, the French their revolution, the Americas their civil war, and the Europeans their world wars. No one seems to learn from anyone else. We sometimes wondered if the Africans, too, had to have their wars.

I asked a friend recently in Canada how his offspring got a job at Sask Tel. He said because he knew someone. In Kenya, if you were of the right tribe and knew someone you had a job. If you did not, it was very difficult to get a worthwhile job on your own merit. Jomo Kenyatta, Kenya's first president, died while we were there. When president, though I am sure he creamed some of the wealth off the top for himself, he let most of it filter through. He also encouraged many Asians and white Kenyans to remain in Kenya. This was a key to Kenya's relatively successful economy. My sense is that Jomo Kenyatta's successor failed in both these areas, and I would not be surprised if this has contributed significantly to Kenya's deteriorating economy.

As a white person, the only time I really felt any tension between the races was from the reaction of a crowd in a cinema. From the older Africans, I often felt a reverse discrimination; because I was white I was treated better than an African. When our first Christmas came round no party was held at Price Waterhouse because certain partners felt they could not mix the races. When our second Christmas came round, the expatriates living in our set of flats hosted a party for any of the staff who wanted to come; we even provided rides after the party back to major bus routes so that staff could get home. Our enlightened partner attended; the rest stayed away and all enjoyed the party.

In April 1979, just nine years after Jim Potter had left Zambia, I was posted to Lusaka, Zambia for six weeks. Nikki came with me. The shortest route from Nairobi to Lusaka would have been to fly over Tanzania. However, because Kenyan aeroplanes were not allowed to fly over the latter's air space, our plane had to fly out over the Indian Ocean, avoiding Tanzania and, after flying over Mozambique and Malawi, landed at Lusaka. I am sure the journey took twice as long as it need have done. We were met by one of the accountants who gave us a ride to the Intercontinental Hotel. On the way he showed us Joshua Nkomo's residence, which, with the residences of two other members of the government, had recently been blown up by raiders from Rhodesia.

Our first impressions of Lusaka were good. What a clean place we thought. The streets are wide, the buildings new, and much of the city has been landscaped.

In Lusaka I led a fairly isolated existence. I moved from the hotel to my work and back again. I was not involved with the

213

partners and staff of Price Waterhouse, apart from those with whom I worked on the audit. It was a very isolated existence, seemingly cut off from the reality of life as lived by most Zambians. I had one trip with Nikki when we flew to Livingstone and then saw the Victoria Falls. We were lucky to see them in full flood just after the rains. They were magnificent.

While I worked, Nikki was free but not as free as she might have been in Canada, for there was a curfew following the bombing of Kaunda's home. Everyone had to be off the streets from 8.00 in the evening till 6.00 in the morning, and to this was added, in the daytime, the intimidating presence of the military, both in Lusaka and at the Victoria Falls. Nikki was able to visit the supermarkets, read the newspapers and make new friends, one of whom was a Zambian who worked at the airport and another a fellow Canadian, a professor from the University of Manitoba who was teaching at the University of Zambia. She also flew to the Luangwa National Park in east-central Zambia. There she spent two very peaceful and pleasant days and nights. Each day she was taken on safari, on one of which she saw her first leopard. She also met a family from New Zealand. The father of the family was a chartered accountant who had lived in Zambia for the previous four years. He said the country had deteriorated tremendously during the previous two years.

Zambia is a landlocked country that was going through some hard times. Most of its supplies came in from South Africa by rail through Rhodesia. The train would stop just below the Victoria Falls on the bridge spanning the Zambezi where the South African crew would disembark and the Zambian crew take over. Except for the freight train, the border between these two countries was closed because Zambia was supporting the 'African Nationalists' who were trying to overthrow Smith's white regime.

Zambia was filled with contradictions. The West was both envied and in the same breath despised. The newspapers were full of venom for the USA and South Africa, yet aeroplanes took off from Lusaka and landed in Malawi to make connecting flights to South Africa. Economically, it was in deep trouble. The Zambians themselves seemed to have neither incentive nor hope. Basic commodities like sugar, milk and flour were either not available or were in short supply. They had to import their butter from New Zealand, their meat from Botswana, and their maize from Kenya. Profiteers would sell these supplies either to Zaire or on the black market, which is where most people bought their commodities. There are three main supermarkets in Lusaka. Nikki visited them all. Shelves were empty; refrigerators and freezers were running, but they too were empty. Sometimes a few shelves were filled with pillows and ping-pong sets from China, just to make the store look full. When a basic commodity became available, queues a block long would form to get whatever was available.

Zambia has a potentially rich economy based on fertile soil and minerals. Most people said that the main problem was the war with Rhodesia and there were no incentives to work. Even in our hotel 10 per cent was added to the bill, the waiter knew this was coming to him, so he did not set out to please his customers.

Editorials in the newspapers condemned the capitalist and imperialist British and American people, who provided them with aid, and praised those of the eastern block, who sent them arms. While we were there, the East German minister of defence, who stayed in our hotel, said, 'We will arm you to the teeth to carry on the struggle for liberation.' The Czechs gave Kaunda a rifle, with which he was photographed on the front page of the newspaper. While the Zambians said all this, they drank South African wine and South African tea, used South African parts in their cars and machines, and transported their goods through Rhodesia and South Africa.

Kaunda seemed to be obsessed with liberation in the struggles of other countries. Rumour had it that Zambia was host to 30,000 freedom fighters, some from Cuba, and Nikki's friend at the airport told us that plane loads of Zambian

soldiers were going to Lebanon and Libya for guerrilla training. No wonder the country was floundering. We noticed that
there was more crime and violence in Lusaka than in Nairobi.

One of our friends, John Rogers, who had lived in Lusaka
for a number of years, told us the following story; it was one
of many. John, by the way, always had a store of firecrackers
in his home. He lived in burglar alley, so called because so
many burglaries had occurred there. He himself had been
burgled three times. On one occasion when the burglars
arrived to clean him out, he threw firecrackers at them through
the window. The robbers immediately ran away, taking only
his liquor with them. John followed them and found them
about a mile from his home. They were already heavily into
the liquor, so he waited until they had finished it and were well
and truly sozzled. He and his houseboy then caught them,
bound them and brought them back to his home, tied them to
a tree, and then called the police. Meanwhile, the surrounding
houseboys and guards all came and started to flog them
because they too had been their victims. Four hours later the
police arrived and took them away for further punishment.
They were lucky to be still alive. Many such victims were killed
on the spot. We had heard of similar incidents in Nairobi.

Chris Gerrard now writes

I have been drawn to Africa for almost as long as I can remember. Even when I was a little boy in Saskatoon staying home
sick from church one Sunday morning, I drew and coloured a
detailed map of Africa to take to Sunday school the following
week. This must have been before 1960, since large green parts
of west-central Africa were labelled 'French West Africa' and
'French Equatorial Africa'. I do not recall whether Ghana was
still the Gold Coast, but all the other British colonies still had
their colonial names.

Although I grew up in Saskatchewan from the age of four, I
knew both sets of my grandparents well. Granny and Grandpa
Gerrard visited us three times in Canada and we visited them

216

once in England in 1960. After Grandpa died in 1969, Granny moved to Oxford in 1973 to be near Kathleen. While studying at Oxford University from 1972 to 1974, I had lunch with Granny once a week during my second year. Although I never spoke much to my grandparents about the details of their lives and work in Africa, the fact that Granny and Grandpa had spent 26 years as medical missionaries in Zambia and Kenya, and that my father had been born in Zambia, was without question one of the factors that inspired me to become a development economist, specializing in the economic problems of developing countries and with a particular concentration on Africa. Once when I broached the subject with Granny in 1972, she dismissed it as passé. On the other hand, in January 1974, when I returned to Oxford from my first trip to Africa, having been to Maua three days before, she almost fell off her chair. For in the 1930s, it had taken her several days just to travel from Maua to Nairobi, let alone England.

Excluding a three-day excursion to Morocco in January 1973, my first trip to Africa was a three-and-a-half-week vacation to Kenya and Tanzania in December 1973 and January 1974. That summer, I had met Mary Miller and her daughter Wendy in Saskatoon. Mary's husband, Roy, was a general surgeon, while she herself was an anaesthetist. They had lived and worked in Kenya since the late 1940s. Now based in Nairobi, they often travelled to mission hospitals to help out in emergencies. Their daughter Wendy was a physiotherapist who had decided to pursue her career in Canada. Their son Brian later trained to be a surgeon in Saskatoon. The family eventually emigrated to Australia. When I intimated an interest in travelling to Africa, Mary invited me to visit them in Nairobi for Christmas, along with an Oxford friend of my choosing.

So Tom Sargentich and I travelled to Kenya in December 1973 during our Christmas vacation. When we arrived in Nairobi, Roy and Mary provided us not only with free lodging in Nairobi, but also with the use of their third car — a Renault

4. Our longest safari was a two-week round trip — southeast to Mombasa, further south to Tanga and Dar es Salaam, northwest to Mount Kilimanjaro and Arusha, further west to Olduvai Gorge and the Serengeti, north to Masai Mara, and back through Narok to Nairobi. We saw dozens of elephants in Tsavo National Park on the way to Mombasa, this being before the major poaching epidemic of the 1980s. We spent Christmas in Mombasa with Colin Forbes, a paediatrician, and his family. Colin was one of my brother Jon's medical professors at McGill University who was working in Nairobi at the time and who later emigrated to Kenya. We spent New Year's Eve in Dar es Salaam with friends of an Oxford friend. Then, during our last few days in Kenya, we drove clockwise around Mount Kenya, stopping in Maua on the second day. There we surprised Margaret Bell, who quickly recognized me as a grandson of the Dr Gerrard who had preceded them at Maua in the 1940s.

I have since travelled to Africa another 34 times. This includes living in Africa on two occasions — once in Addis Ababa from November 1974 to December 1976 and the second time in Nairobi from August 1979 to April 1980 — this second time with my wife Mary and our newborn son Philip.

My first job after graduating from Oxford was with the United Nations' Economic Commission for Africa in Addis Ababa. One of the five regional economic commissions of the United Nations, this had been established in Ethiopia at the invitation of Emperor Haile Selassie. Working in the economic research and planning division, I carried out analysis and survey work of economic and social conditions in African countries, and prepared background papers for the biennial conference of African planners. The preparations for one of these papers took me to Zambia for the first time in May 1976, just as Zambia was beginning its long economic decline. The government buildings that had been constructed during the copper boom of the 1960s were still impressive, but the retail stores were largely empty of durable goods. Like Peter and Nikki three years later, I saw Victoria Falls for the first time in full flood, immediately after the rains. Working at the United Nations' Economic Commission for Africa was a good place to learn a lot about Africa, but not a good place to do much about it. The commission was trying to advocate a regional approach to economic development in Africa at a time when most African governments were extremely nationalistic — in the case of Kenya and Tanzania, even closing their common border to each other after the collapse of the East African Community. Also, unlike other international organizations like the World Bank, the commission did not have any resources to give or to lend to African governments to cajole them otherwise. Therefore, after two years in Addis Ababa, I decided to resume my academic studies by pursuing a Ph.D. in agricultural economics at the University of Minnesota.

After I had completed my course work, but before writing my dissertation, I interrupted these studies to take a consulting job as the agricultural economist on the design team for an agricultural project to improve the storage of grain on smallholder farms in Kenya. Living and working in Kenya for eight months, we travelled to all the major grain producing districts to survey how smallholder farmers were storing their grain, and to collect samples of maize, beans, and small grains to analyse in a laboratory for insect and mould damage. We concluded that farmers were losing roughly 15 per cent of their grain in storage, but, even more significantly, that about 25 per cent of farmers' grain was infected with aflatoxin, a carcinogen that is produced by the storage mould, *aspergillus flavus*, and that causes liver cancer in human beings. Basically, the majority of farmers were placing their grain in storage when it was still too damp, or in solid-wall storage cribs that did not allow the air to circulate and help dry the grain. We ended up designing a rather traditional agricultural extension project that was intended to extend improved post-harvest practices to smallholder farmers.

219

Back in Minnesota after this eight-month assignment, I completed my Ph.D. dissertation on a comparative analysis of grain marketing in Kenya, Malawi, Tanzania, and Zambia. At independence in the early 1960s, all four countries had inherited national marketing boards for marketing staple grains. Since independence, they had all extended their boards' monopoly powers to control domestic prices (to both producers and consumers), to control the movement of grain within their countries, and to import and export grain. I concluded that all four countries were pursuing, not only in name but also in fact, a policy of domestic self-sufficiency in the production of their staple food grain, maize. Since all four countries had a comparative advantage in maize production, this meant that they were taxing their farmers (relative to world prices) in order to keep prices as low as possible for urban consumers, consistent with domestic self-sufficiency. By 1980, the system was breaking down in all four countries — but more rapidly in Tanzania and Zambia — because the latter had been less successful than Kenya and Malawi in promoting broadly based agricultural development in their countries.

After obtaining my Ph.D. I joined the Department of Economics at the University of Saskatchewan in 1981, and I visited Africa only once during the next eight years. This was a two-week trip to Ethiopia with my wife Mary in 1987. Moved by stories and photographs of widespread famine in Ethiopia in 1984, Western donors had provided much food aid to Ethiopia. I was the Canadian representative on a multi-donor mission (headed by the United Nations' World Food Programme) to evaluate the effectiveness of one particular food aid programme — a national food reserve in Nazareth, Ethiopia, to which Canada had contributed. Our team found an unsustainable situation. On the one hand, one government agency — the Ethiopian Agricultural Marketing Corporation — was operating one fleet of trucks and storage facilities to transport locally produced grain (which it had seized from small-scale farmers at roughly one-half the world price) primarily for urban consumers in Addis Ababa. On the other hand, another government agency — the Relief and Rehabilitation Commission — was operating a second fleet of trucks and storage facilities to transport food aid from the Red Sea port of Assab, often to the same farmers whose grain had been seized. The two fleets of trucks were literally passing each other on the highways. Nonetheless, we recommended continuing the ongoing food aid programme. We felt that Western donors would have a greater influence on changing this absurd dual-marketing policy by remaining in the game rather than out of it all together.

Then, in 1989, I started travelling to Africa once or twice a year on behalf of the Economic Development Institute of the World Bank, now called the World Bank Institute. This is the external training department of the World Bank, which organizes and delivers short, one- and two-week courses on a range of development topics, primarily for government officials and academics from countries that are borrowing money from the World Bank. From 1989 to 1994, I was a regular resource person for a series of courses on macro-economic and agricultural policy analysis in sub-Saharan Africa. Then, in July 1994, I accepted the invitation to take over the management of this programme, joined the World Bank and moved to Washington DC. In these two capacities, I travelled to Africa 27 times between 1989 and 1999 inclusive. My wife Mary accompanied me on three of these trips, my son Philip on two, and my daughter Emily on one. On the latter occasion, all four of us travelled together on a four-week trip to Malawi, Kenya, Uganda and Zimbabwe in the summer of 1994.

The World Bank — formally the International Bank for Reconstruction and Development — was founded at the end of the Second World War as an international cooperative to assist the reconstruction of the war-shattered economies in Europe and Asia. With a current capital base of approximately $US 25 billion (to which its member countries have contributed roughly in proportion to their gross domestic products) it borrows money on world capital markets to re-lend to developing countries. While the wealthier developing countries pay market rates of interest, the poorest countries pay only an administrative fee of 0.5 per cent interest.

While the World Bank is therefore not a charitable institution, it does provide a range of non-lending services, usually free of charge, to its member countries, the objective of such services being to enhance the quality of the Bank's lending portfolio. These non-lending services include policy dialogue, strategic work, analytic work, project preparation, and the training courses to which I contributed and later managed between 1989 and 1999.

Basically, I organized two different types of courses in Africa between 1994 and 1999. The first were national-level seminars, primarily for government officials from one country at a time, in association with the preparation or implementation of a particular Bank-supported project in that country. Held on some aspect of agricultural and rural development, I would recruit and pay for (out of my programme budget) both international and local resource persons in order to provide both international and local perspectives on the topic. The government would pay the local costs for accommodation (usually at a resort outside the capital city), meals and local transport. Increasingly, we would also invite representatives from civil society organizations and the commercial private sector, since policy reform, project preparation and implementation have become much more pluralistic in most African countries.

The second type of activity, the 'training of trainers', consisted of regional workshops for lecturers and researchers from African universities and associated research institutions with a view to building up their capacity to conduct national-level training activities with or without our support. Being regional in nature, with participants from a number of different countries, I would pay the full costs (including airfare, accommodation and meals) for one participant from each participating university or research institution to attend these work-shops, while they would attempt to raise the funds for a second participant to attend. Inviting them to these regional activities and working with them on the national-level activities mentioned in the previous paragraph, our objective was to build local capacity that could sustain the programme once the World Bank Institute ended its direct support. We also hoped that participants would use the training materials we had developed in their own regular undergraduate and graduate courses and research programmes.

Holding four regional workshops for the 'training of trainers' between 1996 and 1999 inclusive, and working with these same people on national-level activities throughout the rest of the year, I really got to know the network of African trainers very well. Our activities were not organized like academic conferences in which invited speakers spoke down to their audiences. Rather, we would present a theoretical framework and concepts that would provide structure to a learning dialogue in which we all shared our experiences, issues and options for addressing these issues.

Developing new training material for these activities was a continual challenge. In part to expedite this process, I organized two international workshops in Washington DC, the first in May 1997 on rural infrastructure (such as rural water supply and rural roads) and the second in May 1998 on community-based natural resource management. Both are extremely problematic issues in rural development that are not answered by simple, one-track solutions such as central government provision or private sector provision. Rather, both require decentralizing some authority to local governments and involving local communities in provision and monitoring. After the first workshop in May 1997, I travelled with a video-maker to six countries — Bangladesh, India, Egypt, Mali, Ghana, and Zambia — to make two videos on decentralizing rural infrastructure services in order to communicate to a wider audience the major messages that had come out of the workshop. The first video is aimed at senior policy makers to encourage them to provide an improved strategic framework for rural infrastructure, while the second is aimed at practitioners who are actually responsible for implementing policy and institutional reforms on a day-to-day basis. We then distributed the video and accompanying brochures, in the first instance, to all the participants at the first workshop.

Political and economic development is a long-term process. In the wake of the first oil crisis that began in October 1973, and influenced by the first Club of Rome book, *The Limits to Growth*, published in 1972, I personally wondered if economic development was even desirable during my first trip to Africa in 1973/4. Tom Sargentich and I received our answer very quickly, especially during a one-day excursion to the Machakos district immediately east of Nairobi. There we saw scores of people making woodcarvings for tourists and for export. Without a doubt they wanted economic development and they wanted it as quickly as possible. Who was I, an affluent Northerner, to deny to them the same creature comforts I enjoyed if they were willing to work so hard to attain them?

Therefore, most African leaders give at least lip service to economic development, since they know that their citizens want economic development as rapidly as possible. They were very upset with us at the Economic Commission for Africa in the early 1970s whenever we revised downwards their estimates of economic growth in their respective countries. But the first generation of African leaders also quickly discovered that governing a country is much more difficult than achieving independence.

From the perspective of the end of the twentieth century, I think it is useful to divide the last hundred years of African development into three periods — colonial, immediate post-independence (starting in most countries in the 1960s) and the years after 1981. Political independence was clearly a break, for it was associated with a transfer of power to black African rule, but why 1981? This was the year of the worst economic crisis, continent-wide, most African countries have experienced since independence. World interest rates topped 20 per cent as the US Federal Reserve attempted to rein in inflation and the world prices of Africa's principal export commodities — such as coffee, tea and cocoa — plummeted by 40 or 50 per cent as that year's world economic recession began. While many countries had experienced substantial economic growth in the 1960s, this had slowed down in the 1970s and came to a screeching halt in 1981. Before 1981, most African countries pursued state-dominated, centrally controlled and protectionist development policies. Since 1981, an increasing number of countries have one by one adopted more pluralist, liberal and open development policies.

In the World Bank training programme I managed for five years from 1994 to 1999, we emphasized four major economic and political reform strategies associated with these more open development policies:

- economic liberalization and privatization,
- democratization,
- decentralization, and
- restructuring central governments.

Each of these strategies relates to one of the four major actors in economic and political development. Liberalization of international and domestic markets and privatization of commercial government companies is intended to empower the *commercial private sector* to pursue entrepreneurial opportunities that were previously closed. Democratization is intended to empower citizens to express their voice, to organize themselves collectively in *civil society organizations* (both national and local) and thereby to participate more actively in decisions that affect their wellbeing. Political and fiscal decentralization is intended to empower and strengthen elected *local governments* to provide local public services such as water and sanitation, roads, basic education and basic health services to their local populations more efficiently than central governments are able to do. Restructuring *central governments* is intended to focus their activities on core public services of a national character that none of the other three major actors are capable of providing.

We now have a better idea of what comprises these core public services of a national character. At or near the top of the list are the institutional arrangements for a pluralist democracy and a market economy — what we now call 'social capital'. Both in Kasenga and in Maua, Granny and Grandpa Gerrard encountered and lived in ordered societies with established leaderships, customs, beliefs, norms and values. Even the relatively simple economic and social exchanges that took place in these small rural communities required a certain kind of order — rules about this and that, which, enforced by chiefs and other elders, helped sustain these communities over time.

As these small rural communities were aggregated first into colonies and subsequently into nation-states, three things have become evident. First, while contacts with the outside world and ultimately political independence have brought some benefits, much social capital has been destroyed in the process, resulting in increasing disorder at the local level. Hence Stanley and Margaret Bell had to treat many more trauma cases during their second time at Maua than their first. Second, building and sustaining an ordered society is a much more complex task for a nation like Zambia or Kenya than for rural communities like Kasenga and Maua. Third, the essential reasons why order is necessary for economic growth and development are still the same.

Economic markets represent voluntary exchange, one to one, between two parties, whether individuals or firms. Exchange occurs when one party (the buyer) values the exchanged commodity more highly than the other (the seller). In this way, markets are able to allocate commodities efficiently among buyers and sellers over time, place and form (from raw commodities such as wheat to processed goods such as flour and bread). In small communities, like Kasenga and Maua, where everyone knew everyone else, where exchange was face-to-face and repetitive, and where maintaining one's reputation was important, it was possible for markets to operate efficiently without any formal rules. But, as economic production became more specialized, and as farmers in Kasenga and Maua began to sell their crops in distant markets to buyers whom they did not know, there came a need for more formal rules that are enforced by a third party of some kind in order facilitate such exchanges. Central governments clearly have a key role to play in establishing and enforcing such rules at the national level.

In addition, markets are only able to supply certain kinds of commodities efficiently over time, place, and form — what economists call 'private goods' like a drink of Coca-Cola, which is consumed by only one individual at a time and from which the seller (whether a grocery store, restaurant or vending machine) can generally exclude consumers who are unwilling to pay. Markets function less well or not at all in providing 'public goods' like rural roads and footpaths, which may be used by many people at the same time and for which it is difficult to exclude (for example by means of toll gates) those who are unwilling to pay. Some form of collective action is necessary to distribute the costs of building and maintaining the roads fairly among all users.

Once again, while it may be possible for the chiefs and elders in a certain village to organize the villagers to build and main-tain the roads or the footpaths without any formal rules, it is much more difficult for a national government to build and maintain the national infrastructure (such as airports, seaports and trunk roads) without formal rules and without coercion, such as taxation, to make everyone contribute. These formal rules are themselves public goods, albeit abstract public goods, which require collective action to establish and enforce, usually through the political system, the government administration, and the judiciary.

These processes for establishing and enforcing the rules of

economic and political game are complex. However, all countries that are now developed have succeeded in putting in place new and better institutional arrangements that support each of these four major reform processes — privatization, democratization, decentralization, and restructuring central governments. Good leadership definitely helps. I regard statesmen like Nelson Mandela as individuals who look at things in the long term rather than the short term, who are concerned about the welfare of generations not yet born rather than enriching their own families, who care about establishing a rule of law rather than the rule of men, a rule of law that respects private property and private initiative, and that provides everyone with fair and equal opportunities to better themselves without fear of confiscation while also providing social safety nets for the poor and disadvantaged.

Unfortunately, national governments with the authority and means to prescribe and enforce rules that create an economic climate in which individuals have the incentives to save and accumulate wealth also have the authority, unless somehow checked, to expropriate and redistribute wealth from their political opponents to their political allies. Some such redistribution may be legitimate and unavoidable, for example in distributing the costs of public goods like health and education fairly among all citizens. But, in post-independence Africa, much such redistribution has simply increased the wealth of the president and his closest supporters.

These four major reform processes — privatization, democratization, decentralization and restructuring central governments — are in various stages of implementation in different African countries. Through our work at the World Bank we have attempted to identify each country's present stage of development and political challenges. However, the completion of this development agenda cannot be left to specialists in agricultural development, health, education or any other sector. It also cannot be left to politicians and senior policy-makers in presidential offices or in central integrating minis-

tries like planning, finance and local government. The population at large must understand the agenda, for only then can the
people exercise their newfound freedoms to provide the
necessary checks and balances on both the experts and their
political leaders. I would like to think that fostering such
understanding among the government officials, university
teachers and civil society representatives who attended my
courses has been one of my major contributions to the long-
term development of Africa.

John Gerrard now writes

Chris's work has been very much appreciated by the Africans
whom he served. At the conclusion of his last 'training of
trainers' workshop in Kampala on 25 February 1999, Chief
Olu Makinde from Nigeria, speaking on behalf of the other
representatives, gave the following speech. This testimonial
also reminds me of the letter in which the Baila chiefs begged
my father, Chris's grandfather, to remain in Baila country for
they had grown to look upon him as their father.

> Chris Gerrard has been the manager of the World
> Bank's training programme on 'Policy and Institutional
> Reform for Sustainable Rural Development' since Sep-
> tember 1994. During the last four-and-a-half years he
> has organized 17 activities of various kinds in Africa,
> including this annual series of regional TOT workshops
> of which the present workshop is the fourth.
> Chris Gerrard may be a Canadian, but he has an
> African heart.
> Over the last four years, he has promoted a new
> approach to agriculture and rural development, which
> focuses on institutions and institutional development.
> From him, we have learned a concept of 'institutions'
> that is more fundamental than simply 'organizations'.
> Rather, we have learned that institutions are the 'rules of
> the game', both within and between organizations and

individuals, that create incentives for people to behave in ways that are either beneficial or harmful from the point of view of society as a whole.

We have learned that rules are necessary in order to coordinate human activity in beneficial ways. For without rules there is chaos and confusion. He has encouraged us to look beyond the conventional dichotomy between 'the state' and 'the market', and to include other coordination mechanisms such as collective action and coproduction. He has encouraged us to look beyond the public and the private sectors, and to recognize the equally important roles of civil society organizations and decentralized local governments in the provision of agricultural and rural services of all kinds. For the central government is no longer the be-all and end-all of development. Its role is no longer a direct provider of rural services, but a facilitator of private sector, civil society and decentralized provision of rural services.

Finally, for we who are policy analysts and trainers, he has encouraged us to look beyond the 'substance' of policy and institutional analysis to the 'process' of policy and institutional reform. For the way in which societies reform their institutions is itself an institutional issue. Chris Gerrard has taught us not only how to identify key institutional issues in rural development, but also practical steps in formulating viable institutional strategies and implementing effective institutional solutions in order for the rural sector to play its vitally important role in overall economic development, poverty alleviation, food security and sustainable natural resource management.

What you have taught us may not have had much immediate impact yet. But it will. For what you have sown are seeds for the long term — seeds that will bear fruit in the long term.

Chris Gerrard is now stepping down as the manager of

this training programme. But the programme will continue and he will continue to work on Africa. In the future, when he visits Africa, whether alone or with his family, he will not have to stay in hotels, he will be welcome in our homes.

From all of us, thank you very much for the work that you have done. Please accept this gift [an African wood carving] as a small token of our appreciation for your positive impact on our lives.

13

Africa Calling

My father was nearly 29 and my mother had just turned 20 when a group of meat hungry Africans from the nearby village of Kasenga welcomed them ashore. They did not know what lay ahead, but they knew they had a mission to undertake and they wanted to fulfil it.

My father was well equipped for the task ahead, for he was not only a medical doctor and minister but also a carpenter, bricklayer and builder, and had a keen ear, which would stand him in good stead when learning the language and translating the Gospels. My mother was only too eager to help him in any way she could. She would soon be his scrub nurse in his make-shift operating theatre with the patient lying on the kitchen table; later she would be the nurse in charge of motherless babies; and she would be in charge of the very popular sewing class that Mrs Smith had started.

Having learnt to trust their traditional doctors, the Africans at first were reluctant to bring their medical problems to a strange white man. Even Edwin Smith had had to turn to a traditional doctor when a snake spat venom in his eye, causing him a great deal of pain and, he feared, the probable loss of his eye. Though the traditional doctor had produced a concoction that almost immediately alleviated the pain and restored his vision, when the Africans saw the miraculous way in which yaws vanished in response to my father's needle, and when they saw him look inside people and remove swellings, their expectations rose and the time soon came when, if they were not given the magic needle when they asked for it, they assumed that my father did not want to help them.

When news of his return from his first furlough reached the nearby and even faraway villages, crowds came to seek his help. In Zambia, where the population was thinly spread across the veld, his medical skills were not always fully employed. In Kenya, on the other hand, though the beds were not always fully occupied in the early days, by the time my father had established a reputation, there were often two, plus babies, to a bed and babies were being delivered in hospital rather than in darkened huts with the aid of a hurricane lamp.

It was through watching my father at work that the Africans learnt what he meant when he told them to be good Samaritans and to love and help their neighbours. It was no wonder, when he was transferred to Maua, that the Baila chiefs called him their father and begged him to stay.

The kinds of medical problems with which doctors had to deal changed after my father left Maua. Though malaria, pneumonia and dysentery persisted, malnutrition and kwashiorkor diminished. As injuries inflicted by lions and crocodiles decreased and eventually disappeared, panga wounds became so numerous that they kept one surgeon busy all the time. Also, had AIDS been prevalent when my father was working, he would almost certainly have acquired it through his contact with his patients.

Although medicine was an important component of my father's work, he did not consider it the most important one. When fellow missionary Mr Groves asked him about his work, for example, it was the schools that he emphasized. He told Mr Groves about how Jeremiah, having graduated from the mission school, went to Kafue for further training, and then returned to teach in a mission school and to enrol his village in a catechumen class. He wanted them all to become good Christians. Medicine was like the icing on a cake, something special, but something that needed the body of the cake — schools and churches — to support it.

Schools were undoubtedly the missions' lifeblood. Children did not have to be persuaded to attend school, it was the chief who had to be convinced that more was to be gained by letting them learn to read and write than by sending them off to herd cattle or manage the crops. The children were so pleased to have the chance to learn that if there were no school in their own village they would gladly walk to one with a school, often Kasenga, arriving in time for classes on Monday morning, staying all week and returning home at weekends.

Schools liked to have the missionary call, for a hymn, prayer and story from the Bible always preceded the formal lessons. I remember, when visiting my parents, seeing the children singing with great gusto, 'We are children ob de King, Ebenelly King, Ebenelly King, we are children ob de King, singing as we churney.' Lessons, reading, writing and arithmetic would follow.

Much of my father's time was spent visiting outlying schools to ensure that the children were attending the school and that the teachers were teaching them.

The finished product was not necessarily an angel, but some at least had put a foot on the bottom rung of Jacob's ladder and all, through learning to read and write, had learnt about the new and exciting world beyond their own villages. Many students went on to high school and some even to university — Fort Hare in South Africa, Makerere in Uganda or, for some like Nyerere, as far afield as Edinburgh. The African leaders who graduated from these schools recognized their importance. When Kaunda was president of Zambia he even paid students to attend postgraduate courses. A Saskatchewan teacher who taught journalism in Lusaka after independence remembers her students being paid to attend and each week, after receiving their pay, going straight to the pub to spend it on booze.

Nyerere, too, knew the value of education, taught at one time, and was known by his people as *Mwalinu*, teacher. He believed his people needed education and safe water (when growing up), and freedom and work (when fully grown). We know something about the impact on a black person of mission schools and a mission university from Mandela's autobiography, *Long Walk to Freedom,* which I think is worth recapitulating.

Mandela was a Xhosa and until the age of nine was brought up by his mother. At nine his father died and almost immediately he was taken to the royal residence of the regent, the chief of the Thembu people. There he was brought up in relative luxury. The regent supervised his education and training as he hoped that one day he would become one of his counsellors. Mandela himself often watched the regent listening to and discussing his problems with his counsellors. From this Mandela learnt how to conduct meetings, reach a consensus and formulate a plan of action. After attending the local primary school he went to the Clarkebury Boarding Institute, a high school and teachers' training college run by the Methodists. The principal was the Reverend Harris, an austere man who was always stern when on duty but who relaxed and had a heart of gold when he was in his garden. It was here that Mandela got to know and admire him. In retrospect, Mandela said that the Reverend Harris had been one of the major influences in his life.

After Clarkebury Mandela went, aged 19, to Healdtown, a residential school for boys and girls in Fort Beaufort, which had been founded and was run by Wesleyan Methodists. The buildings and the countryside in which they were nestled were far more beautiful than those at Clarkebury; Mandela called Healdtown an academic oasis. With 1000 students it was the largest residential school for black students south of the equator. The principal, Dr Arthur Wellington, never tired of telling his students that he was a descendent of the great Duke of Wellington who had defeated the French Napoleon at Waterloo and who had saved civilization 'for Europe and for you, the natives'. At Healdtown the fare was frugal, the work hard and the discipline strict. The latter was enforced by prefects, of which Mandela was one in his final year. By the time Mandela left Healdtown he had developed a profound respect for the British and was very grateful to them for having saved civilization and for passing it on to the 'natives'.

After Healdtown Mandela went to the University of Fort Hare, which Scottish missionaries had founded in 1916. It was the only university in Africa for black students south of the equator. It was small with only 150 students. Mandela, being a Methodist, was put in Wesley House. At Fort Hare he spent half his time in the classroom — he was a good, conscientious and industrious student — and half on the playing fields. He played soccer, participated in cross-country running to test his stamina to the utmost and enjoyed ballroom dancing. On Sundays he taught in Sunday schools in the surrounding villages. He was a member of a student committee and had no hesitation in speaking out and standing for what he knew to be right and fair, even when he knew it meant crossing swords with the principal, Dr Kerr, who on one occasion threatened to exclude him from the university if he did not change his mind.

While he was at Fort Hare Mandela acted in a play about Abraham Lincoln. He himself took the part of John Wilkes Booth, Lincoln's assassin, and Lincoln's Gettysburg speech received a resounding ovation from the black audience. Jan Smuts came to Fort Hare to address the students at their graduation ceremony. Though Smuts had fought a brilliant campaign against the British during the Boer War, when the latter was over he became one of their strongest supporters because of the generous terms of their peace proposals.

It was at schools and at the university of Fort Hare, all founded by missionaries, that Nelson Mandela acquired the name of Nelson and learnt how to study, how to keep physically fit, and how to recognize the difference between right and wrong. He also acquired the stamina he needed to hold fast to what he believed to be right and to remain free from bitterness, even after 27 years in prison.

Mission schools did not produce angels any more than our own schools do, but they gave their pupils a chance to grow. They graduated one Mandela, one Nyerere and many other African leaders. They played a part in the awakening of Africa.

My father's erstwhile houseboy Harry Nkumbula was the only graduate from his mission station to have gone into politics. In 1962 Harry and Kaunda joined forces to form a coalition government, but when the elections two years later gave Kaunda a clear majority, Nkumbula became leader of the opposition and Kaunda's sparring partner. It was he who publicly accused missionaries of being hypocrites — not a pleasant thing to say about one's teacher — but then later, when my parents visited Zambia, insisted on seeing my father for a long and pleasant evening fortified from time to time with beer.

There was a time when some members of the family suggested to my father that he should abandon Africa, if only temporarily, for the sake of his children. His answer was short and to the point. 'I didn't decide to be a missionary for the sake of my family,' he said.

Both my parents had a strong sense of their mission. This was to bring the news of the Gospel to Africans, to tell them that there was a God who loved and cared for them, and who wanted them to love and care for each other. This God had also sent His Son, many years ago, into the world so that all people might see how they should live. My parents did their best to show in their own lives what this meant. My father carried this message to the villages. The only sermon I heard him deliver was in Kasenga. His text was, 'He who puts his hand to the plough and looks back is not fit for the Kingdom of Heaven.' Having once put his own hand to the plough, he never looked back.

Once, while walking through the forest in a time of drought he met a woman searching for fruits and berries. When she saw my father she told him she had no fears for she knew God was a loving father who would look after her. My father commented in his letter that he was happy to know that his message was getting across.

The church he built, and for which he and his brothers and sisters paid, was not his crowning achievement, but it was one of which he was very proud. When he returned to Meru and Maua he was overjoyed to discover that there were 55 local preachers and five were called Gerrard.

My father had a great respect for district commissioners and magistrates. They were tolerant and fair and, though many African leaders were PGs (prison graduates), they did not seem to bear the British any ill will. When independence came it came relatively smoothly, except in Southern Rhodesia and South Africa where the white rulers were not prepared to share power with the black people. In passing, it should be said that my father worked happily with the district commissioners and magistrates, both helping them when they asked him, for example, to provide a haven for children rescued from slavery, and he, on his part, using prisoner stretcher bearers to transport sick or injured patients. Laws were administered impartially and some customs (like female circumcision and polygamy) were allowed to stand, but when the government thought a custom needed to be changed, for example burial of the dead, my father was pleased that the government first obtained the approval and support of the council of elders before promulgating the new law.

My father's thoughts on some of these problems are illustrated in the following letter he wrote to my cousin Catherine Bennett. We do not know what she said in her letter to him, but we have a copy of his reply written a year after his arrival in Maua and almost 20 years after first reaching Kasenga.

Methodist Mission
PO Meru, Kenya.
18th April 1935

My dear Catherine,

I am sorry I cannot answer your questions from personal knowledge. Both in N Rhodesia and in Kenya I have lived right in native reserves, so that for example, while in some parts of the continent there may be criticism or even antipathy to British rule, in neither of these reserves have I heard any suggestion of it. Generally they do not understand what is happening. They see the white man is in power. He has taken over the government of their territory, and imposes an annual tax. They accept the situation, though in some years, especially recent ones, they have no doubt found the tax a hardship. In these reserves there is no question of the purchase of land; the people continue with their age-long system of tribal ownership, the power of allotting any piece of land being in the hands of the chief or native council. In some areas neither European nor native visualizes a time when the African will be free from European domination, nor is there any tendency that way, unless it be that in recent years tribal authorities are being allowed more power in their own courts.

I am not familiar with the history and economies of land to say whether native ownership would be a retrograde step, but I should be inclined to think so. At any rate its introduction at this stage would be disastrous in native areas; their own system is much the best for their present economic conditions. It is a big question and lands you up against the whole question of Socialism and Capitalism.

So you know Victor Murray's *The School in the Bush*? You will find in that a lot of good sound stuff, interestingly written on the progress and future of the African. I visualize a time when Kenya, for example, will have

239

European, Arab, Indian and African citizens who share its government and all regard themselves as Kenyaites, working together for the good of the country. That is a long time off, but, meantime it is up to the European to give the African the best he has, let him share his culture, and if it is in him, as I think it is, let him develop till he stands on an equal footing.

I haven't heard the indictment Dr Leakey mentioned. It is likely that some missions would oppose inoculation; there are a lot of old fashioned folk on the mission field. I have met missionaries who object to taking medicine of any kind, though they were not consistent. In Kenya I understand a large proportion of missionaries are fundamentalists, just the type to object to inoculation.

I have not met with any attempts at coalescing native and Christian practices. The tendency has been for missionaries to seize on objectionable features in native ceremonies and make them 'taboo' for Christians with practically little or no attempt to understand the psychological and other implications. In this country, for example, there is an objectionable ceremony in connection with the initiation of girls; there is some mutilation which may involve suffering later when the girl becomes a mother — the churches made it taboo and lost a large number of members. My own inclination is to interfere as little as possible with native ceremonies, and let any changes come gradually as a result of teaching and Christian influence. I believe there have been one or two very praiseworthy attempts to introduce into church life ceremonies on the lines of native initiation ceremonies.

We shall be home soon, and if you have any questions to ask I shall do my best. Probably you know a lot more than I do.

Yours very affectionately,

H. S. Gerrard.

Had my father at this time been told that in 30 years' time Northern Rhodesia would be called Zambia and would be an independent country with its own elected government, he would not have believed it. But if he had believed it, and if his fellow missionaries and the British administration had believed it, they would surely have said to the Africans:

In 1964 you are going to be your own rulers. To do this successfully you will need a trained group of men and women who will govern your country, and who will think of your needs rather than their own ambitions. They will not all have the same aspirations for your country, so they will need to be wise enough to compromise when making their plans for your future. The government will need to enact laws which will lay down what you must not do, steal for example, and what you must do, pay taxes for example, for the government will need money if it is to carry out its work. It will need a police force to make sure that the laws are obeyed, and judges and law courts to decide whether laws have or have not been broken, and if they have what the penalties should be, and prisons for some offenders. You will need more schools, a university and colleges where men and women can be trained to become doctors, lawyers, teachers, farmers, painters, and even politicians — all the skills that are needed in a modern society. You will also need safe water, telephones, a dependable supply of electricity and power.

Thirty years is a very short time in which to learn all these skills. We think it would be wise if we were to start training you now rather than let you flounder when you start ruling yourselves. Better by far for you to learn to swim before you jump into the sea. This is a formidable task for you will have to learn to do in a few years what has taken us hundreds of years, and we are still far from perfect.

I think the mission schools, although they did not know it, were doing just this. We, who love Africa, and the Africans themselves, owe a great deal to those in the British Isles, like Sam Berresford, who supported the missionaries. We also owe much to the missionaries themselves who, like my parents, heard and responded to Africa calling.

Appendix: Family Letters

The following two letters from Grandpa, T. L. Gerrard, to Bert and Doris exemplify his humanitarianism and his wide interests.

> Norfield, Swinton, Manchester
> 8.30 a.m., Sunday 11 June 1933.

My dear Doris and Bert,

We have had a wonderful Whit week for weather — the best I should think for many years. The heat at times and in many places has been terrific (for us) over 80 in the shade in London. In the Manchester Sunday School procession there were hundreds, either lookers on or in the procession, who were overcome and needed assistance. The extreme heat lasted only a few days. Now we are quite cool.

On Thursday morning I went to the office and saw the letters. The only director who turned up while I was there was me. Clement was away with Alice at the house near Colwyn that Peggy has taken for a long holiday. They went Wednesday. Thursday morning Clement left for London for the Hymn and Tune Book Club Committee — a very important meeting. He should have stayed over Friday, but it was not thought quite fair that he should leave Alice alone with Peggy and Trego for more than one day. Clement leaves Alice there. He comes home today. Business is making big demands on him just now, with these three schemes of houses and flats.

It is said we could sell the 300 houses we are starting at Hither Green, within six months, if we could build them so soon. If so it should turn out a very good speculation in two ways. It is helping to find work and it should make a substantial contribution to the company's profits.

I went to London Thursday evening. Before I went, in the afternoon, I walked in the Nonconformist Procession with our Manchester road Sunday school. Then Lilly (the chauffeur) took me to the London Rd station for the 4.40 train. I found, (being Whit week), the train had been cancelled , so I had to wait for the 5.40. It turned out all right. The 5.40 is 'The Comet', a three and a quarter hour express, with only one stop at Stafford, and was due Euston 8.55. The 4.45 was due in at 8.45. Also I had not booked a seat in the Diner. As I was at the London Rd platform when the train came in at about 5.15, I managed to get an odd seat in the Diner. The three other seats at the same table were reserved, I saw, for a Mr and Mrs Wilde [Walsh?] and a master Wilde, who turned out to be their son, a lad of 15.

We travelled for a full hour before we got into conversation. I had made up my mind to set the ball rolling if possible, even if I should have to do most of the rolling. Mother would say that would suit me. Well, we got going, and very well pleased we all were. I told a few stories and showed some of my puzzles. The father and son were keen on the puzzles, and the mother seemed quite interested. Mr Walsh had one or two stories and the boy of 15 was very quiet.

Before we reached London, they had learned that I was a director of J. G. and sons, the famous builders, and I had learnt that Mr Walsh was one of 4 directors (the youngest I think) of a celebrated firm of hat makers of Denton. I wondered if they had made my bowler hat, which I had bought at Lewis's, which I liked very well, and was at a reasonable price. He examined the hat. They had made it. He said it was the best value in the world of that type of hat, and they were the largest makers in the world of that type of bowler hat. When we parted at Euston, he was sorry I was not going all the way with them to Balham. We were kindred spirits and will, I hope, meet again.

I walked to the hotel 'Ivanhoe', arriving at 9.20. My suitcase was a small attaché case — almost feather weight — with all I took in it. I don't know what the porter at the 'Ivanhoe' thought when he took it from me to take it to my room. It was absurd of him to go one way (whether stairs or lift I know not), and I by lift alone to the 5th floor. I never travelled lighter. It was only for one night, and I had to keep the case with me all Friday with my papers for committees and etc. It was a hot day. I had neither slippers nor night shirt. I took off my pants and under vest and reinstated my thin day shirt. I had a good bedroom with an open window and slept well.

On the Thursday evening, about 9.45 Jos Longstaffe arrived from Manchester for the same committees. We chatted till turned 11.00. I had found out that breakfast was served from 7.30. This was too early (7.30) for Joseph. We compromised at 7.45–8.00. I was having breakfast when he turned up soon after 8.00. I had risen at 6.30 and looked over my papers of business for the meeting — at least 20 quarto pages. After breakfast Longstaffe went with me to our job — a building — for the P.O., at the largest letter sorting office in the world. We had a taxi. This gave me 20 minutes on the job — a good talk and inspection with the foreman. We were then only 10 minutes walk from Holborn Hall where our first meeting was to be at 9.30 a.m. It was an ex-PM (Primitive Methodist) Central Finance Subcommittee. At 10.00 the full committee was due. There were only about a dozen at the full meeting. We got through the balance sheets for the year ending Mar 31st 1933. Comm Fund, Hartley College, Children's Fund, S.M.W. and O. Fund etc.

We finished at 12.20. I took a taxi to Sydney Walton's office. He wanted to see me, and I had arranged to call between 12.00 and 1.00. He has beautiful offices, well situated on what was once a bank of the Thames. He overlooks trees, grass and a fine open space. He it was who the other day got the Prince of Wales to speak at a Housing Conference. He also got Sir Samuel for another meeting. He is a publicist [public relations officer]. One Society gives him 500 pounds a year as a retainer fee to help them with their advertising etc.

He is greatly interested in J. G. and sons. I sent him a balance sheet. He called it *wholesome*. He is interested in finance, and may be of service to us sometime.

We left his office about 1.15 by taxi. I dropped him at a Class restaurant. I went on to Westminster for my meeting with the Methodist Church Finance board at 2.00. Before my meeting I had lunch at a small place not far from the Central Hall, recommended by my taxi driver. The place was crowded. The few small tables were full. There were more people standing that sitting. A glass of hot coffee and milk, 2 pence, with an egg beaten, 4 pence. Cakes, tarts, bananas, etc. etc. The 4 people who were serving were kept going at a great pace.

At the counter I got a cup of hot coffee and a fine banana, all for 4 pence. I needed nothing more, I had breakfasted well. I had been in committees all morning, and was going to another committee for the afternoon. It suited me splendidly. It would not have suited your John (our John too), or Raymond.

We had a good Finance board Meeting. Mr Hillis, Jacob Walton, Joseph Longstaffe and self made up the ex-PM [Primitive Methodist] contingent. Mr Hillis scored well in getting a resolution through to enlarge the powers of a small Central Finance Committee to take into its purview the whole of Methodist Finance. This will go to Conference for ratification or otherwise. [The final page or pages are missing.]

The second letter shows T. L. Gerrard in his family rather than his business and public affairs role.

> Norfield, Swinton, Manchester
> Sunday 19 August 1934, 8.15 a.m.

Dear Doris and Bert,

Yesterday mother saw Margaret on the train at Victoria station at 9.45 a.m. for Bootle, Cumberland [now Cumbria] where Winifred, Tom, John and Kathleen are or will be. Though Margaret has had a very happy time with us at Norfield — she says she loves Norfield — she went off quite happily. Mother arranged for her to be well looked after on the train. There were two ladies in the compartment, and the guard promised to look after her. Her wits are so good. She is so alive, alert and intelligent, I could trust her to get there all right. She is so likeable that people instinctively become friendly towards her. Again this last week people can't keep their eyes off her.

She was invited to go with us to the Robertson's party last Tuesday, to commemorate the 80th birthday of Henry Mason. She was quite a centre of attraction. Some one said to mother, what bonny children you have. One day mother took her and Mrs Isherwood and

Mrs Bacon to Southport. There again these two ladies fell in love with her. They arrived before lunch, and Margaret had a bathe in the bathing pool. Granny advised her not to go in where it was deep. She said, 'Oh I can go where it is deep alright.' And she did. Although she had not bathed [swam] for quite a long time, she was absolutely at home, and swam with great ease.

You will imagine we are feeling lonely at Norfield this morning. She has done us good. We must now live with her in memory. If we feel like this, what must you both feel like, so far away, and so long to wait for the sight of her and the feel of her arms round your necks, and the kiss of her lips. Then, too, you have the double loss for the time being of K and M. But I mustn't be writing so much in this strain.

Nothing can deprive you of the joy and satisfaction of having brought into the world three such bonny children, and all so good. People see in M visions of her father. It gives them such a lot of pleasure to see the likeness.

We cannot have everything. We cannot have all we would like. It is good for us that we cannot. Tho' self that is worth the living brings much self denial, we are not debarred from counting our many blessings, and if we count them one by one it will surprise us what the Lord has done.

At Henry's birthday party were Bernard and his wife, Connie and Wilfred and their daughter Celia, Mabel and Harry Stuart, Henry and his wife, we two and Margaret, and the Robertsons. We had bowling and cricket (soft ball) on the lawn, (not at the same time). A few had billiards. There was the pleasure of seeing each other and having a few words.

Connie has written Alice telling of mother's beauty and grace. Several told me how well I look. I doubt if I ever looked better. The tea was the climax, with the birthday cake. John (Robertson) had asked me to make an informal speech of congratulation to Henry. I sketched it out in bed that morning from 6.00 to 6.30. I don't know whether I ever made a happier speech. I offered our congratulations. I said he had not always pleased me with what he did. (1.) When I was a young fellow he visited our house to see my eldest sister. In the end he took her away. She was my favourite sister. We were chums. Two years younger than I. People said we were like lovers. I could not blame Henry overmuch, as I was afraid Annie was a party to it. (2.) He did not always lead me in the way I should go. One night found us both in a crowd outside a Manchester theatre waiting to go in — probably to one of the cheaper seats. I had never been in a theatre before. I had not asked my mother's permission. I dared not ask. I wasn't sure which of us was to blame, but as Henry was four years older than me, I naturally put the blame on him. However, we have never regretted it. We had the great and wonderful experience of seeing Henry Irvine and Ellen Terry in *Faust*.

I said Henry was never rich in money, but I believed he had a small stocking somewhere. But he has always been rich in the affection of others. He reminded me of the man who was appointed to move a vote of thanks to his employer. The employer had had a good year, and had given a seven course dinner to his employees. The oldest employee was a carter, a jovial jolly fellow. After thanking his employer and saying what a good employer he was, and what a wonderful feast he had provided, he said, 'Well chaps aw can only say Goodness and Mercy have *followed* me all the days of my life, but it has *catched up* wi me toneet' (loud laughter).

Everyone seemed in good health, especially Henry, and spirits. Henry and his wife looked the oldest.

Clement and Alice are due home from Bude, Cornwall, this afternoon. Last night they spent at Broadway. (Raymond and Christine are with them). May, (Doris's sister) said her father was considerably better than he had been. She seemed a bit concerned about his financial position. He has had losses. Not but what they are all right at the present, but she wonders what there will be for Flo and her. She did not think there would be enough to live on. I suppose either of them or both of them have something in their fingers. I hope that somehow they will be relieved of any anxiety. May was very chatty. She didn't look too well. I wish one of them had some outside interest. Perhaps it is better as it is, and perhaps I should not have said anything. I shall always be interested in them both.

Love to you both from mother and self, Father.

Monday 20 August 1934

Bert's letters July 17 and July 24 arrived this morning. Full of interest. It will be a new lease of life for both of you. What a chance! What interesting things and people!

Winifred phoned us last night from Bootle. Margaret arrived all right Saturday night. Not without incident. The train did not stop at Bootle. Margaret seems to have acted most sensibly. She was in a compartment alone. She walked down the corridor to another compartment where [there] were people, and told them of her difficulty. They said, 'Get out at the next calling station and take the next train back for Bootle.' She did, and found at Bootle station that John and Kathleen had travelled by the same train. They had been out somewhere and were returning.

Mother says that if she had known that the train would not stop at Bootle, she would not have dared to trust Margaret. She has a good head and a good body, and a happy disposition. We are all proud of her.

Love Father.

The following letter from Father is undated, but was probably written in September 1926, soon after my father returned to Kasenga alone after having left Doris in England to look after the children. He had, after landing in Cape Town, visited a hospital for lepers and, near Johannesburg, a compound in which miners were housed. The letter ends with a commentary on his life as a grass widower and is unsigned.

... utensils occupied some shelves; the floor was as clean and shiny as it was possible for a mud floor to be; the patients were clean and neatly dressed; at one side I saw a sewing machine, and was told that one of the occupants was an expert seamstress, and made many of the dresses worn by the women. Her fingers were too deformed for her to fold down the hem, so she used a table knife for the purpose. Many of the patients are given some occupation, and are paid according to the amount of work they do. Some of them must be comparatively well off, for they are given, on entering, an outfit of blankets, clothes, sleeping mat, and utensils, and all their food is, of course, provided. At one time their food was prepared for them, but it was found that they were much more contented if they prepared their own food; it gave them an interest.

Formerly the place was well guarded, and attempts at escape were frequent. Now, a guard is quite unnecessary. We visited the laundry where some of the women patients had just finished work, and there was a pile of clean, dry clothes. In another house the usual neatness prevailed, and on the floor was a large loaf of bread that one of the occupants had just cooked. An industry in one of the compounds was the brewing of beer, and many an evening, it appeared, the patients had a sort of fancy dress ball, when they came in their best clothes, and spent the time in drinking and dancing. Every thing is done to make the patients contented, by keeping them occupied and interfering with their liberty as little as possible. The asylum includes a crèche, and babies being born being separated at once from their mothers, and brought up by hand. Very bonny and well the babies looked as they lay in the open air with their nets over them to protect them from flies. That week about fifty patients had been sent away cured, and over two hundred were undergoing the new treatment for leprosy, but better than any medicine seemed to be the health restoring properties of clean orderly lives, good food and the clear air and bright sunshine of the South African hills.

My next place of call was Johannesburg. Here, through the good offices of Rev. A. Kidwell, I had the opportunity of seeing something of native life in the compounds and locations. Conditions in these are different. The compounds are rectangles enclosed by buildings in which live the men who work in the mine to which the compound belongs. The locations are native quarters on the outskirts of the town where live men and women and their families. Entering the compound through the gateway between the offices and the manager's quarters, we went across the square to examine one of the rooms. It was large enough to accommodate a score of men, who slept in concrete bunks, sawdust being mixed with the concrete to take off the chill. The manager joined us, and as he talked one was struck with his keenness for the welfare of the men in his care. Taking us into the kitchen, he showed us the large iron boilers in which were cooked stew and thick maize-meal porridge. The diet of the men, he said, had been scientifically worked out. It consisted of meat, fresh vegetables, macaroni, fat of some kind, sugar, coffee, maize-meal porridge, and, as extras, a non-alcoholic brew called *mohau* and mild kaffir beer. The beans, which formed part of the ration, were all germinated before being cooked, thus increasing their food value and making them antiscorbutic.

Before going on to Kasenga on my return from furlough, I had to call at Kafue to attend a language committee. In our section of Northern Rhodesia there are seven missionary societies working amongst three tribes. Each is producing its own literature in a more or less different dialect. We were meeting to see if it was possible to secure some uniformity so that the same books could be used by all the missions, thus helping to cheapen and multiply literature. We were fortunate in having, as a member of the committee, the Jesuit priest, Father Torren who is famous as the author of *A Comparative Grammar of the Bantu Languages*. That book was written forty years ago, and he has still continued his studies through these years, and he may well be regarded as an expert. We were certainly very glad to follow his guidance almost entirely. He was convinced that the various dialects we were considering were so much akin that we were by no means attempting an impossible task, and when the work is completed it will be largely owing to his knowledge, industry and enthusiasm. Two months later he paid us a visit at Kasenga, and in a few days he made himself master of the chief differences between our local dialect and the others in the group, besides pointing out features in the grammar and pronunciation that we ourselves had not recognized.

At Kasenga I began my third term, this time as a grass widower, having left my wife in England to look after the children. As far as the housekeeping was concerned I was not too badly off, having in my cook, Gordon, a hardworking, capable houseboy who had been used to my wife's way of doing things. He needed no instructions from me about keeping the house clean and tidy, or washing clothes. The cooking, too, I have left entirely to him, except that I have given him a few lessons in making whole meal bread. He was away the week Father Torrend was with us, and his substitute was not so good. Our most difficult day was Friday when meat was forbidden and there was no fish, either fresh or tinned. Then I was compelled to study a cookery book to discover vegetarian dishes that were possible with the few vegetables I had. At any rate there was a sufficiency of bread, and the Father was very fond of that.

There is no doubt that the absence of the doctor made a distinct gap in the life of the fold around Kasenga. After eleven years they had become accustomed to him and his hospital, and I was kindly reminded of it by such remarks as, 'You hid from us', 'You threw us away', or 'You left us lonely'. The news of my return spread quickly. Coming from the line people spotted me in the car, and called out, '*Ngu wezu Njelende.*' (It is Gerrard — there are no titles in Baila). Before long the procession of patients called forth the remark from one man, 'They are coming in troops.' At first they came from the nearer villages, but ...

Index

Index

Index

257

Index

263

Index

Watson, Henry, 2
Watson, John, 3
Watson, Will, 1
Wellington, Dr Arthur, 235
Wesleyan, 16, 21, 131
Wesleyan Methodist, 16, 131
West Africa, 202, 216
West Malvern, 159
Westminster Abbey, 27, 152
Winnipeg, 211
Whitehead, Betty, xiii
Woolmer, J., 122
World Bank, 186, 207–8, 219, 221–3, 225, 228–9
World Bank Institute, 221
World Food Programme, 220

World Methodist Conference, 189
Worthington, R. T., 121

York, 1, 43
Yorkshire, 2, 12
Young, Lake, 113

Zambezi, 26–7, 30, 34, 43, 51, 56, 75–8, 162, 170, 206
Zambia, xiii, 1, 27, 32, 34, 90, 96, 130, 161, 163, 166–7, 186–7, 202–8, 213–15, 217–18, 220, 223, 226, 233–4, 237, 241; *see also* Northern Rhodesia
Zambia Airways, 205
Zanzibar, 131
Zimbabwe, 27, 221